TED DEKKER

THE FORGOTTEN WAY

MEDITATIONS

THE PATH OF YESHUA
FOR POWER AND PEACE
IN THIS LIFE

Cover concept by Allison Metcalfe
Cover design and interior layout by Yvonne Parks at www.PearCreative.ca

Printed in the U.S.A.

ISBN 978-0-9968124-0-5

CONTENTS

FOR ADDITIONAL INFORMATION
ON ADDITIONAL PERSONAL AND
SMALL-GROUP RESOURCES AS WELL AS
SPEAKING ENGAGEMENTS, VISIT:

THEFORGOTTENWAY.COM

(SEE LAST PAGE FOR MORE)

BEFORE YOU ENTER

This simple book is a gateway to a simple journey of radical discovery for Christians, laid out in three sections.

The first section, called *The Forgotten Way*, unpacks the conflicts we find on the pathway we call this life. As a matter of sound faith and doctrine, you are filled with the Spirit in this life and saved in the next life, and yet you struggle to be saved from the storms that rise up against you in this life. Although you know that the evidence of those who know God is love and that the fruits of the Spirit are peace and joy, conflict and strife batter your mind while you walk this earth. Read this section and you will surely see yourself on the page.

The second section contains *The Meditations* on the Way of Yeshua for peace and power in this life—that way so easily forgotten by each of us every day. Like a symphony that builds, together they create a whole that must be experienced, not read like sheet music. The meditations are delivered in three movements: (1) The **Truth** of who your true Father is and who you are. Here, the news is good. (2) The simple and only **Way** to find peace, love and power in this life. Here, the news is even better. (3) The **Life** you will lead when you follow the Way. Here, the news is better than you have ever imagined.

The third section contains the *Scriptures* from the meditations and *Reflections* that delve deeper into those references, written by Bill Vanderbush.

Throughout this book, except where noted, Scriptures are taken from the New American Standard Bible.

This is our reformation in Yeshua: to be free from the lies that hold us captive to the old way of being in this world. This is our healing: to *see* what few see. This is our resurrection: having been raised with Christ, to now *be* his body on Earth as apprentices in The Forgotten Way of Yeshua.

The time for our transformation has come.

THE FORGOTTEN WAY

I have called this book *The Forgotten Way* because we, as Christians, so often forget the truth that empowers in this life. And I use the term *Way* because Yeshua's followers called themselves the people of the *Way* in the years after His resurrection before others later began to call them "little Christs" or *Christians*.

I am one of those Christians, and the meditations in this book are written to myself and to my children, and to any who find themselves drawn. They are our constant reminder of those truths we so easily forget each day, leaving us powerless to find peace in the storms that rise against us in this life.

Like Paul the apostle, I find myself the chief of sinners.[1] Just like you, I'm prone to struggle because life happens in cycles of ease and challenge, highs and lows, remembering and forgetting, often in the space of a single day or hour. All that is written here is for me more than for any other. Herein are words that point to the way of freedom.

Following the Way requires no specific affiliation with any particular Christian institutional organization, even though gathering together is a critical element in our journey. The Way is a path of discovery experienced by each of us, together and alone. It is our transformation from victims in a world darkened by deception to overcomers through an awakening to our true identity.

As such, the Way isn't a set of facts or labels or dogma, but a living, breathing journey on which all Christians find themselves.

The journey from hate to love.

The journey from fear to faith.

The journey from insecurity to complete rest and peace.

The journey from crawling to flying.

Being in the eternal realm of the Father's sovereign presence here on Earth, empowered by the Spirit, we will find peace in the storms; we will walk on the troubled seas of our lives; we will not be poisoned by the lies of snakes; we will move mountains that appear insurmountable; we will heal all manner of sickness that has twisted minds and bodies.

Joy and peace are our clothing because they are states of being rooted in Christ, not merely emotions that come and go like the tide. Love will flow from us as living waters, because the manifestation of the kingdom of heaven on Earth *is* love. And when we love, all will know, there goes one who is filled with the Spirit and can fly.

The Forgotten Way is a journey of experiencing that great triumph in *this* life, not only in whatever life awaits us, by awakening to our true identity.

Indeed, we are now, at this very moment, those who can fly. But we cannot *be* who we are unless we *see* who we are, stripped of all the lies that have blinded us. Unless we remember who we are. Unless we actually come to *believe* the truth about our Father and ourselves. This is the journey of transformation, of awakening, of the renewing of our mind.

In the end, the journey is letting go of who we *think we are*, to see and so be who we *truly are* right now, in this moment.

THE CONFLICT WITHIN

If there is one elephant in the room among us who are joined with Christ and filled with His Spirit[2], it is that what we *think and say* we believe and what we *actually experience* are all too often two radically different realities. Ironically, we ourselves are often the last to see this disparity.

We think and say we believe in Jesus, but we are anxious for tomorrow and cringe with fear in the face of the storm. We think and say we love our neighbor and our enemy, but we court jealousy of those who have what we want, and we secretly despise those who attack us.

We are Christians with various emphases in doctrine, yet in our daily lives we seem to be the same, often stumbling in darkness and feeling lost, and judging with anger not only ourselves but all those around us.

The evidence of our lives does not match our rhetoric. Have we forgotten the teaching of John? There is no fear in love.

Have we lost sight of Paul's teaching? He made it plain: The preeminent evidence shown by those who know the Father is this: *love*. And not just any love, but the unique kind that loves enemies, not only those who show us love in return. A love that is patient, showing no jealousy or arrogance, keeping no record of wrong, not seeking its own and not provoked by another's behavior.[3] This is to love as Christ loves, submitting to each other without judgment.[4]

Thus we show all manner of evidence but the one that matters the most.

We show the evidence of profound words to others, speaking truth in the tongues of men and angels[5]; yet if we rise up in anger at our brother we are as guilty as any murderer, as Jesus said.

We show the evidence of informed doctrine and all knowledge, having studied the Scriptures, and yet we do not love the lowest person as Christ, so our knowledge is worthless.[6]

We may give all of our possessions to the poor and surrender our bodies to be burned and have faith to move mountains[7] and heal disease, calling Him Lord[8], yet these profit us nothing if the evidence of His Spirit called love does not rule our hearts.

We call ourselves born again, baptized in water and the Spirit. We are diligent in taking communion, singing in choirs, serving the church, paying tithes, reading the Scriptures, fasting when called to humble ourselves, gathering in Bible studies, attending conferences, going on missions, submitting to authorities, and rehearsing our arguments.

And yet rivers of love, joy and peace do not flow from us like living waters, and so, as Paul said, all of these profit us nothing.

Oh you human. You beautiful, noble child, seeking as best you know how to find your way in this life, how precious you are to your Father! May our love be the only defense we show ourselves and the world.

What matters isn't our stated belief and doctrine but how we live and what we experience in the story of our lives, as Jesus, John, James, and Paul all make so abundantly clear.[9] It's our actual *experience* and *expression* of life that show us and the world what we *truly* believe and to what extent we *truly* love, not what we *say* we believe or whom we *say* we love. If we say we have faith, but the workings of our life don't reflect that faith, that faith is indeed dead.

If our experience in life and our dogma do not line up, we will find ourselves in conflict. We will be powerless and unable to fly.

There is no new doctrine to be considered here, only a fresh perspective and a new experience of our lives. But renewed perspective often changes what we believe about ourselves and the world we live in.

Case in point: If some argue, based on an interpretation of certain Scriptures, that there are no miracles today, but then one day they witness an arm miraculously healed before their eyes (new perspective), or if their own arm is healed (new experience), they will have to reconsider their interpretation of the dogma they once argued with great passion, yes?

This brings us back to the elephant in the room. If what we say we believe (our dogma) and what we experience in life are in open conflict, one of the two must eventually yield.

We all believe the Word of God without question, and that Word is a person named Jesus, through and in whom all that was made exists. When we say the Word is living, active, sharper than any two-edged sword, piercing soul and spirit, able to judge the heart, we are talking about Jesus, who alone is the Word.[10]

We also believe in the inspired words that were written, but our interpretation of those words varies dramatically. Nevertheless, we know that God is perhaps best revealed to children, so His way must be simple. And we know that, as Jesus said, His yoke (which in his day meant *interpretation of the Scriptures*) is easy, and His burden light.[11]

Even as a child intuitively knows a good story and good news, so we look for the good news of the Father in a simple story. We become like that small child so we may know the Father.

Our greatest challenge is that we no longer know who we are as our Father's children, because we have been swallowed up by a dogma that isn't reflected in the actual expression of our lives.

MY OWN JOURNEY INTO THE LIGHT

I grew up as the son of missionaries who left everything in the West to take the good news to a tribe of cannibals in Indonesia. They were heroes in all respects and taught me many wonderful things, not least among them, all the virtues and values of the Christian life. What a beautiful example they showed me.

There, in the jungles of Indonesia, I grew up in a kind of garden of Eden, oblivious to danger and fear. Are we not all born into a kind of childlike wonder and innocence? But soon enough we are cast out of that garden, and there we discover an ominous world full of danger, many of us at a very young age.

When I was six years old, my parents did what all missionaries did in that day and for which I offer them no blame: they sent me away to a boarding school. There I found myself completely untethered and alone. I wept that first night, terrified. I don't remember the rest of the nights because I have somehow blocked those painful memories, but my friends tell me that I cried myself to sleep every night for many months.

I felt utterly abandoned. And I was only six. I was lost, like that small bird in the children's book who wanders from creature to creature, asking each if they are his mother.

Are you my mother? Are you my father?

But I found no father or mother in that boarding school. There was no parent figure whose favor I could earn. I was only a name among many, and most of my meaningful interactions with adults revolved around their disapproval of me when I did something wrong, like not taking my medicine or not being in the right place at the right time.

Shortly after my arrival, I made the mistake of knocking over a pee pot they placed in our rooms each evening because it was too dangerous to use the outhouse at night. My new house father stormed in, quickly identified me as the guilty one, dragged me to the laundry room, and beat me with a firm rubber hose.

I screamed, terrified and bruised, and I knew then to never knock over the pee pot. Or do anything else that would earn me punishment. The sum of my life was measuring up to either avoid terrible punishment or to win favor and so be accepted and loved.

It was simple: If you say, and or do, and or believe the right things, you're golden. If you don't, you're screwed. It all depends on you. Just like with God, or so I was led to believe.

I was adrift, alone, without any tether to my true identity. I was lost, starving for intimacy, desperate to be valued, swallowed by a sea of lonely hearts, thinking that perhaps I was the only one who was lost.

In that strange isolation, without the modern conveniences of things like television or computers (were they even invented yet) I went on the hunt for acceptance and identity in a vast journey of the imagination, that wonderful gift we all have—perhaps the greatest power given to humans.

All of life is a story, you see. This much we all now know. We, each one of us, are the ones who interpret our life situation as a story and we assign meaning to it, based on our own perceptions of the story we weave of our own lives.

In my imagination, I began to escape from the reality around me by creating a reality far more to my liking. How?

Through books. Novels. Comics. These were my windows into worlds of hope in which things were far more expansive and less earthbound than the stark world I saw with the two eyes in my head.

You may not have escaped into books, but you have and still do escape into your interpretation (story) of this life, whether you think it's fanciful or not.

We are all looking for a better way of being in the world, yes? More love. Better health. More Christ-likeness. More job satisfaction. You name it … We all escape into a story of how things could or should be and we're unwittingly doing it all the time.

In the worlds of my novels and comic books, I was always the winner. But in the stark reality of boarding school I was often the loser.

I see now that my entire life has been one long search for identity, intimacy, and acceptance.

I was terrified of rejection, though I didn't recognize it at the time. But of course I feared rejection—my earthly father had unwittingly abandoned me as a child.

Even more, I believed that my heavenly Father had and would reject me unless I presented myself to Him in a certain way or at the least believed the right things about Him. If I didn't, He would send me to a place of terrible suffering forever. It would be like an eternal beating with a rubber hose, only this one would have razor blades sticking out of it.

Unable to fully embrace any father figure, I searched for my identity and acceptance by finding others who would love me, and when I thought they did, I determined my significance by their perspective of me. I did so in sports, thinking if I could only excel, I would be honored. I did so in school, thinking if I could measure up to the expectations of my teachers, I would have meaning. I did so in romantic relationships, thinking if this one person loved me, I would be secure.

I sought for identity and acceptance by trying to measure up to my society's blueprint of what did or did not look cool by wearing the right clothes and trying to have the right body. Or by standing out in a group, which made me somewhat important. Or by sometimes rebelling against the status quo, because this gave me significance in another group.

But mostly by trying to fit in and avoid rejection. I remember coming to the Unites States for a year when I was in the fifth grade. For reasons not clear to me at the time, I was soundly rejected by my grade school class in Montana—only because I was a peculiarity. Even more, I was bullied by those who thought I was weird. They laughed at the way I looked and dressed, made fun of the way I talked, and beat me up on occasion. My stories of eating spiders in the jungle didn't help my cause. I was far too exotic and different for their tastes.

I tried to change my behavior to avoid rejection, but to no avail.

When I returned to the United States in the tenth grade, this time to Chicago, I went to great lengths to find acceptance. I had to prove myself in sports and in social settings or I would surely be rejected. Case in point: The year was 1979 and disco was in full swing, so I latched onto the notion that if I could impress a particular girl with my moves, I would at least find love and acceptance from her.

Despite all of my efforts and practice, however pitiful in retrospect, I failed to impress and did so quite spectacularly. In the end, I felt uniquely unacceptable. Approval depended on my being or doing the right thing, you see, and I could not measure up.

I had to try harder. I had to find the right group. I had to find a home, a girl, the right friends who would accept me as I was. And so I did try harder, but all to no avail.

I see now that in my search for love and acceptance, I slowly began to enslave myself to various identities, which I mistook for my real self in many arenas—sports, church, relationships, career, wealth. These identities became like gods of a lesser kind, all of which I hoped would save me from insignificance in this life.

Somehow, as I grew older, I had abandoned the idealistic triumph I'd found in my books when I was younger. What a shame. It was almost as though I, like Adam and Eve, had fallen out of that Garden of Eden where everything turned out perfect.

I had to find a way in the real world, I thought. So I unwittingly enslaved myself to the gods who promised to accept me in this world.

Can you relate?

The problem was, none of these lesser gods per se came through for more than a little while before failing me. Like blooming flowers, they soon withered and died. The falling in love soon leads to heartbreak; the first-place finish eventually gives way to a loss; the perfect body is soon compromised.

Worse, in addition to my inability to measure up to the standards of this world, I never seemed able to measure up to what I thought were God's expectations of me, mostly regarding the matter of love.

Jesus' teaching was clear: any sinner can show love to those who love them, but true love shows kindness to those who are cruel and dishonoring to you. Paul was plain: true love holds no record of wrong.

Indeed, without this kind of love, all other manifestations of faith and power—even giving your body to be burned at the stake for the gospel—were useless, as Paul wrote in his famous letter to the Corinthians. Love, then, was clearly the greatest power of any, I saw.

So I pressed in harder, determined to be the one who would succeed in earning God's favor by loving as He asked me to love. If I couldn't measure up to the world's expectations, I would give myself to measuring up to God's expectations of me.

But no matter how hard I tried to submit myself to God, I wasn't able to love in this way, you see. Not really. I tried, but in my heart, where it really matters, I was offended by those who were mean and lashed out against me and I judged them in return, thus failing to show true love, without which all else was worthless.

I never doubted my standing in the next life, but I often felt shame in this life, constantly disappointing God in my failure to love as He asked me to love. As such, I was caught in a kind of stupor of unworthiness.

Can you relate?

And as I grew older I became increasingly aware of my failure to demonstrate other powers promised in the Scriptures. Didn't Jesus say plainly: *If you believe in Me, anything in My name and it will be done?*[12] But I *did* believe in Him, I thought. I certainly believed all the right things about Him and had all my doctrine laid out just right in the most orthodox sense. Furthermore, I *was* asking in His name, I thought.

Yet it did not follow that whatever I asked for came to be. Not even close. In fact, not at all, it often seemed. While I heard the victorious rhetoric of others, I didn't seem to have those powers, so I condemned myself.

I was sure that my powerlessness was uniquely my fault. I didn't have enough faith. I needed to try harder and do better. Others seemed to have it all together, but I was a failure.

So I pressed in with greater passion. I got filled with the Spirit; I got a degree in biblical studies; I spent days praying in the mountains; I fasted; I wore the pages of my Bible ragged; I went on retreats; I recommitted my life at the altar over and over; I took communion with utter sincerity; I worshiped in silence; I worshiped with my hands raised; I worshiped to organs; I worshiped to drums; I served as best I could; I shared my faith; I started a home group; I preached on a corner; I went on a mission—I did it all.

I was that kind of person, desperately seeking the approval and favor of my Father in heaven by measuring up to His expectations of what constituted a good son—one who is known for a love that holds no record of wrong and who does the works of Jesus wherever he goes.

And yet while my passion swelled, I still could not quite measure up for more than a day or two, a week, maybe a couple months before feeling once more like a wretch in my heart of hearts.

Can you relate?

When conflict in my relationships challenged all of my notions of love, when disease came close to home, when friends turned on me, when I struggled to pay my bills, when life sucked me dry, I began to wonder where all the power to live life more abundantly had gone. Then I began to question whether that power had ever really been there.

Thinking that perhaps I was following nothing but folklore, I courted agnosticism for a spell. Then, terrified I was making a terrible mistake, I reversed my course and threw myself at finding the truth with even more determination, desperate to discover God's love and power in this life. I often went to the mountains alone for days at a time, walking the fields with tears in my eyes, falling on my face before Him.

Each time I experienced breakthroughs that illuminated my path for a short time. But invariably I settled back into that familiar cohabitation with unworthiness because I still couldn't find lasting peace. I still couldn't measure up.

Somewhere in all the beautiful mess of all my obsessive searching, I began to notice something quite stunning: Everyone else seemed to be in the same boat as me, beginning with those I knew the best and those who seemed to know everything.

Most who claimed to live holy lives were just like me—a fact that was apparent to everyone but them. Like me, they, if dishonored, secretly held grievances for an hour, a day, a week, for months and years even. Clearly, they did not know how to truly love. Their love was no different from the love demonstrated by the rest of the world, beginning with the Muslims that I grew up with who were, in general, as loving in my eyes as any Christian.

Did Jesus not say we would be known as His followers by our love? Did He not teach that jealousy and gossip and anxiousness and fear are just other kinds of depravity? Did He not say that even to be angry with someone or call anyone a fool is the same as being guilty of murder?[13] Not just kind of, sort of, but *really*. The churches I attended were full of murderers, I thought.

Are we not all equally guilty, every day, even those who claim to be most holy while looking down at the less righteous?

How, then, does one find and know love, peace and power in this life when surrounded by such a great cloud of witnesses who only pretend to be clean, like Pharisees who whitewash their reputations while pointing fingers of judgment?

Crushed by what felt like a great betrayal to me, I tried every device known to man to find acceptance and love in all the corners of human experience.

But, like the prodigal, this led me into even deeper pain and suffering. I always thought I was doing my best, and I was in my own way. Even in all my flailing I was passionately seeking acceptance, love, significance, and identity in a world where traditional Christianity seemed to have failed me.

It seems to me that this is true for most Christians.

Haven't you tried your best given your own struggles, your own upbringing, your own mind and justifications at any given time?

Whether your failing is anger with another or anxiousness in your circumstances, have you not sought to find peace?

A RETURN TO STORY

I was in my mid thirties when I first began to consider writing a novel after seeing a friend of mine take a stab at it. If he could do it, I could, right?

Hadn't I found incredible wonder through story? Hadn't those worlds offered me a kind of truth that the "real" world failed to offer me? And wasn't all of life just a story we tell ourselves anyway? We assign meaning to events and make that our story. So storytelling, which is what Jesus did so much of, drew me.

But I didn't know quite how to go about writing a novel. A few years later, I took the plunge and began writing a novel. I'd come home from work each night and lose myself in a story I called *To Kill with Reason*. Six months later, I finished. My first book bound and in my hand.

Problem was, no one wanted to read it ... other than my close friends and family, naturally. Either way, I was determined, so I went about the process of trying to find an agent and I finally convinced one to at least take a look at my novel.

We went out to lunch, and as we sat at the table, I listened with bated breath, hoping to hear that I would be the next Stephen King or John Grisham. But that's not what I heard. Instead, she told me that not only was my novel un-publishable but that, in general, it sucked.

Walking out of that restaurant, I felt numb, crushed. So I did what all reasonable people do given the situation. I gave up. For six months my novel just sat in the bottom drawer, a constant reminder of my worthlessness as a writer.

But I just couldn't get rid of that mad tug at my heart ... seducing me forward. *Try again, Ted. Just try ... Never mind what they say ... You can do it.*

And, after reading an article about a guy named Frank Peretti who had sold millions of books, I wrote another novel. This one was science fiction and I called it *The Song of Eden*.

But no one outside my close friends and family really liked this one either.

Didn't matter, I was hooked now. The writing itself had become my drug and I was addicted.

So I wrote another novel. And another. I learned the hard way— going deep and plumbing the depths of my own soul. I became a sponge for new ways to tell story and for getting those stories into the world.

In the process, a completely new way to approach storytelling began to consume me and my novels took on a new quality. I had no idea how significant that shift in approach would prove to be.

By this point I had an agent, and he'd received nothing but hundreds of rejections over the course of submitting four of my novels.

Everything changed in the writing of *Heaven's Wager*, my fifth novel. I received offers from four different publishers on that fifth book. Ecstatic, I signed a three-book deal, and dove into my next novel, armed with a whole new way to approach storytelling.

Heaven's Wager was published in 2001 with virtually no marketing behind it. I remember going to the bookstore and not being able to find it, and once again I was crushed. I'd published a book but, surely, no one would find it! Regardless, I was committed now, so I suppressed my fears, hurried back home and continued working on my next novel.

A year later I received an email from my publisher: *Heaven's Wager* had hit the bestseller's list. What? How? Word of mouth. It had become a big deal in Canada, evidently.

But of course, I thought... Because I had written it in that new way. I pressed on, and over the course of the next twenty novels, I continued to refine the proven way of storytelling that I'd discovered. It was like that treasure in the field that Jesus talked about. Remember? I sold everything for that treasure and it rewarded beyond my wildest dreams.

My friends, many of whom were way ahead of me when I first began to write, were dumbfounded. How had I managed to succeed so quickly while they were still struggling? Why were millions of readers buying my novels and not theirs? Even my writing coach, who was already published at the time, was perplexed.

I would shrug. "I have an unfair advantage," I'd say to them. And it was true. I had discovered a path that few ever do. I called the advantage *unfair* because most writers don't really get it.

It was simply this: I was writing to find myself. To find transformation. The purpose of my effort wasn't to teach or entertain others, but to find truth myself.

The stories were about me, you see, and since we are all the same, readers were finding themselves in my novels.

I wrote for transformation, and I found it in and through all of my stories. But you must know two things. First, I, like most Christians, was still utterly lost to the reality of my true identity, so the journey out of that valley of darkness was a long one. Truly, my writing was the better part of the journey.

Second, the way out of darkness was actually in. I had to plumb my own fears and drag them slowly into the light. I had to walk through my trance of unworthiness to find my worth.

For fifteen years I pressed in, writing more than thirty books in a solitude I called my prison, driven by an almost maniacal obsession that few I knew could understand, determined to experience my Father as He was presented by Jesus.

Many of my novels weren't terribly spiritual on their surface—some were even banned by church bookstores because they were too dark or too this or too that. I didn't care. I had to be authentic to my own journey.

Readers connected to my authenticity and my books began to sell by the millions. I rejoiced. I was finding my freedom. I was finally "making it." I had found meaning and significance and acceptance.

But those stories had also shifted me, you see? And I quickly found that what I had longed for my whole life wasn't the answer.

The more I succeeded in the eyes of others, the more I realized that success itself was only another prison, fashioned by the values of this world, including the Church. More wealth only demanded I maintain that wealth. More status only begged me to rise higher. And fame . . . What a cruel and jealous mistress fame is.

I remember the first year that I sold a million books in one year. I had made it. My books were in all the airports. I was making tons of money. I was supposed to be super happy, yes? And I was to a point. But I was also disturbed. Ironically, I've never met a truly authentic "successful" person who didn't find their success disturbing on some level. And for me—one who'd obsessed with finding my true identity in this world but not of it—fantastic success quickly became a god that haunted my dreams and laughed at my antics.

I see now that I was being lovingly led to a great breaking because it would allow me to awaken to a new discovery of the very thing I had obsessed after my whole life: true love and freedom.

A new birth.

A DEEPER AWAKENING

It was only then that something deep within me finally did break. It was as if there were two parts of me, and they could no longer live with each other. One part of me was grateful for my success. Another part felt as though I was failing my purpose in life. That I was somehow betraying my Father. I now know that I *wasn't* failing Him, not in the least.

In fact, it was Him—God—who was awakening me and doing so with perfect confidence in me. That awakening began with a complete shifting of who I thought He was.

I remember the day so clearly. There in my office, drowning in a sea of self-condemnation and unworthiness, a gentle question whispered through my mind.

Does your Father not love you with the same love that He asks you to love others?

The room went utterly still. I blinked, unable to comprehend.

What is love? the voice asked.

But I knew, of course. Love was a staggering concept that held no record of wrong and was kind in the face of cruelty. When the evil man attacked, love turned the cheek without offering blame or grievance. This is the love no one knows—the same love Jesus talked about often.

Does your Father not love you in the same way He asks you to love others?

I sat in my chair, stunned, unable to accept the implication that anyone could possibly love me in such a way. I had never thought to ask if God loved me in the same way He asks me to love others.

Then I heard another thought, like a voice but not a voice at the same time.

Let go of all that you think you know about Me, so that you can KNOW Me.

Translation: Let go of your intellectual knowing so that you can *experience* My love (to know in a biblical sense).

As a deeply philosophical thinker trained in theology, deeply dependent on logic and intellect, this invitation should have frightened me. Instead, I began to weep with gratitude at such an intimate offer.

You mean I don't have to figure it all out?

Has doing so ever led you to this kind of love?

No.

Taste Me and see that I am good. I am love. I am Father.

I didn't hesitate. Nothing else mattered to me in that moment, because if it was true that God was this kind of loving Father, I would throw myself off a cliff to fall at His feet in gratitude for such an extravagant love.

And so I did. There, in the night, I closed my eyes, let go of who I thought I was and who the Father was, stepped off a kind of cliff, and I free-fell into that space beyond mere intellect where faith and love are found.

This was my surrender, you see. I let go of my own fear of not having it all figured out; my fear of not having all the right doctrines and beliefs; my fear of not being accepted unless I measured up to the demands of a holy God. I let go of all of that and fell into the arms of trust and love.

It felt like falling into a great unseen mystery, but I was actually falling into the light. I was falling out of a prison—a darkness that had been deepened by my own attempts to make my own light through reason and striving.

As the light filled my awareness, I began to awaken to a whole new reality.

It was then that I began to *know* my Father intimately in the way Jesus talked about *knowing* the Father—a word used for a deep intimate experience between a man and a woman. It was that kind of knowing, not an intellectual knowledge that swallowed me.

There, I trembled at His goodness, because He is infinitely good and complete and could never, never, never be compromised by anything anyone did or thought. Ever. I had been searching for this revelation and union with Him all of my life, since that day at age six when I'd found myself abandoned and then beaten by my house father for knocking over the pee pot.

As I knew my Father in a new way, I began to discover who I was as His son: that I was already all I could hope to be because I was one with and in Christ. My eyes were opened to who I was as my Father's son. I came into alignment with what was already true of me. Falling out of that prison was surely falling out of a false perception of who I was—of who the church had taught me I was, of who the world says I am—and falling into an experience of who I truly was.

It was a shift in perception, not a shift of truth.

All of my striving to *become* had actually hidden the truth from me, because in striving to become, I was only denying who I already was.

Falling off of the cliff into faith, I began to discover that I already had wings. And that I could unfurl those wings. And that to the extent I experienced my Father's love, I could love with that same love. Love *Him* that way. Love *myself* that way. Love *others* that way.

The light of Christ that was already in me and *was* me began to illuminate my understanding. In that light, my perspective of my Father, myself, and Christ shifted dramatically, offering me a whole new kind of peace and love, a totally new way of being in this world. And in that love, the heart of Jesus' teachings suddenly became so clear to me that I wondered how I could have missed them all those years.

My entire identity shifted. For all of my searching, I had not known the full goodness of my Father, nor myself. I wasn't who I thought I was, not at all! It was like waking from a dream to see another reality far truer than the dream I had awakened from. I was experiencing a dimension called the kingdom of heaven, which is already here, beyond what our earthly eyes show us, just like Jesus taught so often. That realm Paul called the *unseen*. Eternity now.

WHO AM I?

Over the course of the next few months, Jesus' and the apostles' teachings came alive to me in ways I had never imagined. Suddenly all those texts I had known for so long all came into focus. And none more illuminated than the many teachings on who I really was as the son of my Father.

It is as Jesus taught, that I am in Him and He is in me, in the same way that (just as) He is in the Father and the Father is in Him. A radical union that He said could only be known with the help of the Spirit of truth, whose primary purpose is to help us walk in that union, something He called *abiding in the vine*. And abiding in the vine is evidenced primarily by our love as we know His love for us.[14]

Yes, I know, it all sounds so … theological. So philosophical and distant, but it's mind-blowing goodness and utterly transformational. It is brilliant and worth dying for. It is, as Jesus taught, all that really matters in this life!

And more, it opens a gateway for powerful writing that will blow your mind. Follow me here …

Paul's teaching on our radical union with Christ suddenly made perfect sense to me. It was Paul who wrote that not only had Jesus died *for* my sin, but that I had died *with* Him. That I had been raised *with* Him. That I was already seated in heavenly places, right now.[15] I was a new creature in Him.[16]

It is no longer me who lives, he wrote, *but Christ who lives in me.*[17]

This was written by Paul, a man who characterized himself as the foremost of sinners. Paul, the man who said he had not attained the perfection of knowing and experiencing his union with Christ, still insisted that we were one with Him and in Him. Paul, a man who struggled with thorns in his flesh, made it clear that he was already glorified with and in Christ.

I suddenly realized that this was true of me as well. It was no longer *I* who lived, but *Christ* who lived in me!

But Paul went even further in his most bold claim in Colossians 3:11 where he writes emphatically of Christ's identity in these terms: *Christ is all. And Christ is in all.*

But how was this possible? Was I not separate from God on some level? Paul was saying no. It defied reason and raw intellect, and can only be revealed by and in spirit. But hadn't Peter said the same thing when he said we are participants in God's divine nature?

This is why Paul insisted that I was already complete (perfect) in Him.[18] You cannot be more complete than complete. What is complete has no further need for correction or it would not be complete. I, the Father's son, was complete because I was hidden in God with Christ.[19] Therefore, for me to live *was* Christ, just like Paul.[20] There was therefore no condemnation for me, because I was in Him and He was in me, as one, in the same way (just as) He was in the Father.[21]

So I found myself asking over and over: If it's no *longer me who lives, but Christ who lives,*[22] then who is this person called Ted, whom I judge and condemn for his constant failure? Who is the man I see in the mirror? He doesn't look like a new creature and doesn't appear to be seated in heavenly places. Who is this guy who stands on two feet, seeking acceptance and significance in various ways?

Who is this man trying to write transformational stories and earning a living writing those novels?

The answer became plain. My seen, temporary earthen vessel, to use Paul's description, was like a character in one of my novels. Like a role that I played for a short time. It wasn't an illusion or evil as claimed by the Gnostics—God forbid. But, clearly, it was passing away—decaying already—and therefore not eternally true. It was like a role in a TV movie.

I had mistakenly put my identity in that role, rather than in my true self so clearly characterized by Jesus and Paul as one joined *with* and *in* Christ.

There was far more to me than what my eyes showed me, just as Paul wrote. In fact, what I saw with my physical eyes was only something that shifted in form and would soon return to dust. That was only my small self, my earthen vessel, like a car I drove around in for this very short life.

The truest me was far more. And I could align my small self with the me who was now one in Christ. Alignment was now my only real journey.

Clearly, I hadn't seen myself the way my Father saw me in the unseen realm. The world seemed to have conspired with the father of lies to keep the eyes of my heart blind to my true identity, so I had spent my life threatened by the world around me. To the extent I believed those lies, I stumbled in darkness.

But what if I could see myself the way my Father saw me? How would I be then?

A NEW JOURNEY

My view of what it meant to be alive on this planet shifted in the simplest and most profound way.

For starters, the state of Christianity, of which I am a part, became suddenly clear to me. If you take all the things that Jesus said would evidence those who were in His way and call it RED, there were very few RED people in the church per se. This included me most of the time. Clearly, whatever way we had been following, it wasn't the way of Jesus. Some of the way perhaps, but not the way that mattered the most. This way that truly mattered would be evidenced by far more than theology.

What we believe is shown not by what we say or even think, but by how we live. To believe in Christ is to "be" and "live" in Him. Thus few Christians seem to actually believe *in* Jesus. They only believe many things about Him.

Perhaps this is what some mean when they say that Christianity at large is the last great mission field—those who think they see while walking in darkness still. They say they are RED, but everyone sees them as GREY, no different than anyone else.

Jesus made it clear, He was the *only* Way to experience the Father and thus manifest true power and extravagant love in this life.[23] Maybe our fixation with the next life has distracted us from following Him in this life.

Either way, there is only one way to awaken to true love and few of we who labeled ourselves as Christian were in that way. You cannot deny the evidence, something He was very clear about.

But I didn't condemn myself or other Christians for any failing. Rather, I began to see that we had simply forgotten and so gone blind to Jesus' core teachings. He invites us all on a journey of being reborn into new awareness and experience of what He called the kingdom of heaven, which is in our very being.[24] We each choose to take or not to take that journey each day. Each hour.

Does your life flow with the evidences that Jesus said would show you were in His way? Do you want the joy, the peace, the love and the power that He promised? Then you get to take a journey to find it, and uncover it, and let go of everything else to realize that treasure as a firsthand experience in the field of this life.

What does that journey look like?

According to Jesus, our journey through this life now is primarily to see who we truly are, as the sons and daughters of a Father who does not condemn us and who loves us far more than we can comprehend. We are His sons and daughters, established in His likeness, flowing with more beauty and power than we have thought possible. As we *align* our perception of who we are with our true identity, we are filled with love, joy and peace.

As we forget who we are, we feel separated, condemned and we condemn others.

To be aligned is to be fully awake to our true identity. You might ask, "How do I know if I'm aligned?" Simply ask yourself this: "Am I concerned with how I am seen by others in any regard? Does others' view of my status, my value, my body, my performance in life, my worthiness or lack thereof cause me any concern?"

If so, you aren't seeing yourself the way your Father sees you and are out of alignment in some regard. You are asleep to your true identity, complete, not needing man's approval on any level.

Thus, we all get to awaken so that our joy might be full.

Our journey isn't becoming more than we are, because we are already complete. Rather, our journey is to awaken to, or align with, who we already are. And as we do that, we find ourselves rushing to our Father's table where His fruits are peace, love and power in limitless abundance.

It is as Jesus taught: our eye (perception) is the lamp of (it shows us) our body (earthly experience). If we see clearly, our earthly experience is full of light. We see beauty. But if our perception isn't clear, the light within us is dark, and how deep is that darkness.[25] Our experience of life is all about the perception of who we are. We are the light of the world, but we cover up that truth and so cannot see it. We condemn ourselves and others, ensuring that we remain in darkness.[26]

This was why Jesus came to bring sight to the blind and set the captives free. He came to change my perception of me as the son of the Father and set me free from my prison of condemnation. To seek and save the lost—me—every hour of every day.

I also discovered that the only way we can see (and be) who we truly are in this life is to let go of our attachment to all other identities. To surrender them. However good they are in form, to the extent they define us, they only block our sight to who we already are as the light of the world.

As we see who we are as our Father's sons and daughters—as we experience His extravagant love for us—our natural experience and expression of life always lead to a staggering kind of love, on Earth as it is in heaven, right now, right here. *Your kingdom come, Your will be done on Earth, as it is in heaven.*[27]

In fact, love is surely the whole point of our union with and in Christ, even as He prayed: *I have given them the glory that you gave me that they may be one, just as we are one.* Why? *So that the world may know that you sent me and loved them even as (in the same way) you have loved me.* It is only in the awareness of how we are loved by the Father and of our union with Christ that we can share that same love.

Then and only then will the world know how they are loved, and that Jesus really *was* sent by the Father.

This is Jesus' version of taking the good news to the whole world. I began to redefine my version to fit His. Love is the missing apologetic we need to show Christ, not more books with bullet points or clever arguments that impress the intellect. Our very being, not any pamphlet or sermon, is the light of the world.

My only problem was covering up that light within me and becoming blind to it myself. Then I walked in darkness. But losing sight of the light didn't change who I was as the son of my Father or the light of the world. It only blocked my own and others' vision of that light and left me to stumble in darkness, judgment and misery. And even then, I was still my Father's son!

All of this was incredibly good news to me, the one who seemed to fail every day in his own efforts to become worthy, just like the Pharisees did with all their laws. Perhaps this is why they called it *gospel*, which simply means "good news." It was far better than I had dared hope.

It all sounds so spiritual, and it is, but it is also the staggering reality of all that is. It was like discovering the atom to me. Or that the world was round even though everyone was saying it was flat back in the day.

I can now see that my Father had been gently leading me to that place of discovering my own identity for over forty years. In fact, it was my own separation from my earthly father at age six that first set me on that journey. It is said that suffering gets our attention. So then, what a blessing, however much suffering I experienced on the path of awakening.

Following such a shift at my core, I dove into new kinds of writing projects. In thinking through all of the books I had written, I could see that in my desperate searching all those years, I had actually been writing about my true identity all along. It was as if something deep in me had always known who I was and who the Father was, and that Truth found its way onto the pages as I wrote authentically, through my struggles.

New stories flowed: *Eyes Wide Open, Water Walker, Hacker, Outlaw, A.D. 30,* and others.

I began to call Jesus by the name He used 2,000 years ago, *Yeshua,* which is the name I use for Him in these meditations, only because it sounds as fresh as my understanding of His teachings.

Again, all the novels I had already written were a beautiful, powerful part of my journey. I had always used that advantage of writing authentically to deal with my own challenges and find transformation in this life. They were all a part of my transformation, which is still ongoing.

But now I understood the heart of my search in a new way.

It's all about identity, you see. Who are you? Really, you live to discover *that.* And when you do, you will see that you are far more than you have imagined.

Although I grew up in the church and spent years studying theology, what I discovered in Yeshua's teachings continued to stagger me.

Once again I wondered, *How could I have missed the fundamental essence of His radically good news to me? How can I now possibly forget?*

And yet I do. As I've said, life consists of cycles of remembering and forgetting, and I, like you, still forget, far too often, every time I get anxious or feel like a victim. And in that forgetting, my view of eternal life is clouded once more until I remember who I am by surrendering who I am not.

FINDING ETERNAL LIFE

Growing up, I always assumed that the term *eternal life* referred only to something that began in the next life, after I died. I also thought that the *kingdom of heaven* was yet to come, after I died. I had learned in many theology classes that the Kingdom was already here and among us and within us[28], but those words never really connected with me in an experiential way. I always found a way to shove my understanding of eternal life and the kingdom of heaven into the next life, because it is *unseen,* to use Paul's language.

I also saw that in Yeshua's own words, to know God is to experience eternal life, not merely in the next life but in *this* life. As He said, *This is eternal life, that they may know You, the only true God, and Jesus Christ whom You have sent.*[29] The word He used for *know* is the same word used for sexual intimacy.

So then I had to ask myself, as I now ask myself every day: Am I *knowing* the Father? Or am I knowing and so believing or trusting something else? It seems that most Christians have a relationship with their theology and their thoughts about God rather than with the Father and the One He sent as the Word who preexisted the world of words.

You can know all *about* any person, but that doesn't mean you *know* them. Even the demons know about God and it profits them nothing.

You can *know about* an avocado and believe things about it by studying it and dissecting it and discussing it in a classroom ad infinitum. But you only *know* (as Yeshua used the term) that avocado when you bite into it and taste it. A child can know the Father this way, perhaps more easily than any adult, which is why Yeshua said we must become like children, even infants, to know the Father and see that He is good.[30]

Taste and *see* that God is good.[31]

Suddenly, I wanted nothing more than to *know* God—Father, Son, and Holy Spirit—because to the extent I *know* God, I also *know* myself in Christ. To the extent I place my identity in Yeshua (believe in Him), I find peace. To the extent that I forget who I am, on the other hand, I only seek for myself where I cannot be found, and I find only darkness once more.

But Yeshua showed us a way to abide in the awareness of who we are in Him and He in us. It is in this awareness that the fruit of His Spirit—love, joy, and peace—flow in, through, and from us as our state of being.

I began to call His way *The Forgotten Way* and I set it to story in *A.D. 30* and *A.D. 33*. At the same time, emboldened by many long discussions with Bill Vanderbush, a speaker and my dear friend, and through many deep conversations with my brother in arms Kevin Kaiser, I began the process of writing a series of meditations called *The Forgotten Way Meditations,* which follow this introduction.

Through dozens of lengthy conversations and meetings with leaders, theologians and seekers from all walks of Christianity, I quickly learned that I was not alone in what I was seeing. Very few of them had the language for it; but in all of my travels I discovered that the hearts of nearly everyone I spoke to—every leader, every son, every daughter—resonated with these simple truths, as if they had known it all along but had somehow fallen asleep to it and forgotten. Their eyes grew wide and they appeared stunned. Invariably, they would then smile.

It's almost as though a deep sleep swallowed the church following the death of the apostles, and we are all just now awakening to what seems so obvious. It's good news. Very good news.

These meditations offer a language for that good news seen in the Word made manifest, who is Christ in us and we in Him, as one.

OUR REVELATION

Among a rising tide of millions of Christians, how we label ourselves isn't nearly as important as how we actually experience and demonstrate Yeshua's incredible power in and as us, beginning with the power to love our enemies. To us, this is what it means to know God and the One He sent. Words only reflect an intellectual dogma, but the expression of our lives shows what we truly believe, regardless of our stated dogma.

How are we to interpret the inspired collection of writings we call the Bible? Is God actually a great spinning wheel in the heavens as Ezekiel saw Him, or was this metaphorical? Do angels still ride in chariots? Did they ever? Is the book of Revelation literal prophecy or metaphorical analogy describing something that happens in each of us? If not analogy, have the events described in that book already happened or will they happen, or both? Is the second coming of Christ a radical shift in which the revelation and manifestation of Christ are revealed in all of creation, or is it going to be a physical, one-time event where Jesus actually floats down from the sky? What is hell and who goes there? Was the Creation story literal in every respect so that when it says God walked with Adam and Eve He had two legs?

Yes. Perhaps. Maybe not. Of course. I'm not sure.

These questions are not the ones we should fight over or die for. Our revelation is for the sons and daughters of God, realizing now that the greatest manifestation of the Spirit in our lives is love—the kind that holds no record of wrong—without which everything else we do is worthless, as Paul made so plain to the Corinthians.

The Spirit of truth comes to show us the Father's love and our union with and in Christ, because only in this awareness can we love as He loves and so show ourselves and the world the love of the Father.

It is a revelation for all of us who, having believed, still experience anxiousness, worry, doubt, sickness, divorce, and anger, and so find ourselves stumbling in darkness.

Our journey is to find peace, love, joy, and all of the fruit of the Spirit in the midst of those storms, because this is The Forgotten Way of Yeshua for this life.

The single question that matters most to us is this: to what extent are we *knowing* God intimately? And by that I mean, are we truly *believing in* the identity of Christ and Christ in us each day? You can't believe in Christ without also believing in who you are, one with and in Him. To believe in Him is to place your identity in Him. It is to believe in your true, risen and glorified self.

As such, the only way to truly believe in the *name* (identity) of Jesus is to let go of our identification and attachment to our own names.

Are we experiencing His extravagant love? Are we showing that love to the world? Are we finding peace in the midst of the storms of this life and so being saved from them?

If so, we know that we are abiding in Him and in our own true nature as the sons and daughters of the Father, in the world but not of it.

If not, we have simply fallen out of alignment and become blinded to our identity once again, perhaps often each day. Then we are not saved from the storms of this life, but mastered by them. And as we know, we can only serve one master: either Christ, or the system of the world with all of its storms.

We, like Paul in Philippians 3:10, long to know *Christ* and the staggering *power* of His resurrection. And as those who have risen with Him, to know the power of our own resurrection in Him, not as a creed that satisfies the intellect, but as a reality that empowers us to love ourselves and others as Christ loves us all.

Do you want to find the peace of Yeshua in the storms of your life? Do you want to walk on the troubled seas of this life? Do you want see His power manifested on Earth as it is in heaven?

PEACE IN THE STORM

Think of your life as a boat on the stormy seas. The boat represents all that you think will keep you safe from death by drowning. Dark skies block out the sun, winds tear at your face, angry waves rise to sweep you off your treasured boat and send you into a deep, watery grave. And so you cringe in fear as you cling to the boat that you believe will save you from suffering.

But Yeshua is at peace. How can He be at rest in the midst of such a terrible threat? When you cry out in fear, He rises and looks out at that storm, totally unconcerned.

Why are you afraid? He asks.

Has He gone mad? Does He not see the reason to fear? Does He not see the cruel husband, the cancer, the terrified children, the abuse, the injustice, the empty bank account, the rejection at the hands of friends, the assault of enemies, the killing of innocents? How could He ask such a question?

Unless what He sees and what you see are not the same.

And what does He see instead of the storm? He sees another dimension in which you are complete and safe and glorified, not subject to harm or fear in any way. He sees the Father, who offers no judgment nor condemnation.[32] He sees life and love and joy and peace in an eternal union with His Father, manifesting now, on Earth, in the most spectacular fashion as we place our faith in Him.

He sees peace in the storm. And so can we. His question is still the same today. *Why are you afraid, oh you of little faith?*[33]

Yeshua shows us the Way to be saved from all that we think threatens us on the dark seas of our lives. Only when we, too, see what He sees can we leave the treasured boat that we think will save us and walk on the troubled waters that we thought would surely drown us.

I wasn't seeing what He saw, you see. I was seeing the storm clouds.

What about you? Are you anxious in your relationships or lack thereof? Do you have concerns about your means of income, or your career, or your ministry, or how others view you in your ministry?

I do, far too often, whenever I forget who I truly am. And then I, too, am afraid and lash out in anger and condemn myself and search for significance and identity in this world once more.

Do you fear for your children? Are you worried about what you will wear, or how others will view you in any respect? Do you secretly suspect that you can never quite measure up to what you think God expects of you? That you are doomed to be a failure, always?

Are you quick to point out the failures of others?

I was, though I didn't see it in myself. As it turns out, it's hard to see clearly when you're blinded by planks of judgment and grievance, as Yeshua taught.[34]

But Yeshua came to restore sight to the blind and set the captives free. The sight He offers allows me to see into the Father's realm and into Himself and into myself, a view brimming with light, seen only through the eyes of the heart.[35]

Our challenge isn't in *becoming* more than we are, because we are already risen and complete.[36] Our challenge is to remember and abide in who we are, each day and each hour.

To the extent we remain blinded to our true identity, we search for significance in all that this world seems to offer us for acceptance, satisfaction, and security.

His way of being in this world is full of joy and love and gratefulness. In His state of being, all burdens are light and each step rests in trust. Contentment and peace rule the heart. A new power flows unrestricted in a great dance between the Father, the Son, the Spirit and yourself, now fused into that staggering relationship.

We were created and reborn out of the infinite goodness of our Father. In that identity we have incomparably great power *during this age* as well as the age to come, as Paul made plain.[37] Are you experiencing that incomparable power in this age?

It is written that in the last days the earth will tremble at the goodness of God.[38] So then I ask you, what kind of goodness would make you weak in the knees with gratitude and awe?

If I was to simplify the teaching of Paul and Yeshua so that a child might understand, they could be found in five simple declarations.

THE TRUTH

1) God is infinitely good, far more loving and gentle and kind to His children than any earthly mother or father imaginable. **God is infinitely complete;** nothing can threaten or disturb Him. Nothing can be taken away from Him, making Him less than complete, nor added to Him who is already complete.

2) You are remade in the likeness and glory of your Father, finite yet already complete in union with Yeshua—you in Him and He in you, risen with Him and seated in heavenly places. Nothing can separate you from His love.

THE WAY

3) Your journey now is to see and align yourself with who you truly are, because you are the light of the world, the son or the daughter of your Father, a new creature flowing with more beauty and power than you dare imagine possible.

4) You will only see who you are and thus be who you are as you surrender your attachment to all other identities, which are like gods of a lesser power that block your vision of your true identity and keep you in darkness.

THE LIFE

5) Love, joy, and peace are the manifestation of your true identity and the Father's realm, on Earth as in heaven through the power of the Holy Spirit.

An expansion of these declarations will be found at the end of the **Meditations**, and this we call **Our Declaration**. Even so, no catechism or lesson will teach us to love or give us peace. Love and peace are states of being that can be found only as we undertake the journey ourselves, which requires experiencing and knowing rather than merely hearing and knowing about.

Any teaching in the name of Christ that strips away the full power of the finished work of Yeshua, which restored us in Him, unwittingly leads Christians back into a kind of blindness and robs us of our power in this life. Yeshua warned of such teachers, saying there would be many. History has proven this to be true in sweeping fashion, and hundreds of millions have surely embraced and still cling to a powerless gospel stripped of unity and love.[40]

Protestants would say that the reformation delivered them from a powerless gospel. But do we show the extravagant love of Christ (which is the greatest manifestation of Christ's power, as written) in greater measure than others?

It seems as though we Christians have developed a nasty habit of leading people into a radical encounter with God's unconditional love, forgiveness, acceptance, and union only to spend the ensuing years teaching them how to become close to God to earn His approval. In this way we unwittingly deny their existing union with and in Christ. Perhaps we are trying to talk them out of their experience of first love because we no longer experience it ourselves.

Perhaps we have forgotten who we are and are no longer being "Christian" ourselves.

The rub isn't evil intention on our part. The rub is that Yeshua's Way of believing *in* Him and *knowing* the Father is 180 degrees from the way of the world, and as such is completely counterintuitive to any system of human logic, both inside and outside of human religion.

The old mind cannot see Yeshua's Way for this life—true vision requires new eyes. The brain cannot understand it—true knowing is of the heart and requires a whole new operating system to process.

This is why, as Yeshua predicted, very few even find His Way.[41] It is said that nearly 70 percent of all Americans have accepted Jesus as Savior at some point, but how many of us have found His Way for this life? How many have been saved from fear and bitterness and anger and the fear of dishonor?

To follow Yeshua's Way is to let go of this world's systems to see and experience a far greater one—one that is closer than our own breath.

It is to surrender what we think we know *about* the Father, so that we can truly *know* Him. It is to let go of who we think we are to discover who we really are.

It is to let go of our continued striving to invite Yeshua into our hearts and instead place our identity in the fact that He has already taken us into His heart.

It is the great reversal of all that we think will give us significance and meaning in this life, so that we can live with more peace and power than we have yet imagined.

When we follow Yeshua's Way, we no longer ask ourselves what we are *doing* for Yeshua, but rather who we are *being* so that He can *do* through us. What we *do* flows naturally out of who we believe ourselves to *be* in any given moment. As we see ourselves in Him, we will be Him to the world because, as John writes, His love is perfected in us, and as He is, so are we in this world.[42] We are indeed His body here on Earth.[43]

FINDING SUPERMAN

In today's vernacular, Yeshua's Way is indeed the way of superheroes. In this sense, was He not the first superhero, and we now His apprentices, born into His identity and learning to fly? Would we not rush to see and experience this truth about Yeshua, our Father, and ourselves through the power of the Holy Spirit?

Think of yourself as Superman or Superwoman. If Superman were to forget that he's Superman, he would only be Clark Kent and Clark Kent can't fly. Only Superman can fly. And having forgotten that he's actually Superman, Clark no longer knows he can fly.

How then does Clark Kent go about flying again?

Someone would need to tap Clark Kent on the shoulder and say, "Umm . . . excuse me, but you're Superman. If you take off that shirt and tie (surrender them), you'll find you're clothed in another suit in which you can fly."

Then Clark Kent would need to believe this is true and align himself with that truth of his identity. Aligning himself with this truth would look like rushing to the phone booth, letting go of his old Clark Kent costume, and flying once more as Superman.

In the same way, as Paul writes, we who are the sons of God, clothed in Christ,[44] have great power and none greater than to love—without which the rest is nothing. But only in surrendering the old business suit (the old identity) do we see who we really are.

Who are you being right now, at this moment? Do you want to "fly" again? Or maybe you want to fly for the first time, because in your life "flying" is loving God with all your heart, loving yourself as you are loved, and all others as yourself. And what a thrill that is!

One again, as Paul wrote, our chief aim now is to know Christ and the power of His resurrection, which is to know ourselves in Christ, resurrected in Him. To know Christ and the power of *our* resurrection.

And in that resurrection we can "fly." We can truly love. In that resurrection, there is no fear, because there is no fear in love.[45]

This is our renewal in Yeshua: to be free from the lies that hold us captive to the old way of being in this world. This is our healing: to *see* who we truly are. This is our resurrection: *having* been raised with Christ, to know the staggering power of our resurrection in Him and to be His body on Earth as we follow The Forgotten Way of Yeshua.

This is our manifestation: to love as He loved.

The time for our transformation has come.[46]

YOUR JOURNEY FORWARD

Do not conform to the pattern of this world,
but be transformed by the renewing of your mind.
ROMANS 12:2

Ask and it will be given to you; seek and you will find;
knock and the door will be opened to you.
Which of you, if your son asks for bread, will give him a stone?
Or if he asks for a fish, will give him a snake?
. . . How much more will your Father in heaven
give good gifts to those who ask Him!
MATTHEW 7:7, 9-11

A few words of guidance before you begin the Meditations.

The prophet Ezekiel was among the first to write about a radical personal encounter with God, high and lifted up. His writing shook the religious establishment of his day. How could God be encountered so directly outside of the Temple, and without the help of a priest? More, how could God be described in such strange terms, as a wheel within a wheel?

Still, many people longed to have a relationship with God like the one he described. To know God so directly—so personally—made the establishment as nervous then as it has throughout history and still does today. How can this be? A deep, personal relationship with *God*, not with dogma or with institutionalized religion, is at the heart of Christianity.

The wall between mankind and God, erected by the church and heavily reinforced for over a thousand years, began to crumble during the Reformation. Many periods of renewal and revelation in the five hundred years since have further demolished that wall of separation. Perhaps the most significant one occurred in the early 1900s, when explosive personal encounters with God defied the traditions of men. The movement to know God experientially continues to accelerate today as more and more believers find true peace and love and power. Such gifts come only from knowing God intimately and sharing His divine nature through identity in Christ.

So today we seek Him directly, not as the Gnostics—extremists who believed the physical world was either evil or totally inconsequential (much more on that in meditations 8 and 9)—but as eternal spiritual beings in temporal earthen vessels, fully integrated with this world. *In* it but not *of* it.

Has any church more fully experienced the power of the gospel than the one that first embraced Yeshua's spirit in the twenty years following His resurrection? This church did not have any of the gospels or the epistles to argue about or defend. And yet perhaps far more than we, its members lived and breathed the power of *being in Christ* on Earth.

Those sacred writings that we now have are called the Scriptures, and they point to Christ, but they are not the Word who is Christ and Christ manifested in us.[47] Let us worship Christ alone, not the words or the religious dogmas that point to Him. If we worship doctrine, we will have unwittingly made a god out of something other than God. Then we will not understand our need to *know* (experience) Him intimately. We will be no different from the religious leaders during the time of Yeshua who would not yield to Him.

Take comfort, because we know, as Yeshua said, that God reveals Himself to children, so His way must be simple. We know that His yoke (His interpretation) is easy and His burden (what is required to follow that interpretation) is light.[48] So we look for the good news of the Father in a simple story, and we become like children so that we may know the Father.

Along the journey, try not to condemn yourself for not being more "successful" in your attempts to follow the Way than you are. Self-condemnation only pushes you deeper into despair and unworthiness and toward substitutes for His love. Substitutes like judgment of others or false comforts.

Instead, remember that you are the son, the daughter of the Father and He does not condemn you. When you see yourself as He sees you, neither will you. Rather you will be drawn to Him.

THE BEAUTY OF UNCERTAINTY

The process of transforming the mind from old ways of thinking to new ways is called *metanoia* in Greek: *meta* (to change or go beyond) and *noia* (one's mind or knowledge). This is translated as *repentance* in the King James. *Repent* (transform your thinking) *because the kingdom of heaven is here*. For this we must become like little children, trusting the Father, no longer bound by fear.[49]

Why? Because in our own minds, stepping into the deep waters of new thinking feels utterly uncertain and requires faith in Him, not in our old minds. As such, that uncertainty is a beautiful thing, because it is the gateway to faith that goes beyond intellectual understanding.

Think of your old mind as a shore on one side of a lake or a river, and your new, transformed mind as the shore across that river. The only way to reach the other side is through the river of change, which is filled with intellectual uncertainty. Or think of the process of renewing your mind like stepping out of a boat that you think keeps you safe from the troubled sea.

Entering that river necessarily means letting go of the things that you think keep you safe. Stepping off the shore or out of the boat will cause objection and fear because the old mind is like a god who demands our allegiance.

Entering the waters of change requires surrendering who we *think* we are and what we *think* we know about the world so that we can discover who we *truly* are and so find faith to walk on the troubled waters in this life.

The old mind almost always speaks first. It speaks loudly. It is suspicious in the least and vicious in the worst and, make no mistake, it isn't interested in our liberation because our freedom means its death. Indeed, that old mind is the old identity that we must surrender in order to discover who we are.

Yeshua calls to us: *Come to me. Trust. Have faith in me, not in your boat.*

His promise cannot fail: *If you ask for a fish, I will not give you a snake.*

His word to us is clear: *Perfect love casts out all fear* and *God is that love.*[50]

Therefore, have no fear. To fear that God might punish us for our questions is to vastly misunderstand His goodness. The reason why so few of the Muslims I grew up with would reconsider their dogma was because they feared God's punishment. But we have no need to entertain such fear, because our Father loves our questions as much as He loves us.

He will not give us a snake if we ask for a fish. He will not lead us into darkness if we ask for the light.

Furthermore, fear of being rejected by others is only to enslave ourselves to them—this has surely been one of my greatest struggles in life. History proves that anyone who questions their denomination's dogma brings down the wrath of those entrenched in that dogma. Every doctrine is a heresy in someone else's doctrine. And so it goes, round and round. The Internet is full of Christians who spew accusations or offer "holy" defense of their doctrine.

But we don't need to be concerned about what people think of us. What our Father thinks of us is all that matters. Our Father is infinitely gentle and, as Yeshua said, *He Himself is kind even to ungrateful and evil men.*[51] How much more does the Father smile on us when we seek the truth, however clumsy our search might seem?

When we humbly surrender our intellect's need for certainty, we find faith, the faith of a child in his Father. When we stop leaning on our own understanding, we become truly open to *knowing* God, rather than only *knowing about* Him.

I've never met a sixty-year-old who believes all the same things in every respect that he did when he was thirty. Not one. Views on child-rearing or love or judgment or a hundred other issues invariably change. Beliefs change. So let's not to be too dogmatic at any age. We might very well be arguing with a future version of our own selves.

Instead, may we extend grace to ourselves and to others, and take the journey alongside each other in humility. May we open ourselves up to knowing our Father intimately rather than defending what we think we know *about* Him.

We are in Christ and Christ is in us, as one. So we will ask the Holy Spirit to bring into our full awareness the life, the peace, the joy, and the love that are already our true nature in Christ. We will ask Yeshua to guide us, and we will trust Him. He will not lead us into danger. We will step out of the boat. It's the only way we will ever walk on the troubled waters in this life.

HOW TO EXPERIENCE THE MEDITATIONS

Do you remember Yeshua's parable of the great banquet to which the master invited all to come and dine? But everyone was too busy, yes? They had bought property and houses and had just gotten married and were thus too preoccupied to attend. They were on their honeymoon or celebrating the great blessings of this life. And so no one came to the banquet.

In Yeshua's parable, the master then called the outcasts to come, and they did. Their joy was made full.

It is said that Potential is Actualized through Intention and Devotion. PAID. As Yeshua said, we reap what we sow.

We can think of our Intention and Devotion to awakening into our identity as the son or daughter of the Father in the same way. We have been invited to see ourselves as our Father sees us and so feast at the table of peace, love, joy and power each day. The choice is ours to make each hour, each moment.

Are we too distracted to come? No. And so we devote ourselves to this great awakening for the joy set before us in this life.

To meditate, as the Scriptures say and as I use it in this guide, is to quiet the mind's incessant chatter and lies so the heart can hear truth. For he who has ears to hear, let him hear.

Each of the following meditations will take you only a few minutes to read. Twenty minutes in quiet contemplation each day is a very small investment to make in your transformation, and yet even this will reward you far more than you might expect. Find a quiet space the same time each morning or evening, and rest in the good news that will surely change the way you see God, yourself, and your world.

The meditations are organized in three sections: *The Truth, The Way,* and *The Life*. Each section contains seven meditations. These are by no means an exhaustive inquiry into the nature of all things, but rather an immersive journey into the heart of those staggering truths that set us free.

ALIGNMENT

I am the Vine, you are the branches
Remain in Me as I remain in you

At the end of each meditation you will find a simple exercise of *alignment*. To align is simply to come into the experience of who Yeshua says you are through agreement. It is to *see* and so *be* who you are in truth.

To align is to come into the vine truth, which is Christ in you. To remain in alignment is to abide in the vine and so to know Christ and the power of our resurrection in Him.

Here, our joy will be full, and *only* here, as He said. Here, we walk on the troubled waters of these lives and find peace, power and a staggering love for all.

Everything we say, do and think aligns us with darkness or light, love or grievance. Thus, everything is a spiritual practice, whether we are aware of it or not. We are constantly, in every moment, aligning with one way of being or another. The choice is ours to make each moment of each day.

You can also think of coming into alignment as coming into obedience with one system or the other. As a horse comes into alignment with its master, the two are in one fluid motion without conflicting wills. To the extent the horse resists, there is struggle for the horse. When we align with the truth, we lay down our resistance to who Yeshua says we are and so make Him our master. To make Him our master is for *us* to master this life, because we are one in Him and He in us, as one.

But when we resist the truth of who Yeshua says we are, we slip back into alignment with the old man and are mastered by fear or anxiety. We already are the light of the world. We already are one in and with Christ. *Christ is all*, Paul wrote in Colossians 3:11, speaking of all God's children. All includes you and me. Believing it, or aligning with this truth, becomes our journey now.

Oddly, Christians have no problem agreeing that we are *New Creatures* who are glorified, as Paul writes, but many have a problem with any notion of our divinity in Christ. They say that the old man we were is dead; that as new creatures we are the holy ones (saints) and have risen already in Christ. But they are afraid to say share in Christ's divine nature.

This, even though Peter makes it clear that we "participate or share in His divine nature" (2 Peter 1:4).

The human is not divine, naturally. Our fingernails and our bones are decaying and temporal, as Paul wrote, not divine or eternal. But our resurrected nature in Christ surely is divine. To deny this is to deny Christ in us. Yet we speak as if the new creatures we are, are somehow still separated from God and bound in a trance of wretched unworthiness.

Some theologians like to say, "Yes, we are glorified and complete because so many Scriptures make it plain, but that can't be. So we will say *already but not yet.*" Which is like saying "kinda-sorta, but not really."

But now we will say *really*. And awakening to that reality is what allows us to experience this life as Yeshua said we would, in His way. We might say, abiding in *the-vine* is to experience the *de-vine*. Christ in you. You in Him. One.

Think of yourself as an *aspect* of Christ. Not *the* Christ, but certainly a divine, new creation, who is one with and in Christ. We are not *equal* to God nor *are* we God. We are an aspect of Him in Christ. We share His divine nature.

This is what Christian means to us.

If we misunderstand who we are as the reborn ones, we will only continue to live in our old-man selves. When we abide in that old self, His love does not flow through us as He said it would. We become powerless, regardless of our dogma.

If Paul's and Yeshua's many claims of our true nature in Christ found in the meditations sound too good to be true at first, it's okay. The old mind can't fathom the great mystery of two becoming one and is rooted in the old law of condemnation and separation. But we *will* see as the eyes of our hearts are opened. Oh, how we will see! And as we do, our experience of life here on Earth is radically transformed.

Our journey now is bring our *jar-of-clay self* or *seen self* or *temporal self* or *tent self* or *outer-man* self (some of Paul's many terms for your body and brain) into alignment with our *new-creation self*, who I will choose to call our *eternal self.* Paul calls this process transformation. *Be transformed by the renewing of your mind.*

Eternal self is simply a term I have coined that means the true you who is risen and one in Christ. The eternal self is that identity that participates in Christ's divine nature. Our jar-of-clay or earthen vessel self, with all its personality and preferences, is a beautiful gift but is temporal and quickly gone, like dust in a breeze.

To align to your new-creation self or your *eternal self,* you get to let go of your identification with the *you* you've always thought of as you, a practice that Yeshua spoke about often in the most adamant of terms, as you will see.

We are far more than just our bodies and our brains, and as we awaken to our true identity in Christ—as we align ourselves with who our Father says we are—we will naturally find peace and power in the storms of this life. We will naturally begin to love all that He has created, including our bodies, as gifts given to enjoy rather than instruments that enslave us in condemnation and judgment.

Who do you experience yourself as mostly during each day? Your eternal self, or your earthen vessel self? When we align with our eternal, risen self, we are free. When we do not, we are captive once more.

And so our journey is to awaken into who we are as the sons and daughters of our Father, enabled by the power of the Spirit. It's the only way to *know* Him and so to experience His eternal life flowing through us during this life.

FINAL THOUGHTS

Remember that all teachings and guides are like road maps. They have many signposts and markings that point the way, but in the end, they are only a map.

We can look at the map, study the path, argue over the directions, and read or write endless blogs about the path. We can study all the markers and signposts, build shrines to them, wage wars over them, even worship them. Many do.

But we must remember that these meditations, like any guide, only point to Christ; the words, like all words and all Scriptures, are not Him. Christ is the Word and the Way, quickened in our hearts by the power of the Spirit.

We must each get on the road ourselves and go where the signposts direct us, or that map is useless to us. In the same way, this guide invites us to leave the shores of our old mind and venture into the river of transformational change to discover the mind of Christ in which love and peace have their dominion over all.

Do you remember the parable of the ten virgins?[52] Each was making her way to a great celebration with oil lamps, but five of the ten fell asleep and let their oil run dry. When the time came, these five had no flame to light their way.

The other five could not share their oil with those who had fallen asleep. Why? The simple meaning is plain: we cannot borrow the oil of our neighbor's transformation. Each of us is responsible for our own journey; we best not grow weary and fall asleep or we miss out on His banquet—the kingdom of heaven—which can be experienced by us today and always.

Keep in mind Yeshua's parable of the sower as well.[53] Once a seed of truth comes to us, the father of lies can snatch it away so that it doesn't take root. If that seed does take root, it can be choked out by the cares and worries of this world. Then it will not bear the lasting fruits of love, joy, and peace in our lives. But if we till the ground of our hearts and nurture and protect that seed, the truth will bear much fruit.

In the end, our Father, who is far greater than we can possibly imagine, will draw us to Him through His Spirit, even as we are drawn to Him now. In Him, we are far more loved and powerful than we can possibly imagine. The good news we will encounter on our journey is a bright sun that will chase away the dark clouds of our old mind, exposing the stunning truth. With new strength we can leave behind all of the vain lies that have enslaved us, and we will rush toward our Father. Let us be glad and hurry! We must not delay one more day.

Every step we take toward the truth is a giant leap in awakening. Simply becoming aware of who we are and why we do the things we do or feel the things we feel saves us years of struggle, even if we don't imMeditately experience the effects of that new awareness.

So let us continue our journey home, to the truth, every hour and every day.

It is the only journey that truly matters.

I write to myself and my children,
and to all the sons and daughters of the Father.
May we awaken to the only Truth, the only Way, the only Life.

THE
MEDITATIONS

I

THE TRUTH

Yeshua made it plain: *I am the Way, the Truth and the Life.*

In the first section we will enter seven meditations on the simplest *Truth* about, first, who the *Father* is (meditations 1-3) and, second, who *you* are, as the son or the daughter of the Father through Yeshua (meditations 4-7).

These constitute the first and second declarations of The Forgotten Way.

THE FIRST DECLARATION

God is infinitely good, *far more loving and gentle and kind to His children than any earthly mother or father imaginable.* **God is infinitely complete**; *nothing can threaten or disturb Him. Nothing can be taken away from Him, making Him less than complete, nor added to Him who is already complete.*

THE SECOND DECLARATION

You are remade in the likeness and glory of your Father, *finite yet already complete in union with Yeshua—you in Him and He in you, risen with Him and seated in heavenly places. Nothing can separate you from His love.*

ONE

LOOK! HOW MAGNIFICENT IS YOUR FATHER!

Then God said, "Let us make man in Our image, in Our likeness . . ." Then the Lord God formed man of dust from the ground, and breathed into his nostrils the breath of life; and man became a living being.

GENESIS 1:26; 2:7

For in him we live, and move, and have our being.

ACTS 17:28

MEDITATION

Let me tell you a story. A spiritual teacher is walking with a small boy in the savannah one sunny afternoon. He uses a walking stick because his bones aren't as strong as they once were. The child holds the old man's free hand because in the boy's eyes, the teacher is a giant and can save him from any danger.

Today's lesson is on God the Father. The teacher has brought the boy to a field frequented by lions. Seeing a pride under a tree, the teacher stops and points to a lion who stands alone, watching them. He turns to the boy.

"Imagine that God is a strong lion, and the accuser, representing all of evil, is a hyena," he says. "Tell me, can the hyena hurt the lion?"

"Yes," the boy says. "He can chase him and, with many others, take him down."

"Well then, let's make the lion bigger, because God is infinite. Let's make him as big as the field. The hyena, being finite, does not grow bigger. It is still the same size. Now can the hyena hurt the lion?"

The boy thinks for a moment. "Yes, he could bite the lion's foot," he says.

"Then let's make the lion bigger. As big as the whole savannah. Can the hyena now hurt the lion?"

The boy thinks hard for a long moment. "Well . . . Maybe . . ."

"Let's make the lion as big as the whole world and the hyena now only a tiny speck on the field. In fact, let's make the lion as big as all the worlds. As big as the whole universe. Now . . ." He turns to face the boy, staff planted in the dirt before him, his gaze steady. "Can the hyena on that field, who is still the same size, much smaller than a single atom on the surface of a billion suns, hurt the lion?"

"No," the boy says, eyes wide with wonder.

"Can the hyena threaten the lion?"

The boy shakes his head. "No."

The teacher looks off to the horizon and draws a deep breath through his nostrils. "Can the hyena even *bother* the lion?"

The answer is plain to the boy. "No," he says.

The teacher looks down and offers an approving nod. "Always remember, this is how big and powerful your Father is. The only thing bigger is His wisdom and His love for you, because God *is* love and you are His son. The hyena can only bother those who do not know who they are."

Where did you come from? What is your origin? But more, *who* is your Father? You must know the answer if you wish to experience your true identity on this earth.

You were fashioned in the image of God, who is Father, Son, and Spirit, and who spoke to *Himself* at the foundation of the world, saying, *Let us make man in Our image.* And thus, the Scripture tells us, you were made in the *likeness* of God.[1]

God is both infinitely transcendent and infinitely close, closer than your own breath. This we know when we taste and see that He is good. This we know from countless Scriptures.

But who was God before He first created the fabric of time and space and all that is in this universe? If God is infinitely perfect and complete now, has He not always been? Was He lacking before He created the world? Was He ever like so many false gods, frail and in need of completion, or lonely and in need of followers? No.

Furthermore, can anything be *added* to what is already infinitely complete and perfect? The answer is plain even to the old mind.

But even more, can anything be *taken away* from the One who is infinitely complete and powerful? Can God be compromised? Can any power anywhere make Him less than perfectly complete?

No. Nothing can be added to God, who is already infinite and complete in perfect love, and nothing can be taken away to diminish Him in any way. Ever.

Can anything even pose a true *threat* against such an infinite Being? Can He *feel* threatened? Can He *be* threatened? Is your Father vulnerable in any way? Does He fear and fret for His safety?

Can your all-knowing and complete Father ever expect one outcome and yet be surprised by another, as a god made in man's likeness might? Hoping for one outcome but getting something less brings disappointment. Your Father has known from eternity past all that will ever happen—so can He ever be disappointed?

Is this the weak Father you belong to? Never. Do you see how powerful and complete your Father is?

But let's take it even further. You know that God intimately knew you before the foundations of time and space. Before the beginning, He knew everything there is to know about you for all of eternity.[2]

Even at the foundation of the world, you existed in the mind of God as a thought. And God's thoughts are as real as any physical manifestation of them. Thus, outside of time and space, you have always existed. And in that same way, you were predestined before the foundations of the earth to be His son, His daughter.[3]

In the beginning was the Word. A word is the expression of thought. Everything that has ever existed (including you) was made by and through Him. In Him was life, and that life was the Light.[4] Thus, as Paul put it, in Him you live and move and have your being.[5]

Do you begin to see just how infinitely powerful your Father is? He is not a lesser god that has been made in the image of man's religion.

And as for evil, it is like that tiny, tiny, tiny hyena, barking its accusations against you and your Father, stalking those who will listen to its lies, consuming them with misery.

Don't try to comprehend God's magnificence—your brain is too small. Instead just rest in this one thought today, because it is enough to radically shift your perspective from anxiety to confidence that fills your life with joy.

Come to your Father as a child full of simple faith in His goodness. Be in awe. Be glad and rejoice. Do not fear. Nothing can hurt your Father nor you as His child.

CONTEMPLATION

Imagine that you are with your Father high in a castle. Together you sit at a banquet table spread with a feast of delights. But before you can eat, you hear the snorting of horses outside. Startled, you throw your chair back and hurry to the window. There you see marauders in black cloaks like wraiths, rushing for the walls.

Frantic, you run from window to window. "Father," you cry, trembling in fear. "The enemy is at the gate to destroy us!"

He looks over without rising and sees what you see. "Those?" He says with great calm. "They cannot hurt me." Your Father looks into your eyes. "And you are My son." He lets the statement settle and then nods at the table. "Sit with Me."

You blink once, remember who He is and who you are, and the sound of the rushing horses suddenly fades. By the time you reach the table, they are gone.

But of course! Who can prevail against your Father? Who can threaten Him? Who can even bother Him? No one. And you are His son; you are His daughter.

So be at peace. Return to sit with your Father at His banquet table once again.

PRAYER

Father, I come before You in humility and ask You: Are You vulnerable? Are You infinite? Are You afraid of what might attack and threaten You? I am often afraid. Am I safe as Your child, or do I need to protect myself? Can I trust You?

I thank You, Father, for Your glory and power. Nothing can change Your infinite intentions, nor threaten even a single desire in Your mind! I am in awe of You and what You have done in making me in Your likeness. What a beautiful, beautiful Father You are.

ALIGNMENT

That I might know my Father who cannot be threatened

As an analogy, think of alignment as you might resonating with a tuning fork. When you have two tuning forks in a room and one begins to vibrate, the other will also begin to vibrate if it's tuned to the same frequency. They resonate. They abide in each other's frequency.

As you align yourself with your infinite Father, you will resonate with His frequency—His character, His Being—as His son or daughter. This, now, is your journey of awakening to who you are. This is joining with His song in resonance.

As an illustration, think of your Father seated on a high mountaintop. There, His presence is like a tuning fork that vibrates in the frequency of infinite love and power.

We will call the valley below the mountain *the valley of the shadow of death*, in which darkness, although but a shadow, is experienced by you in the low frequency of a thousand fears and self-condemnation.

Your journey is to align yourself with Him, high and lifted up. On that mountain peak, there is no threat. No malice. No lack. Only light, love, joy and infinite creative power. On the mountain peak, your perspective of the valley below shifts dramatically. Peace floods your heart and mind.

In truth, your purpose isn't to escape this world by running up a mountain. Rather, your purpose is to experience your Father *in* this world. It's why you are here. Though you are not *of* this world, you are still *in* it, and for good reason. Our illustration of a mountain is only a useful way to think of alignment.

Align with your Father today. Join in His presence and resonate with His power and love today. In aligning yourself with Him, you will see that you, who are hidden in God with Christ, cannot be harmed.

Say this today: *Today, I say yes to aligning myself with my infinite Father, who cannot be threatened or ever compromised in any way. Today, I know that I am made of His fabric as an aspect of Him, in the world but not of it. As I align with my Father, I know myself as the son, the daughter of the Father.*

Oh, what manner of love is this that I should be called the son, the daughter of such a Father![6]

TWO

THERE IS NO FEAR IN LOVE

There is no fear in love; but perfect love casts out fear,
because fear involves punishment,
and the one who fears has not been perfected in love.
1 JOHN 4:18

Neither death nor life, neither angels nor demons,
neither the present nor the future, nor any powers,
neither height nor depth, nor anything else in all
creation, will be able to separate us from the love of God
that is in Christ Jesus our Lord.
ROMANS 8:38-39 NIV

MEDITATION

In the previous meditation you peered through a small window and began to see just how incomprehensible is your Father's infinite power. Now you will see how close and loving He is to you.

Before you can know who you are, you must know your Father. But when I say *know*, I do not mean to know *about*, rather to know *intimately*, which is what Yeshua meant when He said "this is eternal life, to *know* the Father."[1]

To *know* is to *experience*. A child, perhaps more easily than an adult, can know the Father this way even if he knows very little about the Father's dogma. In fact, dogma often gets in the way of experience. Perhaps this is why Yeshua said we must become like children, even infants[2], to know the Father and experience the goodness of eternal life now at hand.

Again, you can know all about an avocado, but until you taste it you don't really know it at all. When you actually taste Him, you will see that your Father is good.[3] Anything that is not good is not Him.

In a world gone mad with twisted visions of love and fear, it is easy to be blinded to your Father's unconditional love. When this happens you feel shame and separation, because blindness distorts what you think you know about Him.

Today you will see differently, because Yeshua came to bring sight to the blind. Open your eyes in the light of love, which has dispelled all darkness.

Consider what is written: *Perfect love casts out fear.* God, being perfect in love, cannot fear. It is said that all negative emotions are rooted in fear, and this is true. If so, what are God's feelings for you? How can God, who is infinite and cannot be threatened by anything so small as a finite evil, ever fear what cannot threaten Him?

Can He, who knows all things to come, fear a loss in the future? How small or big is the Father you have made God to be? And should you fear His punishment? *There is no fear in love . . . because fear has to do with punishment, and whoever fears has not been perfected in love.*[4]

As you grow in true love, you will fear less—your Father least of all. Indeed, you cannot truly love your Father and fear Him at the same time. *There is no fear in love.*

To be in *awe* of your Father is a beautiful thing, and this was how the fear of God was often understood by the ancient writers.[5] So be in awe of your Father's infinite love, which has cast your sin infinitely far from you, as far as the east is from the west.[6]

In spite of this, nearly everyone subconsciously fears a God whom we have tried to adequately serve and please. We are afraid of not measuring up to a Father who demands a standard far too high to be reached. Fearing we are never quite good enough for our Father, we keep Him distant and unapproachable.

The lie that you cannot measure up will create a terrible anxiety gap deep in your heart. This subconscious, insidious fear creates the feeling of vast separation between you and your Father.

Perhaps you fear your Father because you have made God in your own image. Maybe you see Him as an earthly father with undesirable human attributes. This view is deeply embedded in deception.

Do you think that your Father is like the worst of earthly fathers, given to fits of rage when He is upset? Is He impulsive and vindictive, in need of anger-management classes? Do you think your Father fears your failure or your mistakes and wrings His hands with worry?

If so, you've made God in an image of man and given Him a small heart, a God who loves His children even less than you might love your own precious infant. But this is in error. Have nothing to do with such low and destructive views of your infinite Father, regardless of who perpetuates those views.

Many people have been led to believe that Yeshua's primary purpose was to rescue them from the Father's wrath. But as Yeshua said, *If you have seen Me, you have seen the Father.*[7] Yeshua and your Father, though distinct, are one. If He and His Father are one, why would He need to save you from Himself?

What kind of children would draw intimately close to a Father from whose wrath they must be saved? Or what man can manipulate a woman to love him using fear?

How small and pitiful is the love of such a false god. This kind of "love" is not good news. This is the lie of Eden's serpent, which brings shame and judgment. This is the lie that leaves you secretly despising God, because you fear He would crush you.

It was because Yeshua knew that we would make God in our image that He said so plainly, *Call no man on Earth father, for your Father is in heaven.* Instead, begin to see your Father as Yeshua saw Him and so called Him *Abba. Daddy.*[8]

Today, unmake the god you have made in the image of any earthly Father, and let His infinite love cast out all of your fear of Him.

CONTEMPLATION

The good news of the Father will always awaken your desire to rush into His loving arms, because He alone truly accepts you as you are, right now, not only if you become something more.

The good news is that you are saved by what He has done, not by what you have or haven't done. The good news is that your Father's love for you is mind-numbing and sure to evoke stunned awe. As Paul wrote, *Neither death, nor life, nor angels, nor principalities, nor things present, nor things to come, nor powers, nor height, nor depth, nor any other created thing, will be able to separate us from the love of God, which is in Christ Jesus our Lord.*[9]

What is true love as characterized by Yeshua? A love that is kind to those who resist you and are cruel to you, because, as He said, even evil men love those who love them in return. But true love turns the other cheek.

Does your Father not also turn His cheek in the same way He asks you to, or does He, like the gods made by the world, seek an eye for an eye and require your love to show you a conditional love?

What is true love as characterized by Paul? It isn't provoked by others and keeps no record of wrong. Does your Father not love you with this same kind of love that He asks you to love others?

Are you unsure that you can be loved so unconditionally? Then go to your Father and ask Him if He loves you this way. When you feel His love, you will begin to acquire that same kind of love for yourself and be able to love others as yourself.

God is staggering in His precision and completion. Nothing about you remotely resembles a mistake. If you were the only human alive, He would be flowing with rivers of love and pride in you and for you.

Think of the most loving father of a baby just learning to walk. The child stumbles and scrapes her knee, but is the father disappointed in her? Is he upset by her?

Imagine that child knocking over a small vase that she's been warned not to touch. Does he scream at the child, outraged at the mess? Imagine that child now six years old, learning to tie her shoes. If she fails, does the father slap her across the room?

Never! And how much more does your true Father love you?

See yourself as that small child learning to walk, to navigate the Father's house, to tie shoes. Your Father will come to you and gently lift you up and show you a better way.

PRAYER

Father, thank You for Your inexhaustible love, from which nothing can remove me. I worship You and You alone, not the fiction of a lesser Father. I have no words to express my awe for You. Never again will I see You as my earthly father or any earthly father. I am now Your son, Your daughter, and I always will be. I stand in awe of Your beauty, Your kindness, Your overwhelming love seen in the Light. Open my eyes that I might see You as Yeshua sees You, that I might call You Abba.

ALIGNMENT

That I might know my Father, and know no fear

At any given time you choose to align yourself with either the flow of love, or the shadows of fear. The choice is yours. But you know this: God is love and in Him there is no fear. You are the light of the world, complete in Christ in whom there is no darkness. Love is who your Father is and who you are in Christ. So today you will choose to align your experience of this life with your Father and with your eternal self in Christ.

As you climb up the mountain to align with your Father in our analogy, you will see that fear resides only in the valley of the shadow of death from which you rise. There is no fear in love, because perfect love has cast out all fear.

Say this today: *Today, I make my claim in agreement with Yeshua that I am reborn of my Father who is love and light. In Him I have no fear. Only my old mind still feels fear and insecurity as I align with it in the valley below. But today, I rise up the mountain and I align myself instead with who I am as the son, the daughter of my Father.*

In this, I say yes to my experience of who I truly am, free from all fear. In this, I say yes to Christ and to myself as the new creation in Christ.

THREE

THE STORY OF YOUR FATHER

You prepare a table before me . . .
Your goodness and love will follow me all the
days of my life, and I will dwell in
the house of (my Father) forever.
PSALM 23:5-6 NIV

MEDITATION

The previous meditation began to explore the vastness of your Father's love for you. Though the father of lies wants you to believe that your Father is like a human father whose love is conditional, this lie will enslave you in a prison of doubt and fear.

Consider the Father once more, this time through Yeshua's view of the Father in a story He told about the kingdom of heaven and two prodigal sons. Read it carefully, even if you've heard it before.

There was a father who had two sons. The younger one said to his father, "Father, give me my share of the estate." So the father divided his property between them. The younger son then set off for a distant country and there squandered his wealth in wild living.

After he had spent everything, there was a severe famine in that whole country, and the younger son began to be in need. So he went and hired himself out to a citizen of that country, who sent him to his fields to feed pigs. He longed to fill his stomach with the pods that the pigs were eating, but no one gave him anything.

When the son came to his senses (some translations read *came to himself*) *he said . . . "I will set out and go back to my father and say to him: Father, I have sinned against heaven and against you. I am no longer worthy to be called your son; make me like one of your hired servants." So he got up and went to his father.*

While he was still a long way off his father saw him and was filled with compassion for him. He ran to his son, threw his arms around him, and kissed him. The son said to him, "Father, I have sinned against heaven and against you. I am no longer worthy to be called your son."

But the father said to his servants, "Quick! Bring the best robe and put it on him. Put a ring on his finger and sandals on his feet. Bring the fattened calf and kill it. Let's have a feast and celebrate. For this son of mine was dead and is alive again; he was lost and is found." So they began to celebrate.

Meanwhile, the older son was in the field. When he came near the house, he heard music and dancing. The older brother became angry and refused to go in. So his father went out and pleaded with him. But he answered his father, "Look! All these years I've been slaving for you and never disobeyed your orders. Yet you never gave me even a young goat so I could celebrate with my friends. But when this son of yours who has squandered your property with prostitutes comes home, you kill the fattened calf for him!"

"My son," the father said, "you are always with me, and everything I have is yours. But we had to celebrate and be glad, because this brother of yours was dead and is alive again; he was lost and is found" (Luke 15:11-32, NIV).

This is *your* Father as well. How gracious and loving He is.[1]

Consider: The father's younger son wanted to find himself apart from his father's house, so he asked his father for his portion of the estate. He needed to finance his journey, you see.

This is what happens when you seek identity and significance apart from your Father, even though you already have everything in Him.

The father, knowing his son would lose his way, could have discouraged him. He could have been filled with anger and dread. Instead, he allowed his son to take the journey without condemnation.

Consider: The first prodigal indeed lost his way, then came to himself; he returned, expecting to grovel like a servant. Though the son condemned and berated himself, sure that he was unworthy to be called a son any longer, the father rejoiced. His son, who once was dead to his true identity as a son, was now alive to it. Rather than join his son's condemnation, the father ran to him while he was still far away, threw his arms around him, put his robe on his son's back, a ring on his finger, and ordered a great feast of celebration.

The second son, having been faithful to the father all along, condemned the first son and so refused to enter his father's house. Judgment made this young man the second prodigal. But the father judged neither one of them. He longed to feast with both of them, because all he had was theirs, as he said.

Yeshua clearly tells us that *the Father judges no one.* And He follows up this radical statement with more: *Neither will I accuse you before the Father. Your accuser is Moses* (the law) *in whom your hopes are set.*[2]

But that law, as Paul wrote, came into being so that our failure in trying to live up to it would increase our transgression and we would all see that our only hope is to depend on the Father's grace.[3]

This is the fulfillment of the law: its failure to accomplish what only grace can through Yeshua.[4]

The Father judges no one. He will lovingly correct us, even as a mother would lovingly correct her young child learning to walk, and you might call this judgment. But His correction never takes the form of angry retribution like an earthly father's correction might. It simply directs you in the way of walking and then running and then flying.[5] Even as the child of an earthly father is born to run, so you, the child of God, are born to fly. His correction will guide you so that you can.

In the story of the father, the loving father offered no wrath, no judgment, only correction of his son's self image. *You* are *worthy to be called my son!* He offered no punishment, only an embrace, a kiss, a robe, a ring, sandals, and a feast.

So the son went into the father's banquet, and they feasted together in delight. Truly, in the father's eyes, the robe and the ring were always the son's to wear. The house was the son's to enter, and the table was his at which to feast.

When you are like the first son, searching for yourself in all the world, remember your beautiful Father. He holds your robe and your ring and your seat at His table even now, eagerly awaiting you to celebrate who you truly are, *right now.*

When you are like the second son, condemning others, remember that your Father pleads for you to join in His banquet of delight.

CONTEMPLATION

Think of the world of flesh and law as the system of the world in which *for every action there is an equal and opposite reaction,* which is one of the laws of physics we all learn in school. In this world you know that you will reap what you sow. So if you hit your finger with a hammer, that finger will break or bruise and throb with pain, right? In truth, you hit your fingers with hammers all the time, whenever you do something that harms you, body, mind and soul.

But make no mistake, neither your Father nor Yeshua judges you for hitting your finger with that hammer. The *hammer* judges you, and how ruthless is that judgment.

If you don't want a broken finger, stop hitting it with a hammer because you will indeed reap what you sow. If you eat too much, you will suffer the consequences; if you get angry at other Christians for their doctrine, you only feel the misery of your own anger; if you tear down your spouse, you only slash at your own heart; if you ingest the wrong chemicals, your body and mind will pay a price.

So stop it. Or don't. You can either stop hitting yourself or not, depending on how much pain you want to inflict on yourself.

Both prodigal sons in Yeshua's story inflicted pain on themselves, one by chasing the pleasures of the world apart from his father and one through judgment. Both suffered as a result. But the father judged neither.

Yeshua's call to you is clear: rather than hurting yourself, rush to your Father's table because He doesn't judge you and His table is set with the finest foods and fruits that will give you life rather than misery.

Either way, you are loved as the son, the daughter of the Father who judges no one. *Remember, what you believe about yourself never defines you; only what your Father believes about you truly defines you.*[6] *Your beliefs and perceptions, however, do define the experience you have in this world.*[7]

Today, as you are drawn to return to your Father's side, rush to Him without fear. How long will you wallow in your own self-condemnation while your Father awaits to celebrate your identity as His son, His daughter? The Father's only correction will be to reaffirm His son's place through an extravagant display of position and celebration.

Waste no time. Rejoice today in your communion with your Father.

PRAYER

Merciful, infinite Father, I enter into Your holy realm today and sit at the table spread for me. Surely Your goodness and love follow me all the days of my life. Never again will I fear Your rejection of me as Your son. Never again will I doubt Your unending love and kindness.[8]

For I am Your son, I am Your daughter. Nothing in heaven or on Earth can separate me from Your love. You are my Father, infinite in love and power, unchanging forever, threatened by none.

Today I will rest in the knowledge of what is true.[9]

Today I will not forget who my Father truly is.

ALIGNMENT

That I might know my Father, and myself as His son, His daughter

Your view of your Father will necessarily determine your view of your own identity. Aligning your view of yourself with *His* vision of you will dramatically shift your experience of life in the valley of the shadows below, called *this world* in our illustration of the mountain.

Today bring your own perception of reality in alignment with His. Know that all He has is yours, as He says. Know that His ring is upon your finger already; His robe is upon your back.

There, in the high place, His presence is like a banquet spread before you, and there you will feast on love, joy, and peace.

You are His son, His daughter, and you always will be no matter what valley you find yourself in now. Your eternal self is already hidden with Christ in your Father, as one. That is who you are.

Feast with your Father at His table of delights in alignment today and be saved from the shadows of death in the valleys of this life.

FOUR

THE STORY OF YOU

The First Adam

Then God said, "Let us make man in Our image,
according to Our likeness, and let them rule over (the
world)." Then the Lord God formed man of dust from the
ground and breathed into his nostrils the breath of life . . .
The Lord God commanded the man, saying, " . . . From
the tree of the knowledge of good and evil you shall not eat."
GENESIS 1:26; 2:7, 16-17

The Second Adam

The first man Adam became a living being
(and brought death)
the last Adam became a life-giving spirit
(and died to restore life).
1 CORINTHIANS 15:45 ESV

You

Therefore just as through one man sin entered the world
. . . even so through one act of righteousness
there resulted justification of life to all.
ROMANS 5:12, 18

MEDITATION

As we have seen, to know who you are, you must first know who your Father is—infinite and loving beyond comprehension.

Now let me tell you the story of your own origin.

In the beginning, the Word was with God and the Word was God, and all that exists was made by the Word—the expression and manifestation of God in and through His Son, Yeshua. God, being infinitely complete and needing nothing, spoke to Himself and said, let *Us* fashion mankind in *Our* own likeness.

So God formed the first Adam from the earth and *breathed* His likeness, His Word, into this man.[1]

By breathing His life into mankind, God glorified His identity on Earth, saying, *I have glorified My name.* And thus Adam, although not *the Son of God* became *the son of God*, as Luke writes.[2]

Adam and Eve, though they were not God, were made in the *likeness* of God. Made like God, they became the manifestation of God's identity on Earth.[3] In Eden, that garden of perfection, they shared their Father's will. In other words, they were aligned with God in heart and mind.

Thus the first Adam, as the son of God, *knew* God. He was intimate with God, walking with Him in the garden, knowing God as closely as a man knows his wife. Adam and Eve had no grievance against anything because they knew only goodness. They knew only light and no darkness. They experienced no shame of being naked, no judgment of good or evil. Nothing was better or worse than anything else. The Father's will was done on Earth as it was in heaven.

They ate from the Tree of Life; they tasted (experienced) the very nature of God and saw (perceived) that He was good. Indeed, in Him *there is no darkness.*[4] And they, being in the likeness of God, were also in the light. They were only good.

But there came a deceiver, the father of lies, in the form of a serpent that told them they could be *like* God if they ate the fruit of the knowledge of good and evil against the will of their Father. This was the serpent's first lie, because they already *were* like God, you see. They were already made in His likeness.

Think of the fruit of this knowledge as large and two-toned. Half of it is as black as the deepest night, and half as bright as a million suns. This fruit is the knowledge of separation, of opposites, of judgment, of good and evil.

Seduced by the prospect of being equal to God, Adam and Eve thought, *Not Your will but mine*, and they consumed the knowledge of good and evil.

And when they did, their eyes were opened to darkness. No longer did they experience only light. Blinded to the light, they imMeditately judged themselves (shame) and blamed each other (judgment).[5] This is how darkness—also called evil, blindness, or grievance and judgment—overtook the world through the first Adam.

When you were born, millennia later, you suffered the consequence of Adam's decision. You had no choice in the matter. How powerful then was Adam's choice. His one act enslaved every human soul.

But this descent into darkness is only the first half of your story. The second half brings good news that undoes the darkness.

Because there was another Adam, far more powerful than the first. The second Adam, named Yeshua.

Yeshua, the very Word that first spoke everything into existence, came as Light to shine into all of the darkness.[6]

Yeshua came to put the first, fallen Adam in you to death and restore your identity in your Father. When Yeshua approached His death on Earth, He cried for all to hear, *Father, glorify Your name* (Your identity). And a voice from heaven, sounding like thunder, said, *I have glorified My name* (His identity in making mankind in His likeness) *and will glorify it once more.*[7]

So it was that Yeshua went to the second garden, called Gethsemane, to undo what Adam had done in the first garden, called Eden, so that the Father's identity could be glorified in mankind once more.

There, in great travail and trembling before the Father, Yeshua reversed the first Adam's choice. Where the first Adam had said, *Not Your will but mine*, Yeshua said, *Not My will but Yours.*

Having surrendered His own will, He went willingly to the cross. There He echoed David's cry in Psalm 22: *My God, my God, why have you forsaken me?*[8] Did Yeshua think God had forsaken Him? No. Rather, He was identifying with all of humanity's lament, feeling separated from God. And like David, who reversed his lament in that same Psalm, so Yeshua fulfilled David's prophetic declaration by putting that lament to death once and for all, crying out for all to hear, *It is finished!*[9]

So the first Adam in you died with Yeshua, making the way for you, a new creature, to rise from the grave with Yeshua. This is how you have been restored to the Father's glory and likeness once more.

More, Yeshua also restored the realm of heaven on Earth. He set you free from the law of sin and death and restored you to the law of life, as it was in the garden before the fall.[10]

It could be said that where God put man in the garden long ago, He has now put the garden into man, to experience communion with and in Him. He has made you the light of the world with Him. You are the son, the daughter of the Father *with* Him.[11]

In the beginning, God glorified His identity (His name) by creating man in His likeness. In Yeshua's resurrection, God glorified Himself a second time by restoring you to His likeness. This is what the Father meant when He said, *I have glorified My name and will glorify it again.*[12]

And He did, by restoring His identity in you through Yeshua. Can you see the glory of Yeshua's death and resurrection?

Life comes only through Christ—there is no other way. He alone is the Truth, the Way, the Life. No man may know the Father but by Him. He is the only path.

Is Yeshua *less* powerful than the first Adam, who brought death to all? Who is Adam that anyone could think he has more power than Yeshua? Who is the serpent that you should cringe under his lies? Yeshua crushed that serpent's head and brought life to you.

As it is written: *Just as* (in the same way that) *through one man sin* (darkness) *entered the world . . . even so through one act of righteousness* (Yeshua's Light) *there resulted justification of life to all.*

Do you see how powerful Yeshua's victory was in crushing the curse of Adam? As the son or the daughter of the Father, your reunification with God in Yeshua is as certain as your fall. Anyone who suggests that Yeshua's power to restore is less than Adam's power to condemn clings to the same lie that first deceived Adam.[13]

Yeshua came as Light into all darkness. He undid the great deception and restored the world to fellowship with the Father. We now see God as in a mirror, and later, face to face.[14]

So rejoice in the certainty of your own salvation! You have been restored by Yeshua, whose unshakable power has far more authority than the first Adam or the serpent.

This is your story, the one so easily forgotten.

Yeshua, the anointed One, crushed death in one fell swoop. He redeemed all that was lost to the Father. He is the Light who gives you the eyes to see once more if you so choose. In Yeshua, you too are now the light of the world. Because of Him you may once again taste from the tree of life and see that your Father is only good.

CONTEMPLATION

But the news is even better than this. Because, as it is written, the Lamb of God (Yeshua) was slain *before* the universe was formed. And if Yeshua was crucified before the foundation of the world, He surely rose then, before time began. How is this possible? Because in the realm of eternity, there is no time.[15]

More, you were destined to be in Him *before* the world was formed.[16] How secure are you, then, chosen in Him before time began.

And, having been restored, it might be said that only blindness now prevents you from seeing who you truly are in Yeshua. As you come to your senses, like the prodigal son, and realize who you are as the son or the daughter of the Father, you will experience Him once more, like that same son.

No matter what you have done (judged your brother) or not done (refused to sit at your Father's table), the banquet feast awaits your choice at this very moment. You are joined with Yeshua because He has restored you.

So then, awaken from your sleep, because the news of Yeshua, the second Adam, and the story of who you truly are in Him, right now, is good indeed.

PRAYER

Father, beautiful Father, words cannot express my awe over how You fashioned me in Your likeness. Yeshua, my Savior, my life, what You have done staggers me and leaves me breathless before You. I was lost, but now I am found; blind, but now I see more clearly. And what I see is far too good for my corrupted mind to fathom!

All of creation will fall before You in awe for what You have done. You created this world, then entered it as a human so that I might once again walk in Your garden, with You and in You, in the Father, in the Holy Spirit.

Open the eyes of my heart to see as I bow before You today.

ALIGNMENT

That I might know Christ and the power of His resurrection
That I might know Christ and the power of my resurrection in Him

Today, align yourself with the reality that there is no struggle in Christ. There is no darkness in light. It is finished. Although you may choose to experience the darkness in the valley below the mountain, it holds no power but that which you give it. Death is now but a shadow. It is finished! The victory is already won.

All that remains is your choice in any given moment to align with the truth of who you are in the light, or not. Awaken to who you are, a new creature, the *eternal self*, risen and glorified and complete in Him as the light of the world already.

Say this today: *Today I will choose to awaken to a life of peace in the storm, free of all struggle, because that struggle is finished. As I align myself to this truth, I experience love and joy and peace in the face of all that would seem to deny the truth of who I am as the son, the daughter of my Father.*

Today, it is finished. And I claim my freedom from all deception that would say otherwise.

It is finished. Death has no sting; it is only a shadow. I can see the shadow or I can see the light. Today I choose to align with and see the light, because it is as Yeshua told me: I am the light of the world. His words do not lie. I am risen, I am glorified, I am the light of the world because Yeshua says I am.

FIVE

SEEING WHO YOU ARE

*I have been crucified with Christ; and it is no longer I
who live, but Christ lives in me.*
GALATIANS 2:20

*And God raised us up with Christ and seated us with
him in the heavenly realms in Christ.*
EPHESIANS 2:6 NIV

*If anyone is in Christ, he is a new creation. The old has
passed away; behold, the new has come. There is therefore
now no condemnation for those who are in Christ. In
Him you have been made complete.*
2 CORINTHIANS 5:17 ESV; ROMANS 8:1 ESV;
COLOSSIANS 2:10

MEDITATION

Draw close once again to the Father with your renewed mind and reborn sight. Your path is not to change who you are in Christ, but to see and know yourself as you already are in Him. You cannot *experience* who you are until you first *see* who you are.

Seeing who you are right now, as your Father sees you, is the means of true sight, which is enabled by the Holy Spirit, who is your helper.

The first glimpse you have of yourself as your Father sees you will surely still your heart. Few Christians ever see who they truly are in Yeshua and so remain blind on their journey, but the time has come for you to see more clearly.

So then, how does your Father see you right now?

Remember: you were formed by the very breath of God in His likeness. God is spirit, and those who fellowship with Him do so in spirit (as spiritual beings) and in truth (through Yeshua, who is Truth). As we will explore in part two, you are not primarily a physical being having spiritual experiences; you are primarily a spiritual being, born of the breath of God, having a physical, temporal experience in your body, which is a wonderful and blessed temple of His Spirit and yours.[1]

Remember: you have always been *complete,* known in the mind of God and chosen in Him even before the foundation of the earth. Then, seduced by the serpent of lies, the first Adam tasted the fruit of the knowledge of good and evil and entered a kind of madness called sin, which is the darkness that separates us from the light. Blindness. As a result, you came into the world lost, able to see nothing but the darkness of that separation, which condemns and judges and wallows in shame.

Remember: Yeshua, the second Adam, reversed the effects of the fall and brought you back into the same fellowship you had with the Father before time began. That correction has been made. It is finished, as Yeshua said before He breathed His last. It is complete.

Remember: in truth, as Paul wrote, nothing can separate you from the love of God in Christ.

And yet, even having believed, you still often find yourself blind, groping around in darkness, condemning yourself and your brothers, clinging to those things that have promised to give you significance and acceptance in this life.

There is a teaching of Yeshua that confounds everyone but those who see with new eyes. He said, *Be perfect, as your Father in heaven is perfect.*[2] Why does Yeshua ask perfection of you who are fallen? How can He expect you to become perfect in this life? Would He ask the impossible?

But He did not say *become* perfect. He said *be* perfect. And that mystery is unveiled in Yeshua Himself. For you are now in Him, and He is perfect.

This is the great mystery of reconciliation on the cross. Although you have heard that Yeshua died *for* your sin, which is true, you must now hear a truth far too counterintuitive to be grasped with the mind alone. It is this: you died *with* Yeshua.

Hear your brother Paul: *I have been crucified **with** Christ; it is no longer I who live, but Christ lives in me.*[3]

See what Paul saw. The old you that was born as son of Adam no longer lives. But your flesh tricks the old mind into thinking it does, and so you stumble in darkness, blinded by the world to your true identity.

And this is only the beginning. Paul, caught up in the heavenly dimensions, saw an even greater mystery. Hear his emphatic declaration: *And God raised us up **with** Christ and seated us **with** Him in the heavenly realms in Christ.*[4]

Do you see? You were indeed crucified *with* Yeshua. You were raised *with* Him. And you now are seated with Him and in Him in the heavenly realms—the Father's realm, which is now closer to you than your very breath.

As Paul wrote to the Romans: *For those whom He foreknew, He also predestined to become conformed to the image of His Son, so that He would be the firstborn among many brethren; and these whom He predestined, He also called; and these whom He called, He also justified; and these whom He justified, He also glorified.*[5]

Do you see? You were foreknown and destined to be who you are now: conformed to the likeness of Christ, justified and glorified.

Remember, Paul characterized himself as the foremost of sinners. Paul, the man who said he had not attained the perfection of fully knowing and experiencing his union with Christ, still insisted that we were one with Him and in Him. Paul, a man who struggled with thorns in his flesh, made it clear that he was already glorified with and in Christ.[6]

Think on this staggering truth: *You are in Yeshua.*

You were raised not only *with* Him, but *in* Him. As such, you are a new creature. Old things have passed away; all things have become new for you. There is therefore no condemnation for you. You have been made complete.[7]

Read Paul's words and let them sink into your heart: *See to it that no one takes you captive through philosophy and empty deception, according to the tradition of men, according to the elementary principles of the world, rather than according to Christ. For in Him all the fullness of Deity dwells in bodily form, **and in Him you have been made complete**, and He is the head over all rule and authority (Colossians 2:8-10).*

And what is complete but that which no longer needs any correction? Are you complete in Christ, or are you incomplete? Are you glorified or not glorified? Let's be clear—it is finished; you are glorified and made complete already. Only your awareness and experience of that completeness are in any way lacking.

You are complete. Not *perhaps*, or *maybe*, or *sort of*. Not in any kind of esoteric doctrinal way, but truly, really. In a more real way than the accuser—who trades in the traditions of men and empty philosophy—wants you to know. Any other teaching is deception.

Can this be true? To be complete in Yeshua, who is perfect, is to *be* perfect, or He Himself would not truly be complete. Is this how your Father truly sees you now, even as you read these words? Yes.

You may ask, then who or what is this person called (your name), who is filled with shame and fear of loss and is prone to illness?

Again, our truest selves reside in what Paul calls an *earthen vessel* or a *jar of clay*, which is temporary and will pass away,[8] as we will soon see.

In the next life you will have a "spiritual body," as Paul wrote, but in this life your body is temporal. Make no mistake, your physical body is a beautiful gift, the temple of the Spirit, neither evil nor inconsequential as claimed by the Gnostics. It is wondrous, conceived of by the mind of God, precisely crafted by an infinite Creator.

It is also, like all things that are seen in material form, bound by the laws of physics (thus physical) and is already decaying as you sit reading these words. It will not last in its current form any more than Paul's physical body lasted. In truth, it is dying already and will return to the ground soon.

But what is eighty years in the scope of eternity? No more than a blink of an eye. This is the lifespan of Paul's and your own earthen vessel. Like a costume, it will soon be shed and fall to the ground.

Your spiritual being, on the other hand, is eternal. The eternal you, seen with the eyes of the spirit, is, with Christ, the light of the world, already seated in heavenly places and glorified in Him.

As you become intimately aware of your eternal self in Yeshua, you will soar in that light. When you forget, you will find yourself stumbling in darkness.

Will you place your primary identification in your eternal, risen self, or will you still identify primarily with your earthen vessel and all that is temporal?

CONTEMPLATION

It could be said that the only problem you will ever face in this life is failing to truly believe in the name of Yeshua. But many of us have misunderstood what it means to "believe in the name" or to "believe in Yeshua." Even the demons believe that Yeshua is the Son of God, and it profits them nothing.[9]

In the time of Yeshua, a name was one's full *identity*. To believe in the name of Yeshua means to put your identity in His identity. It means to trust that Yeshua has remade and renamed you through His death and resurrection (and yours with His). Place your identity in His and you will be saved from fear in the storms of this life, because in Him, you are safe.

Or would you rather undermine the resurrection by saying Yeshua did not make you complete in Him? Would you deny the full power of the cross and your resurrection with Yeshua?

In so doing you confess only a form of godliness while denying its power.[10] If you deny the truth of who you are, you will project your own self-condemnation and guilt on the world. You will be enticed to look for salvation in all the empty promises of this world or through a false kind of religion.

There is no need to remain captive to these deceptions.[11] When you dare believe the truth of who you are now, you will no longer cling to all manner of vain imaginations. You will stop looking for what you think this world can offer to save you, for you are *already* complete in Him—beautifully complete.

Then, as promised by Yeshua again and again, you will learn to master this life rather than be mastered by it. Then you will walk in freedom and relish all of creation and its many gifts for you rather than be enslaved by them.

Again, your true identity cannot be understood with your intellect alone. Don't try to grasp it with your old mind. You are saved by grace through faith, and to have faith is to trust what your natural eyes cannot see. The eyes of faith grant you a new kind of sight, an ability to see who you truly are.[12]

What great love the Father has lavished on you! See yourself through clear eyes as your Father sees you, and all of life will change in one instant, because you will love yourself as He loves you in the light of the second Adam. Give in to blindness and you will see the darkness and shame of the first Adam.

Seizing its opportunity, the accuser joins your lower nature and screams at you, knowing that if you see the truth of your true identity, you will be instantly freed from your suffering.

Paul was no madman; he saw the truth. Indeed, Adam became a madman, but his error has been undone by Yeshua. It is time to see as

Paul saw, stripped of that madness called darkness, then caught up in the realm of the Father.

Paul was blinded when the light of Christ took his sight for three days so that he could see beyond this world. Do you remember what Yeshua said to him, speaking as Light itself on the road to Damascus? *I am sending you to them to open their eyes and turn them from darkness to light.*[13]

Allow the Spirit to reveal *that* light to you.

When you see clearly, the idea of searching the darkness for a way through this life will seem absurd. For you will know that you have already found the Way. His name is Yeshua. In Him you are now complete.

Who, then, condemns you? Neither your Father nor Yeshua. Only yourself, your brothers, and the accuser.[14]

Today is another day for liberation from the accuser's lies, which have held you captive in the darkness though you are already in the light. The prison door is open and you are free. Open your eyes and see.

See who you are, then *be* who you are: safe at your Father's side with and in Yeshua, perfect, even as your Father is perfect.

PRAYER

Thank You, Father, for the great gift of salvation, which has made me complete. I am in awe that You would restore me to Your side as Your own. I will now trust only in You.

Yeshua, my sight is blinded far too often by the lies the world shows me. Even my brothers whisper their doubt. I long to see myself only as You see me. My trust is in You and no other because I am in You and You are in me.

Holy Spirit, quiet the voice of the accuser, who denies my identity by speaking his endless lies. Offer me comfort. May I hear only Your truth and walk in Your peace, which surpasses all understanding.

Today I stand whole and complete, for I am new, I am risen, I am in Christ.

ALIGNMENT

That I might know Christ and the power of His resurrection
That I might know Christ and the power of my resurrection with Him

Think once more of the mountain top on which your Father's presence resonates in the infinite frequency of love and peace and creative power. And think of you, still walking through the valley of the shadow of death below the mountain top. You have longed to climb there, to His side , and to feast at His banquet of delight, devoid of fear and anxiousness.

But today you awaken to a staggering truth that takes your breath away. You are already there on that mountain top, hidden with Christ in your Father, in union with Him!

You are there in Christ. And He is here with you, in the valley, as one. In truth you are already risen and glorified with Him. This is your eternal self. It is who He says you are.

In reality, your truest self has no fear because she *is* the light of the world and *is* love and *is* glorified already! There is no fear in love.

In reality, she is not even a she, because there is no male or female in Christ. In reality, she, who is you, is seated in that heavenly place already at perfect peace in this very moment. That is who you are.

You experience the fear of darkness—the shadow of death—in the valley below only because your old human self, or low self, or earthen vessel self, still clings to identification with the valley of shadows below. You have placed your faith in them. But those shadows are only deceptions that blind you to who you are as the new, risen, eternal self.

Yeshua does not lie. You are in Him and He is in you as one. You are risen. You are glorified. Follow Him or follow another, the choice is yours. But we will follow Yeshua.

As you align with your Father, and with Christ, and with your self in Christ, you will resonate in one song, one frequency, one light, one love—that staggering, infinite power that changes your perception of all that you see on the horizon beneath you in that valley called this world.

Today you can choose to follow the Way who is Christ by aligning your identity with your eternal self who is risen with Christ. The old you is dead and you experience struggles only because you still believe in that old you, rather than believing in the name of Christ and who you are in Him.

Say this today: *I have risen with Christ. It is no longer the old me who lives. I am glorified and complete. Today I align myself with the name—the identity—of Christ and myself in union with Him.*

In doing so, I come into alignment with who He says I am. In doing so I believe in the name of Christ.

SIX

THE GREAT MYSTERY

The Father . . . will give you another Helper . . .
that is the Spirit of truth. In that day you will know that
I am in My Father and you in Me
and I in you.
JOHN 14:16-17, 20

Father, the glory which You have given Me
I have given to them,
that they may be one, just as We are one; I in them
and You in Me . . . that the world may know You sent
Me, and loved them, even as You have loved me.
JOHN 17:22-23

MEDITATION

There is no greater gift you can possibly hope for or receive in this life than to know and abide in Yeshua's staggering declaration of who you are. To know this is to experience the eternal realm flowing with love and peace. All struggle ceases with the awareness and experience of this truth.

Through Paul's words you have heard that the old you died with Yeshua and that you rose with Him as a new creature.

You have heard that, being saved in the next life, your journey now is to find peace and power in this life by aligning your identity with and in Yeshua.

And now hear an even deeper truth about you and Yeshua.

He said, *I am in the Father and he is in me.* And to make it perfectly clear He also said, *If you have seen me, you have seen the Father.* The Father and the Son and the Holy Spirit are one.[1] We call this the mystery of the Trinity, which defies all logic but is true. Three distinct aspects or personalities of one, each unique but in no way separate. The human mind bound by space and time is incapable of understanding this mystery.

An analogy might be found in nature. In the realm of subatomic particles, quantum physics shows us that all atoms and subatomic particles can be and are in more than one place at the same time. Furthermore, one thing can be two different things at the same time. Not just in theory, but truly. The fact that they are not bound by space or time also defies all logic, like the Trinity. Yet this reality manifests in all of nature as one of the core underpinnings of quantum mechanics.[2]

Einstein called this "spooky science," and even he could not accept it. How could one thing be in two places at the same time? Following his death, however, the theory was proven, not once, but many thousands of times. It's happening all the time, everywhere. Indeed, it could be said that the theory of quantum mechanics is now the most proven of all scientific theories. It is as certain as the truth that the earth is a sphere, round rather than flat.

And yet no one knows *how* it works. It just does. Without quantum mechanics, there would be no televisions or computers or cell phones. Almost all of modern technology is based on it, even though it makes no sense to the natural mind, which is limited by the linear dimension of time and space. Yet scientific observation and evidence demonstrates its reality in staggering fashion.

In a similar way, the Trinity is at the heart of Christianity even though it defies logic. Few Christians talk about the Trinity because it seems to be an impossibility. And yet our faith rests on it; it is perfectly true and, indeed, it is the only way that Yeshua could be fully God and fully human at once.

The Trinity is also at the core of what makes you who you are today.

It is as Yeshua said: *I am in the Father and he is in me.* Press two fingers closely together, side by side. Is one in the other and the other in the one? No, you still see two fingers. So then, press them closer. You still see two, not one.

If you could find a way to make the two fingers one, so that all you see is one finger, then they would be in each other in the same way that Yeshua is in the Father and the Father is in Yeshua.

They are One.

How can this be? And yet we see a similar truth in quantum physics beyond time and space, even though we can't seem to wrap our minds around such a concept. We can't understand the Trinity, but we accept it as truth.

But Yeshua revealed this same truth about you. Hear Him: *In that day* (when the Spirit reveals truth to you) *you will know that I am in my Father, and **you are in me and I am in you**.*[3]

That Yeshua should speak of you and Himself in the same way He speaks of Himself and the Father staggers the mind. How can this be? Are we not wretched, defiled creatures separated from a distant Father?

God forbid. No.

The truth is, He is in you and you are in Him. You (one finger) are in Yeshua (the other finger) even as Yeshua is in the Father and the Father is in Him. One.

Believing in the name (identity) of Yeshua is to put your identity in His identity, He in you and you in Him. As one.

Now so many of His teachings make sense! What you do to your brothers, you do to Him. Why? Because He is one with them.[4]

In knowing God we experience eternal life, He said.[5] And again, by *know*, He means experiencing our union with God. This is what it means to be in Christ, joined as one, grafted into the Son, even as a branch is grafted into a vine and made part of that vine.[6] This is the tree of life found in the first garden (oneness), in contrast to the tree of the knowledge of good and evil (division).[7]

Our brother Paul makes this incredible union even more plain by comparing it to the union of marriage: *"Therefore a man shall leave his father and mother and hold fast to his wife, and the two shall become one flesh." This mystery is profound, and I am saying that it refers to Christ and the church.*[8]

You are the church. The bride. If you were the last person alive on Earth, you would still be the church. Singular or plural, it doesn't matter.

Christ has joined Himself with you, the bride, and the two of you have become one. It is indeed a profound mystery.

So how can you know the Father? By entering into union with Him through Yeshua.

One in Yeshua. Grafted into the Trinity. A branch of the vine. Restored in the tree of life as part of the tree. And which part of a tree is *the* tree? Not one part, but the leaves the branches and the trunk as a whole—you in Him and He in you.

This is how you died with Him. This is how you were raised with Him and in Him. This is how you are now, at this very moment, ascended and seated in the Father's realm, one with Yeshua, even as Yeshua is one with the Father.

This is good news.

But there is even more. Think once more how God first glorified His identity by making Adam in His likeness, and then how He glorified His name once more by reversing the fall and restoring you through the second Adam. Hear Yeshua's elaboration on this mysterious truth:

Father, the glory you have given me, I have given to them, that they may be one, just as we are one, I in them and you in me.[9]

You do indeed have the glory that the Father gave to Yeshua. Paul confirms this when he declares that you have been glorified already.[10]

The powerful mystery of your restoration and union with God in Christ will forever change the way you view yourself and the world you live in.

How can you not love yourself now? How can you not love your neighbor as yourself? How can you stoop in misery and bemoan your life unless you do not believe in your identity in Yeshua?

It is true that pain and hardship are unavoidable in this life. But suffering is optional and the prerogative of the old mind.

Only the old mind and the deceiver stand against the truth of your true identity. They lie with silver tongues, tempting you to believe that you have not been remade in the likeness of your Creator, the Word, Yeshua.

Today, listen to the voice of the Spirit within you, because you are the body of Christ, joined with Him, reborn unto the Father. Surely, this is your incarnation now.

When you see this truth in the Light, all the darkness that has clouded your mind from the great and glorious truth of who you are will vanish. Walking in Yeshua, you will do as He did. You will find peace in the storms, you will move the mountains of trouble that rise before you, you will tread on that serpent who lies with a forked tongue.

Remember: it's never what you believe about yourself that defines you; it's your Father's opinion of you that defines you. Your opinion of yourself only defines the experience you have in this life.

Indeed, to believe *in* Yeshua is to believe like Yeshua. To believe *like* Yeshua is to believe in your risen self, because your were raised with and in Him.

Today, see yourself as He sees you, in Himself, for only then can you truly find great joy in all He has made for you. Only then can you truly enjoy the beautiful gift of life in your earthen vessel, however temporal it is.

Only then can you transcend that temporal body and fly.

CONTEMPLATION

Take a moment and remember once again the story of an office worker named Clark Kent. You are him. But in this version, you don't know you are Superman, so it never occurs to you that you can go to a telephone booth, strip out of your shirt and tie, and fly.

Though still Superman, you don't experience the life of Superman because you are trapped in limited awareness called Clark Kent. Only when someone taps you on the shoulder and informs you of who you truly are, under that office dress, do you even think to fly. In essence you are blind to your own identity until you awaken to the truth.

Much of the time we Christians find ourselves living according to our Clark Kent identity, not our identity in Christ. Thus we fear all that can threaten us.

Today, don't be afraid. The Father has drawn you to Him. His Spirit empowers you to awaken to a new experience of life in Yeshua as the son, the daughter of your Father. Fly, dear one. Fly . . .

Yeshua says to you: *You are the light of the world.* Believe who you are and be that light—it will guide your path as you trust.

You share Yeshua's glory. See that light shining and rejoice with all the angels who rejoice over you. For you were lost, but now you are found. You were blind, but now you see.

PRAYER

Yeshua, I join with You in Your prayer to the Father. I am now resurrected in You and glorified in You. I am in You and You are in me, even as You are in the Father and He is in You. I humbly kneel before You in eternal gratefulness. What a beautiful Savior You are!

Give me eyes to see and ears to hear the truth through the power of Your Holy Spirit. My heart rejoices and my spirit soars as I remember what You have done and who You have made me to be.

Although I forget so often, help me to remember who I am. You, Yeshua, are The Forgotten Way. But today I will forget no longer.

ALIGNMENT

That I might know Christ and the power of His resurrection
That I might know Christ and the power of my resurrection
in union with Him

As you climb the mountain in alignment with the name of Christ who is in you and you in Him, your perception of the world below changes and love fills your heart. And yet, many times your faith in the name of the valley below calls to you and you hurry back for what you think will keep you safe. This is to believe in your own name, rather than His name.

Your name is not evil, neither is the valley below. But in attaching your identity to these, you subject yourself once more to the laws and shadows of the valley called this world. In doing so, you feel separated and cut off from the power of Christ and your true identity in Him.

Whenever you cling once again to your old identity, you deny the name of Christ and you deny the truth of your own identity in Christ. And so you will find yourself in fear once more, as soon as the small securities of that valley reveal their failure to give you lasting peace.

But do not condemn yourself for your perpetual denial of Christ and Christ in you. You are aligning with Him quickly and awakening from a long slumber that has kept you bound to the shadows of death.

Rush to your Father's table today. Align yourself with Christ. Be who you are as the light of the world, risen from the shadows of fear and judgment today.

SEVEN

SONS AND DAUGHTERS OF THE FATHER

See what great love the Father has lavished on us, that we
should be called the children of God!
And that is what we are!
1 JOHN 3:1 NIV

For you are all sons [and daughters] *of God*
though faith in Christ.
GALATIANS 3:26

Because you are his sons [and daughters], *God sent forth*
the Spirit of his Son into our hearts, the Spirit who
cries out, "Abba, Father!"
GALATIANS 4:6 NIV

For the creation waits in eager expectation for the
children of God to be revealed.
ROMANS 8:19 NIV

MEDITATION

How simple is the Way of Yeshua, which leads you into peace and power. How unforgiving is the way of the world, which will always deliver you to misery. As we have learned, what the first Adam did to bring separation between you and your Father, Yeshua, the second Adam, undid. As a believer, your challenge now is simply to see what is already true about you and your Father.

When you, through the eyes of the Spirit, change how you are *seeing*, you will notice a massive shift in how you are *being* in this world. Doing flows naturally out of who you believe you are.

When Yeshua spoke of His Father, He employed the language of a little child, calling His Father "Abba." How offensive this was to those who refused to even write the name of God for fear of His judgment. But Yeshua spoke of His Father in endearing terms that defied the conventional understanding of God.

Because you are in Christ and He is in you, you too are the child of the Father. You've heard this over and over again. But more meaningfully, you are not simply a child, but the son, the daughter of God.

Why is it hard for some to embrace this truth? To say *child*, they rejoice. To say *son*, they hesitate. Why? Perhaps because they do not think they are worthy of such an intimate bond. Perhaps because they secretly fear such a union. Perhaps because the accuser cringes at the mystery of such a privilege, which prevents him from being a god in your life.

Nevertheless, this is now your great honor. You are seated with your Father already as *His son,* as *His daughter*, right now—though the world of flesh and bone can't see this truth. Again, hear what our brother Paul saw in the Spirit:

For you are all sons [and daughters] *of God through faith in Christ. Because you are His sons* [and daughters]*, God sent forth the Spirit of His Son into our hearts, the Spirit who cries out, "Abba, Father!" For the creation waits in eager expectation for the children of God to be revealed.*[1]

Can there be any more doubt? This is your true identity: You are the son, the daughter of the Father.[2] The distinction between a son and a servant is one of inheritance and ownership. A son inherits the authority of his father, one with him through blood. So you, too, have far more authority than you can possibly imagine as son, as daughter of your Father.

In your old mind you think of your identity primarily in terms of the roles you play. I am a writer, you say. I am a student. I am an engineer. I am a carpenter. I am a mother, you think. I am a father, a wife, a husband, a musician. A Baptist, a Pentecostal, an American, an Australian.

Yet what are these roles but sandcastles that will soon be washed away by the coming tide? They are the simple roles you play in this life, like roles in a movie; they are not *who* you are.

This is why Yeshua explicitly taught you to call no man on Earth father, for your Father is in heaven.

This is why Yeshua explicitly taught that you should never be attached to your role as mother, father, son, husband, or wife in this world, which we will see in much greater detail later. To the extent you are attached to them, they distract you from your true identity.[3]

Rather, you are eternal, the son or daughter of your Father in a present and eternal dimension called the kingdom of heaven. Like the first Adam, who was the son of God, you too are the son, the daughter of God, and you have been made complete through and in Yeshua. Your Father is the King of this kingdom called heaven now within and among us.

In denying that you are the son of your Father, you deny the power of the cross.

Only when you believe you truly are a child of God will you be able to follow The Forgotten Way of Yeshua, particularly as it relates to your relationships, which make the biggest waves on the troubled sea of your life—beginning with your relationship with yourself.

But there is even more. If you are the son of God as Paul insisted, then Yeshua is your brother. Though you do not possess the same attributes or position as Yeshua, in Him you have indeed become His brother, His sister.

Truly, your Father knew you before the foundation of the universe, and predestined you to be His son, His daughter in Yeshua, who is your brother. As such, He is the firstborn among many brothers and sisters.[4]

When you identify yourself as the child of your true Father and the brother or sister of His Son, Yeshua, you will rest in perfect comfort because you will have found your true identity. This physical life with all of its roles and identities that keep you in a state of anxiety will be seen for what it is: a temporal experience you're having as a spiritual being.

CONTEMPLATION

Imagine yourself seated high in a castle at a table prepared for a feast. There is your infinite Father, who cannot be threatened. There is the Spirit, the kindest Comforter and all-consuming power imaginable to you. There is your elder brother, Yeshua, the Word who spoke you into existence, without whom you would be lost in the first Adam's death.

But you too are son. You too are daughter, honored at the table, made perfect in Yeshua. You are indeed clothed in His robes. And on your finger, your Father's ring.

Here you have nothing to fear. What can possibly approach this castle and threaten the Father or you?

Close your eyes and dare imagine such a new identity, clothed in Christ. What trouble here on Earth can possibly distract you from who you are?

You gaze upon your Father, you look at the Son filled with His Spirit, and you need say nothing, because you are in awe of all that you see, all that they are, all that you are in and through them.

PRAYER

Father, I come before You today in awe of the love You have lavished on me that I should be called Your son, Your daughter.

I am Your child through Yeshua, who gave his life that I might die with Him and be reborn as Your own offspring. And so my heart now cries out, "Abba! Father!" And I, along with all creation, groan inwardly for all Your sons and daughters to be revealed. Give me sight to see the truth today, and the strength to remain in the full assurance of who I am.

ALIGNMENT

That I might know Christ and the power of His resurrection
That I might know Christ and the power of my resurrection in Him

Whenever you feel anxious or angry or dishonored in any situation, know that it is only because you have fallen out of alignment with who you are as the one who cannot be harmed. You are hidden in God with Christ. You are risen and glorified. Only your feelings and body can be harmed, and these are not who you are in Christ.

But never condemn yourself for being out of alignment. The Father does not condemn you.

Rather, be grateful that you can see that you have strayed off course and are missing the mark. Like a red light on the dashboard of your life, the shadows you experience only tell you that you've lost your alignment.

Today, align yourself once more to who you are as the eternal self, already one with and in Christ. As you do so each day, you are being transformed by the renewing of your mind. This is now your journey. Take it with joy and without self-loathing. It is taking you home to the awareness of who you are and what He has done to make you who you are.

THE TRUTH: SUMMARY

In this first section we have entered seven meditations on the simplest *Truth* about who the *Father* is and who *you* are, as the son or the daughter of the Father through Yeshua.

These constitute the first and second declarations of The Forgotten Way.

THE FIRST DECLARATION
Meditations 1-3

God is infinitely good, *far more loving and gentle and kind to His children than any earthly mother or father imaginable.* ***God is infinitely complete***; *nothing can threaten or disturb Him. Nothing can be taken away from Him, making Him less than complete, nor added to Him who is already complete.*

THE SECOND DECLARATION
Meditations 4-7

You are remade in the likeness and glory of your Father, *finite yet already complete in union with Yeshua—you in Him and He in you, risen with Him and seated in heavenly places. Nothing can separate you from His love.*

II

THE WAY

Yeshua made it plain: *I am the Way, the Truth and the Life.*

In the second section we will enter seven meditations on the *Way* of Yeshua, which is, first, to *see* who you are in the eternal realm of the Father's presence now at hand (meditations 8-11) by, second, *surrendering* all other identities (meditations 12-14).

These constitute the third and fourth declarations of The Forgotten Way.

THE THIRD DECLARATION

Your journey now is to see who you truly are*, for you are the light of the world, the son or the daughter of your Father, a new creature flowing with more beauty and power than you have dared imagine possible.*

THE FOURTH DECLARATION

You will only see who you are and thus be who you are as you surrender your attachment to all other identities*, which are like gods of a lesser power that block your vision of your true identity and keep you in darkness.*

EIGHT

THE TALE OF TWO KINGDOMS

The kingdom of God is not coming with signs to be observed; nor will they say, "Look, here it is!" or, "There it is!" For behold, the kingdom of God is in your midst.
LUKE 17:20-21

If we are insane, it is for God,
and if we are conventional it is for you.
2 CORINTHIANS 5:13 (ARAMAIC BIBLE)

Though our outer man is decaying,
yet our inner man is being renewed day by day.
2 CORINTHIANS 4:16

MEDITATION

You have seen the truth that the Father has spoken over you: You are the son, the daughter of the only Father who has no vulnerability and cannot be threatened or compromised in any way. He invites you to dine at His table, where all He has is yours. Your brother, Yeshua, undid the curse of Adam's deception and has restored your union with Him. Now He is in you and you are in Him, a new creation full of His goodness and His radiance. You are the light of the world.

Your challenge now is to see what is already true about you.

Once again, it is not what you believe about yourself that defines you; it's what your Father believes about you that defines you. What you believe about yourself only defines the *experience* you have in this life.

It's possible that you haven't yet experienced your true identity, however undeniable it is. Don't let this worry you. The truth is already setting you free from the darkness.

As you begin to follow Yeshua's Way, it's critical that you awaken to another simple truth: the physical world your eyes have shown you is only a small part of reality. A far greater and more beautiful reality exists right now. Yeshua called this reality the kingdom of heaven, the kingdom of God, eternal life.

Eternal life is this: to know God and the One He sent.[1] But what is eternity? Paul puts it plainly: it is that which is not transient or temporal, which means temporary and passing. It is the vanishing of time, not the elongation of time, because eternity is beyond time with no beginning and no end. Just as God is not bound by time, neither is His kingdom. Thus, eternal life is a dimension, not a destination in time and space.

Yes, there is a deeper experience of the Father that you will only discover in another age, because now we see Him as though through tainted glass, but then face to face.[2] And yes, in another age there will be a new manifestation of creation called a new heaven and a new earth.

But this future reality isn't what Yeshua was referring to when He repeatedly emphasized that the kingdom of heaven is *here* and it is *now*.

What does this mean?

Consider His teaching:

Now having been questioned by the Pharisees as to when the kingdom of God was coming, He answered them and said, "The kingdom of God is not coming with signs to be observed; nor will they say, 'Look, here it is!' or, 'There it is!' For behold, the kingdom of God is in your midst (within you).*"*[3]

What kingdom exists inside of you and around you at this very moment? One that is unseen with earthly eyes.

The natural mind creates spatial separation between this place and that place—*Look, here it is,* or, *There it is.* We tend to think of the dimension called heaven as being somewhere else—in the sky, in another galaxy far away. But this is not the kingdom of heaven that Yeshua was talking about.

The eternal realm of heaven has come into all darkness as the Light of the world. This Light does not stand beside darkness, or around it, or in one small corner of it. This Light has come *into* all darkness, as John writes.[4] Paul makes it clear when he wrote, *In Him all things hold together.*[5] Every atom. All. Show me a place where you think Christ isn't, and He will show you only your blindness to Him there, because He is there.[6]

What good news this is!

Yeshua spoke of the sovereign realm of the Father in staggering terms that defied the human conception of the world. The kingdom is within, without, everywhere, among us, and now at hand.

Even as the *location* of the kingdom of God defies our spatially limited understanding, we also fail to grasp the *scope* of His kingdom. The realm of Light called the kingdom is also *eternal*, meaning it has no beginning and no end.

When Yeshua says, *This is eternal life, to know the Father*[7], He speaks of experiencing the eternal dimension of the Father's love now, in this life, in all of its fullness.

Two kingdoms: one that flows with peace and power and most of all love, and one that is darkened by condemnation and judgment.

Two kingdoms: one that is concerned with alignment with God and joy in the Spirit, and one that is concerned with food and drink and all that seems important to the body, as Paul wrote.

Two kingdoms: one that is eternal, without beginning or end, now *unseen* by physical eyes, and one that is *seen* and temporal and passes away.[8]

In Christ you can experience eternal life now, in the world but not of it.

Similarly, there are two selves for you to contend with: the new self that knows the Father and abides in His realm even now, and the old self that clings to this world of flesh and bone through relationships with everything else that is temporal.

This is why Yeshua said to both love yourself and to hate yourself.[9] (By *hate* he meant "to utterly dismiss any attachment to," as we will soon see.) Furthermore, he taught that you must deny your *self*. The question is, which self? The self that is risen? Surely not.

Two kingdoms and two identities. In each case, His teaching is clear: one must be surrendered to see and experience the other. You cannot serve two masters.

This teaching of Yeshua was so widespread that within a few years of His resurrection the heresy of Gnosticism arose. This misunderstanding of Yeshua's teaching claimed, on the one hand, that the material world was evil and to be abhorred as taught by the Greeks; or, on the other hand, that it was of no consequence at all, which led to hedonism. Many Gnostics even denied that Christ had come to the world in the flesh—how could He have been in flesh if flesh is evil? they reasoned.

This fallacy captured the hearts of many Christians who had heard Yeshua's teaching first or secondhand, because it was close to the truth.

Close, but utterly wrong.

The body is not evil as the Greeks claimed. Nor is it inconsequential. It is a beautiful gift, majestically created like all of creation, the temple of the Holy Spirit, the earthen vessel of your spirit who worships God in spirit and in truth.

Still today, some are so afraid of Gnosticism that any talk of the distinction between body and spirit makes them run for cover and cling to the flesh. They have thrown the baby out with the bathwater, so to speak, and have dismissed the staggering power of their identity as spiritual beings in Christ.

It is as Paul wrote regarding the Light of the glory of God: *But we have this treasure within earthen vessel* (our bodies) . . . *Although our outer man* (the body) *is decaying, yet our inner man is being renewed day by day . . . We look not at things that are seen, but at the things that are unseen; for the things that are seen* (our bodies and the material world we now know) *are temporary, but the things which are not seen* (spirit, the kingdom of God) *are eternal.*[10]

What is the purpose of any vessel? To hold something. Does that make the vessel what it contains? Surely not.

Clearly there is a significant distinction between your inner self (eternal spirit) and your outer self (earthen vessel). Find your inner self and you will have found the eternal you.

The only practical way for you to embrace your identity as the son or daughter of God, already risen and glorified and established in the eternal realm at this very moment, is to embrace the distinction between *that* inner you, which is eternal, and the outer you that you see as a temporal, transient body.

Two identities: one that is seen with earthly eyes as the outer you, and one that is unseen as the inner you.

Two identities: one that is an earthen container or vessel, and one that abides *in* that vessel.

Two identities: one that is of the physical body, which returns to dust, and one that is spiritual and will one day take on a spiritual body, not confined to the physical laws currently known, and as such, not "physical" as we know it.

Grappling with Paul's clear teaching that we are already risen and glorified, many theologians have coined the phrase, *already, but not yet.* But what does *already, but not yet* mean except *not really?*

The truth is, you *really have* died and *really are* already resurrected and *really are* glorified with Christ. Which self has risen? A new self, which is your true identity integrated with the body you see with your earthly eyes.

The truth is, as Yeshua clearly taught, that you must deny your attachment to *self*. Again, deny which self? The self that is not risen, prone to fixation on the things of this world. The self that looks solely to the material world for salvation from the troubles of this life.

The truth is that you contend with two selves: one in spirit, and one in flesh, bound by the law. If you fixate on the flesh, you will find yourself bound by the law, just like the Pharisees, judging yourself and others for any marks in their flesh.

To the flesh self, it seems insane to die to its own understanding of *self*. As Paul wrote, *If we are insane* (beyond reason and rational thought) *it is for God* (the eternal dimension). *And if we are conventional* (speaking with reason) *it is for you* (it is to relate to flesh and bone).[11]

And again he wrote, *From now on, therefore, we regard no one according to the flesh. Even though we once regarded Christ according to the flesh, we regard Him thus no longer.*[12]

The Word became flesh, dwelt among us in the flesh, and rose again. Now Christ is no longer confined to the physical boundaries of space and time, which is how many of us are in Him and He is in many, as one and at once.

To follow The Forgotten Way is to put on the mind of Yeshua, which is beyond space and time and known by the inner man—spirit. As you do, you will experience (know) your Father and your own true identity in Christ.

This is the tale of two kingdoms and two selves.

Which are you knowing today? The inner or the outer? The seen or the unseen? The skin of this world or the realm that flows with love and power?

CONTEMPLATION

Imagine for a moment that you are a child standing on a wide beach with brilliant white sand. On this beach, you get to build sandcastles either alone or with your friends. Big ones and small ones, and really tricky ones that are super elaborate and take many days or weeks to build. One of the sandcastles is large enough for you to live in, like a fort. How fun that is!

And so you build sandcastles with great enthusiasm, fully aware that at any moment, probably sooner than later, a big wind or wave will wipe out some or all of your sandcastles. But this doesn't worry you because you will just build another one. Either way, your stay at the beach will one day be over and you will leave it. But for now, you jump around with delight and play and build.

Why? Because that's why you are here—to build sandcastles! And you love it. How beautiful are those sandcastles that reflect your Father's creative intent.

Do you ever mistake yourself for the sand and cringe at the prospect of being wiped out by a wave? If you do, you will suffer with the crumbling of that sand. But that is not who you are. You are the boy or girl on the beach, enjoying and using the sand. You are neither the sand itself nor the sandcastle you live in, which is temporary and will soon wash away.

You are *on* the beach, not *of* it.

In the same way, you are *in* the world, not *of* it.

You are the eternal child of the Father, here for the express purpose of enjoying life in this incredible world made by your Father; you are not the earthen vessel that is made of sand, which will soon wash away with a wave.

Look at your hands, and then all around you. Everything that is seen with your earthly eyes is the sandcastle that is perishable, yet what a gift it is. But it isn't who you are. Your true identity is eternal and unseen by earthly eyes.

Most think they are the sand and so cringe in fear when the wind blows, or they throw sand at any who come to threaten their sandcastle.

And so they suffer. They have found their identity in the wrong reality. How needlessly, then, do they live in fear?

In the same way, there are two dimensions at hand, and your experience in this life is dictated by the dimension you identify with as your primary reality.

To the extent you think you are the sand or the sandcastles you build—your relationships and wealth and pleasures and enemies and houses and cars and clothing and religion—you will be filled with anxiety when the wind and waves come.[13]

To the extent you are aware that you are the son or daughter of the Father, on the beach for the express purpose to build sandcastles, you will build them with pleasure.

The beach is stunning and such a wonderful gift, so live in and build your sandcastles. But never mistake yourself for any earthen vessel that will soon return to dust in this life.

TAKEN FROM THE LORD'S PRAYER

My Father, who is of the eternal realm, full of power and love far beyond my comprehension.

May the expression of Your love and power be manifested here in my earthly experience in the same way it is known in Your eternal realm.

May Your sovereign will be manifested in every waking experience of my life even as it is in Your sovereign realm.

Give me what I need to live on Earth—food, shelter, and clothing—even as You give to the birds of the air and the flowers of the field.

May I know that I am one with You as I let go of the offenses I have against any other. Lead me not into the temptation to place other gods before You, and deliver me from the deception that they can save me. I am saved already in You.

For Yours is the kingdom, and the power and the glory forever.

ALIGNMENT

That I might know Christ and the power of His resurrection
That I might know Christ and the power of my resurrection in Him

We have used the image of sand castles to represent our earthen vessels. They are neither evil nor inconsequential, but beautiful gifts given for you to experience this life. But that doesn't make you the sandcastle.

No, you are the one from the mountain, the kingdom of heaven. You are risen and glorified. You are in the world, but not of it.

And yet you have aligned yourself with that vessel and mistaken it for who you are, subject to rust and decay and illness and death. But today you may choose to align with the truth of who you truly are as the son, the daughter of the Father.

Say this today: *Today I choose to realign my experience of life with my eternal self who is complete in Christ. I am only experiencing life in this earthen vessel. Today, I look around and see the temporal form of all that is seen and I know that it too is passing and therefore not eternal. Today, I choose to align myself with the kingdom of heaven, which is my true home, even now.*

NINE

WHAT DEFIES EARTHLY EYES

God is spirit, and those who worship him
must worship him in spirit and truth.
JOHN 4:24

If anyone be in Christ, he is a new creation:
Old things are passed way; All things are become new.
2 CORINTHIANS 5:17 KJV

MEDITATION

We have learned that the kingdom of heaven is at hand, among us and within us. There is also the world, the earth, which is the dimension that we see and experience with earthly eyes and our old mind. But let us think once again on how we experience these two realms.

As you know, the physical world as you experience it in body is bound by the laws of physics, thus we say it is *physical*. When something happens that defies these laws, you call it miraculous, or *of the spirit*.

Are you a physical being or a spiritual being? As you have seen, both, yes?

Today we will revisit and expand upon this critical understanding. Without it you will not be able to grasp the truth that you have been raised with Yeshua, are already glorified, and are seated in heavenly places at this very moment.

Again, most still mistakenly believe that they are primarily physical beings having spiritual experiences as they open themselves up to those encounters. But to forget that you are primarily a spiritual being is to misunderstand your identity and be in danger of worshiping the flesh, which decays.

In truth you are not a physical being having spiritual experiences; *you are a spiritual being integrated with a physical experience*—an experience that will come and go in what amounts to no more than a single breath in the scope of eternity.

Consider this question: Is a child born with Down syndrome in any way compromised or at a disadvantage as the daughter of the Father? Can she not be whole even though her body and mind are seen to be challenged? Does the body she live in compromise her spiritual union with the Father in Yeshua?

No. So then there is a distinct difference between her body and her spirit.

Consider this question: Was Yeshua (who came in flesh that was subject to decay) still confined by the same temporal body *after* His resurrection?

Yeshua showed His injured hands and feet to Thomas to make a point because Thomas did not otherwise recognize Him[1], but was the rest of His body still savaged by the beatings He experienced during His crucifixion? Was His face still brutalized from beatings and His back still mangled from the whip? In the average human body, forty-one million cells die every minute—is this true of Yeshua's body today?

Have not even angels shown themselves in human form, as it is written? Is the human body in which they appear their eternal form, or do they merely show themselves as human for our sake? If angels can change form, can Yeshua do so as well today?

These are mysteries, but one thing is certain from what is written: Yeshua, who rose from the dead in body, was resurrected in a body that wasn't confined to the same physical laws of decay that once defined that body in the flesh. He showed Himself as He saw fit, able to appear and vanish at will, and He now lives in millions at once, bound by neither space nor time.

The body you live in now, on the other hand, *is* subject to decay and it will soon lie dormant and lifeless in a grave. Paul calls your current body the *natural body,* which is perishable and temporary. Even more, he wrote, *flesh and blood cannot inherit the kingdom of God.* Your natural body, he said, will one day be transformed into another kind of bodily expression not subject to decay. This he called a *spiritual body,* which is *imperishable.*[2]

But you still live in a *natural body,* which will soon return to dust. Find and open the grave of Paul and you will see that it has decayed—indeed, its atoms are now scattered to the four corners of the earth. But Paul was not defined by that perishable body any more than you are.

It is as Yeshua said: *You* (as spirit) *live in the world* (of flesh and blood) *but you are not of it.*[3]

It is as Paul said: *All that is in Christ is a new creation.*[4]

Is your outer self a new creation today? Did you receive a new body when you believed? No, because your body is still flesh and decays still, even if you are healed of a disease.

But your inner self is a new creation and is your true identity in Yeshua.

Do you finally see that the body you currently occupy is an earthen vessel that will return to dust; a *fragile tent* that will soon wear out and be blown away by the wind, a *natural body* that is decaying already—that which is *temporal* and *transient* and *perishable* and *cannot inherit the kingdom of God*, to use Paul's words? Even healing is only a temporary postponement of the natural death that awaits the body in this life.

This is why, as he said, we must *fix our eyes not on what is seen* (by earthly eyes), *but on what is unseen, since what is seen is temporary, but what is unseen is eternal.*[5]

The moment you become fully aware of this truth, you will feel a dramatic shift. No longer are you compelled to secretly worship your own flesh as a god, nor will you desire to worship all that the world offers you. Instead, you will begin to identity with the eternal you that is already risen from the dead and glorified in Yeshua and as such is already at perfect peace and knows how to love as He loves.

The world of flesh, however beautiful a gift it is for a short time, necessarily ends in physical decay and death just like Paul's and Peter's. Even flowers wilt and die. So why do you set your hope on being saved by all the means of the flesh?

Take a moment and look at your fingernail. You trim it, you might bite it and spit it out. How is your fingernail different from a blade of grass? Is your fingernail your eternal being? Is it risen and glorified in Christ, or does it decay like a blade of grass?

You are not your fingernail or your arm or your body; you are the righteousness of God in Yeshua, seated in the heavenly realm even now.

Again, let me be clear: this is not to say that the body is evil, meaningless, or nonexistent. God forbid. But you must understand Paul's differentiation between the temporal earthen vessel you live in (your outer self) and your eternal spiritual self. Too many people, fascinated by the materialism spawned by human reason and physical science, inadvertently glorify the physical body above its true place.

Instead, fix your perception on what is unseen by human eyes. *Set your mind on things beyond, not on the things that are on this earth*, as Paul wrote, *for you have died and your life is hidden with Christ in God.*[6]

Set your mind on the kingdom of heaven and all these things will be added to you, and what is not added to you doesn't matter because you are already complete in Him.

Consider what you place your hope in. You will see that the flesh is too often your god, and you its slave. You look for security and significance in your body and its appearance; your house and its value; your education, your clothes, your food; your relationships with mother, father, wife, husband, children; your status and position; your job and all your possessions.

This is the world of *mammon,* or money, that single symbol that speaks of all flesh and bone. Though they are gifts from your Father, the things of this world can become your master.

You must know that everything in form is perishable—your body, your money, your house, your food, your relationships—all beautiful gifts, created by the Son of God for your pleasure and His. But you can only delight in them when you let go of their mastery over you. Then you will love your body and all God's good gifts in a way you have never imagined.

But when your flesh clings to them as gods, they replace your Father. They war against you and you feel alienated from Him. The temporal has taken the throne and thrown down God. When you idolize your physical life, it becomes your god and you become its slave. Thus, you put your idols before God and suffer their tyranny. What an impossible fate you face, knowing that soon it will all end in the grave.

It is as Yeshua said: *You cannot serve two masters.*[7]

Your spiritual being and your physical self are often at odds with each other because you can serve only one master: your Father or the world. Spirit or flesh. You decide in each moment which world you will identify with and so serve.

Either your body and the world will master you, or you, as the son, the daughter of the Father, will overcome the world in and with Yeshua. You cannot have it both ways.

But there's good news: the physical world does not define you. As a spiritual being, your identity is perfectly safe in your Father's arms. He meets all your needs. To the extent you are not blinded by the world, beauty and love flow naturally for you; judgment and condemnation are strangers.

When you see yourself as a spiritual being and let go of the mastery this world has over you, you have dominion, even as Adam had dominion over the earth, which is your inheritance.[8]

When you no longer cling to this world—when you are no longer enslaved by it—you can then enjoy it as the gift it was meant to be. The true beauty of all you see will open up like a flower and a smile will fill your face. Then you will see that Yeshua's burden is light and His yoke is easy. Then you who are weary will find rest.[9]

The world of flesh and bone is not evil, nor is it an illusion. The illusion is that by serving the system of this world, you will be saved in this life. In truth, it will keep you in death. Seek first the realm of God's presence, and all these gifts in the world will be added unto you.

So then let go of the mad idea that you are *not* a spiritual being having a temporary physical experience. Be freed from the prison that enslaves you, and find beauty in all you see.

CONTEMPLATION

There was once a woman walking on the path beside the jungle. Suddenly, a tiger jumped out, snarling, and the woman ran, terrified for her life. The tiger gave chase, and just as it was about to catch her, she came to a cliff.

Without thinking, she jumped off the cliff and grabbed onto a vine, just beyond the reach of the tiger. Hoping to escape, she looked down, and there, to her horror, she saw yet another tiger, snarling in the ravine beneath her. There was no escape.

Her predicament worsened when two mice—one white and one black—climbed onto the vine above her head and began to chew through it. It was only a matter of time before they severed her lifeline and sent her plummeting to the tiger below.

Then the woman took her eyes off the mice and the tigers, closed her eyes, and slowly settled. As she did this, she came to herself. And when she opened her eyes she saw beautiful, ripe strawberries on the cliff right in front of her.

So she plucked those strawberries and ate them, and how sweet they were!

You are the woman, and the tigers are all that threaten you in this life. They are your grievances about the past (the tiger above) and your fears of the future (the tiger below). The mice, white and black, are day and night, representing the passage of time. It's only a matter of time before your outer body meets its death.

This is the kingdom of the world in which you find yourself every day, for it is as Yeshua said: in this world you will have trouble.[10]

But, like the prodigal son who came to himself while in the pigpen, you can also come to your true self. When you do, you'll be surprised to find another reality right in front of you, lush with strawberries, which represent the kingdom of heaven.

Taste and know that the Lord is good.

The troubles of your life—finances, relationships, body issues, attacks on you by others, jealousy, anger, anxiousness, illness—will always surround you. It is your choice whether to keep your eyes on them and so live in fear, or to put your eyes on the beauty of your Father's sovereign presence and find peace. Your true identity is part of that dimension.

Only by living in the Father's realm will you be able to truly enjoy your body, your house, your spouse, and all that God has given you that is perishable.

If this thought brings you joy, you are discovering who you truly are.

If it brings you anxiousness, take courage. Even your attempts to know who you are will be richly rewarded. Your freedom is at hand.

Seek and you will find. Knock and the door will be opened.[11] Your liberation is certain because your Father's promises cannot fail.

PRAYER

Father, I come to You as Your child, seeking to know who I am. Show me Your sovereign realm; show me how You see me, which is as I truly am. Open the eyes of my heart that I might see.

Yeshua, You promised that all who seek would find. Let me see now with the eyes of Your Spirit what You see.

Today, I will not be mastered by the lie that this world can offer me significance in this life. I rest now in the certainty that I am a spiritual being temporarily having a physical experience in this life.

I worship You, Father, in spirit, which is truth, because You have made me complete in Yeshua.

ALIGNMENT

That I might know Christ and the power of His resurrection
That I might know Christ and the power of my resurrection in Him

Yeshua said, *In this world you will have trouble, but have courage because I have overcome this world.* Why should *His* overcoming give *you* courage?

Because in Him you too have overcome. Align with the you who has overcome in Him today.

In any given moment, including this one, you are aligned with one master named Christ in you, or you are aligned with the system of the world called the law, the valley of the shadow of death. In Christ, there is no struggle between good and evil because He has already overcome. It is finished.

But to the extent you put your faith in this world to give you significance and honor, it still blinds you to your true identity and thus masters you. And so you find yourself out of alignment with your true identity as the son, the daughter of the Father.

Today, bring the presence of your Father, in whom you are hidden, to your experience of this earth. May His kingdom come and His will be done in this valley as it is on the mountain. This is to know and experience your Father and your self in Christ, here, in this life.

Say this today: *Christ alone is my foundation, my solid rock, the absolute truth of who I am. All other ground will sink and fail me in this life. Today, I align myself with who I am in Christ, free from the law of sin and death and alive to the law of grace who is Christ. Today I know Christ and the power of His resurrection, and I know myself and the power of my resurrection in Him.*

I am in Him; in Him I am.

TEN

SEEING IN THE DARK

Though seeing, they do not see.
MATTHEW 13:13 NIV

*The eye is the lamp of the body; so then if your eye is
clear, your whole body will be full of light. But if your eye
is bad, your whole body will be full of darkness. If then
the light that is in you is darkness,
how great is the darkness!*
MATTHEW 6:22-23

MEDITATION

There are two kingdoms that call for your identification. Only in one can you find true love and peace: the kingdom of heaven.

This begs the question: how, then, can you place your identity in the kingdom of heaven and thus experience His true love and peace? How can you see and know your Father's sovereign presence right now, while you are still on Earth?

Yeshua made the way clear: *No one can **see** the kingdom of God unless they are born again.*[1]

Many think of being born again only in terms of a single, isolated experience. Yes, such an experience, which leads to a fundamental conversion of your perspective, has eternal value. But *seeing* God's kingdom is also a daily journey on a narrow path that few follow.

It is as Yeshua said: unless a man is born again he cannot even *see* the eternal dimension. But just because you *can* see, doesn't mean you *are* seeing.

Your journey now is to see yourself and your Father the way that Yeshua does. For this you must become like an infant, as if reborn with the simple faith of a young child who sees and trusts his father without question. In this way you will see the realm of God's sovereign presence now, in this life, not only the life to come.

Yeshua spoke continually, in many different ways, about being able to *see*, because it is perhaps the single greatest challenge in this life. But even as the first Adam's eyes were opened to darkness, making him spiritually blind, so in the second Adam, Yeshua, who came to give spiritual sight to the blind, you can now see.

Consider one of His most direct teachings on blindness: *The eye is the lamp of the body*, meaning that your perception is what determines your experience as a body in this life.

He continues: *So then if your eye* (perception) *is clear, your whole body* (your bodily experience in this life) *will be full of light. But if your eye* (perception) *is bad, your whole body* (your bodily experience in this life) *will be full of darkness. If then the light that is in you* (the light that you already have and are) *is darkness, how great is the darkness!*[2]

Do you see? Light or darkness; which are you perceiving? If your sight is clear, you will see light, beauty, and wonder all around you. This is the eternal realm of the Father, called the kingdom of heaven. If your sight isn't clear, you will see darkness and offense and grievance.

It is as Yeshua said: you are the light of the world. You cannot gain more light than you already have—Christ is already in you. Indeed, when you cry out for more of Him, you are actually crying out for more *revelation* of Christ already in you.

You cannot gain more light, but you can remove that which blocks your sight of that light.

If you are not seeing His kingdom of light at any given time, you need only to remove that which clouds your vision, as you will soon learn.

To make His point clear, Yeshua said, *If your eye causes you to stumble, throw it out!*[3] It is better to have only one eye and be fully aware of the eternal realm than to have two eyes and be cast into terrible suffering in this life.

It is as Yeshua said: *Though you see* (with your old eyes) *you do not see* (what is really there).[4] Indeed, whenever you live in condemnation and fear, you aren't seeing with new-born eyes. Do you think the world of hatred and fear and shame and powerlessness are a part of your Father's realm? Does darkness reside in His kingdom of light that is now within and at hand? No, because as Yeshua said, *In the Father there is no darkness. He is only light.*[5]

Again, think of your life as a boat on the stormy seas. The dark skies block out the sun, the winds tear at your face, the angry waves rise to sweep you overboard and into a dark, watery grave. So you cringe in fear as you cling to that boat, which you believe will save you.

But Yeshua is at peace. How can He be at rest in the midst of such a terrible threat? When you cry out in fear, He rises and looks out at that storm, totally unconcerned.

Why are you afraid? He asks.[6]

How could He ask such a question? Has He gone mad? Does He not see the reason to fear?

Unless what He sees and what you see are not the same.

What does He see instead of the storm? Peace. He sees another dimension, which this world is subject to and wholly integrated with. He sees the Father, who offers no judgment or condemnation. He sees life and love and joy and peace in an eternal union with His Father, which is manifest now, here on Earth, in the most spectacular fashion.

In this way, to *see in the dark* is to find the path to transformation.

Again, you can choose to see one of two worlds: the troubled possibilities of the storm, or the true reality of your Father, brimming with light and peace. You will see either the kingdom of heaven or the kingdom of this world. In the first there is truth and no darkness; the second is full of deception spun by the accuser who is the father of lies.

If you see lies instead of truth, the dark clouds have blotted out your sight of the sun. But the sun still shines, waiting to be seen with Yeshua's vision, which is now your own.

Think of all your troubles as storms that rise up to crush you in this life. As Yeshua said, *you will have trouble*—there is no way to stop it from coming. Pain will come in many different circumstances, even as pain came to those early followers of Yeshua who were persecuted and slaughtered.

Pain will come and it is real, but in Yeshua suffering is optional because He bore your suffering as His own. Though you, like David in his great twenty-second Psalm, cry out, *My God, my God, why have You forsaken me*, in the midst of your great trouble, you too like David can conclude your lament by seeing the truth in that same Psalm—*God has not despised or scorned the afflicted one; He has not hidden His face from him!*

It is only your perspective that shows you such darkness instead of the light. In Yeshua you are that light, risen from the grave and seated in heavenly places already. Identify with and in Him instead of the storm and you will find peace.

At any given moment you will serve and so be mastered by the reality in which you put your faith. You cannot serve two masters.

Most of the time, you see a dark world that seems to threaten you. If you believe the threat, you are blinded again to the kingdom of heaven, in which you are saved. And so you live in fear.

If you surrender your attachment to this world and fix your eyes on Yeshua, you will see light and find peace in the storms of life.

CONTEMPLATION

Consider this true story of how one can see but not see. In the late 1970s, the genocide by Communist leader Pol Pot and the Khmer Rouge army left millions dead and many maimed, among them over two hundred blind women who came to the United States as refugees.

One peculiarity was observed among this particular group of women, many of whom settled in Long Beach, California. Their eyes appeared healthy. Brain imaging determined that their visual systems were functioning normally. There was nothing wrong with either their eyes or their vision centers.

Curious, researchers dug deeper and learned the truth. All of the women had witnessed terrible suffering—the murder of their children. Together they had subconsciously chosen not to see anymore. Over time, they had all gone blind. "Their minds simply closed down, and they refused to see anymore," researchers told the *Los Angeles Times*.

A tragic story. And not so different from the darkness that now blinds the hearts of most to the staggering realm of the Father, even now.

If pain can blind, Yeshua's love can bring sight to the blind. Through a renewing of the mind, empowered by the Spirit, you can see peace in the storm. The eyes of your heart will be opened, and you will know the presence of the Father now on Earth as it is in heaven.

Close your eyes and consider any area of trouble in your mind and say to yourself, *There is more to this situation than what I see.*

Spend time in quiet reflection. Know that if you could see the way Yeshua sees, all the offense you now perceive would go away; all the threats would become harmless swells in a sea that cannot harm you.

Don't you want your vision corrected to see this light instead of darkness? Ask the Holy Spirit to give you this sight—the flesh cannot heal distorted vision.

Confess your intention aloud: *I want to see as Yeshua sees, that I might be free from the darkness that has blinded me. I want to see peace instead of this troubled storm. I want to see light in the place of darkness.*

This single act of faith offered to the Holy Spirit, who comforts and strengthens you, will give you new sight in an otherwise dark world. The shift will set you free and fill you with relief and joy. Be glad, then. Today is the day of new sight.

PRAYER

Father, though my eyes are so often blinded by this world to the truth of who I am and who You are; though I see darkness and stumble, I offer myself on Your altar of holiness today, asking You to restore my sight and the joy of my salvation. Help me see myself as You see me, cherished and saved into Your light, which is now my own.

Give me sight, that I might see.

ALIGNMENT

That I might know Christ and the power of His resurrection
That I might know Christ and the power of my resurrection in Him

Think once more of our analogy of climbing the mountain to know your Father and your eternal self hidden in Him with Christ, complete and risen.

Only as you climb higher in your mind's eye does your perception of all you see change. Now you are seeing with the eyes of Christ. What once appeared to be a terrible cliff is now but a scratch on the valley floor, put there for the purpose of helping you to learn how to climb. All that once terrified you is now seen in a new light, for in Him all things are made new.

When you align your sight with the sight of Christ, it is as He said: you see light rather than darkness.

But here is the truth: Your eternal self already *has* the sight of Christ. She is glorified already. Align your earthen vessel sight with your eternal-self sight and you will see the world differently.

Say this today: *Today I choose to let go of all that blocks my sight of who I am as the one who is risen and glorified in Christ. Seeing with the eyes of Christ, the shadows of death and darkness vanish and I see light and love. Yea, though I walk through the valley of the shadow of death, I will fear no evil, because that death is finished.*

In His light which is now my own, I can see.

ELEVEN
SEEING IS BELIEVING

First take the plank out of your eye,
and then you will see clearly.
LUKE 6:42 NIV

You are the light of the world. A town built on a hill
cannot be hidden. Neither do people light a lamp and
put it under a bowl.
MATTHEW 5:14

Truly, truly I say to you, whoever believes in me
will also do the works I do . . .
Whatever you ask in my name, this I will do.
JOHN 14:12-13 ESV

I pray that the eyes of your heart may be enlightened
so that you will know . . .
The riches of the glory of his inheritance . . .
The surpassing greatness of His power
toward us who believe . . .
In this age but also in the one to come.
EPHESIANS 1:18-21

MEDITATION

We have learned that perception, or seeing, as Yeshua called it, determines your experience in this life. If your vision is clear, your earthly experience will be full of light, but if your vision is not clear, you will see darkness, like storm clouds on all sides.

You will see tigers instead of strawberries, offense instead of grace, fear instead of love.

You will be anxious for tomorrow, though Yeshua says there is no need to worry about what you will wear or eat tomorrow.[1]

You will cringe in fear when the harsh taskmaster called life comes to knock on your door, demanding to see what you have done with your lot in life, as Yeshua taught in the parable of the harsh taskmaster.[2]

You will see the trouble that you have in this world as if He has not overcome it—though He has[3], and you have as well, because you have risen with Him.

So you ask, *Why don't I see clearly?*

Yeshua made the reason plain: You do not see clearly because you are seeing through the flesh's eye, your old mind's eye. And what distorts the vision of the flesh's eye?

That old eye is blinded by the planks of offense and grievance. These are the planks of condemnation that Yeshua was referring to when He said, *First take the plank out of your eye, then you will see clearly.*[4]

Do you remember the story of the first Adam? The first thing Adam and Eve did after eating the fruit of the knowledge of good and evil was to judge and condemn themselves for being naked. Then Adam blamed Eve, and Eve blamed the serpent. So it was that grievance entered the world, indeed the fruit of the fall *is* grievance.[5] Grievance against yourself and against your brother and against the world.

For this reason, darkness and anxiety in all their forms are all too often what you see. They haunt your memories of the past and rise with each new offense to threaten you again and again.

Though you are the light of the world, condemnation and grievance are like a bowl that covers up and hides your light.[6] You hide yourself just like the first Adam did when he judged his nakedness, then covered up his true, authentic identity.

The first person you condemn when blindness covers your true vision is yourself. Instead of your true self, you see a victim who must be protected from the storm, or satisfied with pleasures to numb the pain.

Remember: in Yeshua's light, you *are* light, remade in His likeness. When you condemn yourself, you deny who you are and so are judged by your own judgment, not God's. It is as Yeshua said: *The Father judges no one . . . Neither will I accuse you before the Father. Your accuser is Moses* (the law and systems of the world) *in whom your hopes are set.*[7] This is why Yeshua said, *Judge not, and you will not be judged.*[8] If you judge yourself or others, you and they stand accused by a law (the law of Moses), which, as Paul said, is dead.[9]

And by judgment, I mean condemnation borne of grievance, not the determination of opinion, preference, or truth. The first will darken your world; the latter is only part of being human.

Think of the light that has come into the darkness like a sun that shines brightly upon and within you. But clouds of grievance block your sight of it. They keep its rays from warming your body. The sun is never extinguished, but you can no longer experience its effects.

Your spiritual practice is to remove all the clouds of darkness and offense and judgment that block your experience of the truth. Positive thinking is valuable but limited in its effect for you. Instead, find and remove all the negative thinking and deception that distort your vision of who you are. Then your whole body will be full of healing light.

Walk in the light even as He is in the light. In Yeshua's light, all darkness flees. In His light, which is now your own, all shame is replaced by honor, all grievance is traded for forgiveness, all sorrow is turned to joy, and all pain becomes but a shadow that passes before the sun. When you follow the Way of Yeshua, you see light.

Yeshua made it plain: *If you follow me, you will never walk in darkness.*[10]

When you forget His Way, you wander into blindness.

In blindness, you no longer believe who you are. You stop placing your identity *in* Yeshua. Instead, you believe the serpent's lie that you are not made in the likeness of your Father. You must become like God, the lie goes, through the knowledge of good and evil, condemnation and grievance, protection and blame.

But today you take a giant stride in your journey of seeing yourself as you are in Yeshua's sight, and believing in Him. You will also believe in yourself as the son, as the daughter of the Father, for you are in Him, and He in you.

In the light of Yeshua, seeing is believing.

Paul made the matter clear to us all: *The eyes of our hearts* (spiritual perception) *must be enlightened* (cleared to see the light) *so that we can know* (experience) *the glory of our union* (our inheritance) *as the holy ones* (saints). *Then we will know* (experience) *the surpassing greatness of Yeshua's power for us as we believe, in the present age and the age to come.*[11]

How simple it is to see. Like looking at a prism, shift it only two degrees and you can see the full spectrum of color. He who has eyes to see, let him see what is already there to see.

How simple is it to hear. Like a radio dial, turn it only one degree and your static will turn to a symphony of gladness. She who has ears to hear, let her hear what is already there to hear.

Though you may be blind to the stunning realm of God's sovereign presence here and now, be glad, for Yeshua came to bring sight to the blind. Gaze upon His kingdom but for a moment and you will remember. Then your world will be filled with light.

All that you need today is the awareness that whenever you are filled with anxiety and fear, it is only because you have been blinded. The darkness you see with your old eyes hides the beauty of His light all around you. Are you willing to see once again?

Seeing is indeed believing.

CONTEMPLATION

There was once a very wise, old teacher whose sole purpose was to teach a small boy the truth of the kingdom of heaven. It was he who taught the boy that his Father was like a lion as big as the sky, and evil was like a tiny hyena on a field. Do you remember the story?

Today he will show the boy who he is in his Father's eyes. So he leads the boy by the hand to a small pool in the forest. It's a special trip for the boy, because he has never been to the pool. There the old teacher stops and gazes around the edges of the pool, where several sticks extend from the water. He points to one of the sticks and asks the boy a simple question.

"Do you see that twig poking out of the water?"

"Yes," the boy says.

"Is it crooked or is it straight?"

The boy leans over and peers at the stick. "It's crooked," he says.

"Is it?"

The boy looks again and sees that the stick indeed bends under the water, so he nods. "It's crooked."

"Pull the stick out of the water," the teacher says.

The boy squats and gingerly plucks the stick from the water. He stares, confused.

"So . . ." says the old man. "Is the stick crooked or straight?"

"It's straight!"

"And it was straight before you pulled it out. The water only distorted the image and made it appear crooked. In the same way, this world of offense and grievance will distort your vision of yourself, making you look crooked when in truth you are straight in the eyes of your Father."

Like that stick, your own vision of yourself is only distorted by what you think you see with the eyes of your flesh.

PRAYER

Father, may the revelation of Your kingdom come to me, now on Earth, as it truly is in Your realm.

May the eyes of my heart be filled with light so that I can experience the glory of my union with You as Your holy son, Your holy daughter, through and in Yeshua. Then I will know the surpassing greatness of Yeshua's power for me as I place my identity in His identity, and believe who I am in Him.

I worship You, and You alone, placing no other god before You to block my vision of who You are, of who Your Son, Yeshua, is, and of who I am in Your likeness.

ALIGNMENT

That I might know Christ and the power of His resurrection
That I might know Christ and the power of my resurrection in Him

Regardless of what you think of judgment, know this: It is no longer yours to give. It no longer serves you. It is the law of the valley below the mountain, the very fabric of death itself. It is the opposite of the law of grace that rules the mountain.

When you judge your enemy, you only attack yourself. When you judge wrinkles on an aging face as less than beautiful, you only judge the wrinkles that will soon be on your own face. In judgment, you reap what you sow, in equal measure.

Though you might never be totally free from judgment in this life, you can align yourself with the intention to see with the eyes of Christ and devote yourself to the path up the mountain from where all is seen in the light.

Above all, you may agree to see yourself as He sees you, rather than live in the trance of condemnation and self-judgment that crushes you in the valley of shadows. In His sight, there are no shadows because in Him there is no darkness.

And neither is there in you who are risen and glorified.

Align yourself with true sight today. It is yours already. See with the eyes of the eternal you who is in Christ. See the world in a new way. Surrender all judgment and align yourself with grace today.

Set your mind on these things above—align your mind with a higher way—and notice how your spirit soars. Now you are experiencing eternal life.

Now you are following The Forgotten Way of Yeshua.

TWELVE

SEE LIKE A CHILD AND BE FREE

I praise you Father . . . that you have hidden these things from the wise and intelligent and have revealed them to infants.

MATTHEW 11:25

Truly I tell you, unless you change and become like little children, you will never enter the kingdom of heaven.

MATTHEW 18:3 NIV

Trust in the Lord with all your heart and lean not on your understanding.

PROVERBS 3:5

MEDITATION

It is time to see with new eyes how simple it really is to know the truth. And when you know the truth, that truth will set you free.

When you know the truth, there is no need to condemn. No desire will be unsatisfied because you are whole already; no pain will define you. You will have nowhere to arrive, only a place to be, right now, safely resting in knowing your Father.

Here is the secret: your problem isn't that you know too little. It's that you "know" far too much—of the lies that stand in direct opposition to knowing your Father.

Joining the truth by releasing the lie is now your path. There is no turning back.

Think of an infant, newly born. Is he not still completely dependent on his mother, even still united with her? It is now known that for the first year of infants' lives, they do not see themselves as distinct from their mother. They have no sense of separation or unique identity apart from their mother. The two are one.

In the same way, to know your Father and Yeshua is to be united with them in heart, trusting them without logic or intellect, like an infant who does not see themselves as separated from their mother.

How simple is an infant's life. How simple is knowing your Father. Just become like a little child as Yeshua taught—surely He knew what we are just learning about infants—thus His words on being born again and becoming like a child.

Consider His repeated teaching: *I praise you, Father, Lord of heaven and earth, that you have hidden these things from the wise and intelligent and have revealed them to infants.*[1]

What a bold statement. The world values the opposite. To remain infant-like is offensive to the natural mind, which insists on being god through intelligence and language. Infants have no language. They have trust. They are united with the one who brought them into the world.

Does a child require intelligence or dogma to climb into his Father's lap? No. The child climbs without thought, seeing only safety. Yes you must put away *childishness* and feast on more than milk, as Paul said, but never set aside your *childlikeness*, because you are remade in the *likeness* of your Father.

Unless you change and become like a little child in simple trust and united identity, as Yeshua said, you will never step beyond the system of the world evident to your natural eyes and enter into the eternal dimension beyond.[2]

If you have seen me, you have seen the Father, Yeshua says.[3] Distinct but one. Does this mean to see Yeshua's body is to see the Father's body? No, because God is Spirit and those who worship Him worship Him in spirit and in truth. Thus to *see* Yeshua in spirit through faith is to *see* the Father.

So then, how can you see like a child and trust once again? In the same way as Yeshua, surely: to see yourself as the son, the daughter of the Father in Yeshua, even as an infant sees himself as one with his mother.

In this way, through faith, heaven is manifested in earthly form as it is in heaven.[4] This is how Yeshua saw and manifested calm in the storm.

When you let go of all that you think defines you and fall into your Father's arms, you are believing *in* Yeshua by placing your identity in Him. Let go of what you think you know about the dark, stormy seas in this world and instead believe in Yeshua. Turn your newborn eyes back to Him and discover trust once again.

This is your surrender: to let go of all of the world as you think you know it. That surrender of the system of the world might seem costly, but what is that cost compared to your gain? Truly you are only letting go of deception to walk in power and freedom. You are surrendering *into* the light and freedom, because the truth will set you free.

Consider Yeshua's teachings: *Count* (be aware of) *the cost before following me*.[5] And more, *What good is it for a man to gain the whole world* (the old system of the world) *and lose his soul* (his connection to his Father).[6] And even more, *Let go of all that possesses you to possess the treasure in the field, the pearl of great price, the kingdom of heaven now at hand*.[7]

If you instead treasure your earthen vessel, which decays, and the world, which even a moth and simple rust can destroy, you will suffer that same decay and destruction, because where your treasure is, there your heart is also, as He said.

So count the cost that is no cost at all. Become like a child and trust your Father. Let go of your fixation with the ground and climb into His arms—He will fill you with wonder and love beyond comprehension.

You might still think the waves will crush you if you let go of what protects you in this world, though Yeshua says they won't. You might think you'll sink beneath the water if you step out of the boat, though Yeshua says different. So much of what you think will keep you safe is only grievance and distraction that block the light of truth and keep you in darkness.

RENEWING YOUR MIND TO BE LIKE A CHILD

It is said that *most spiritual growth comes through unlearning*. Unlearning what? Unlearning everything the world (including religion) has taught you that is in conflict with what Yeshua says is true.

As you unlearn those lies, you are *transformed by the renewing of your mind*, as Paul wrote.[8] As you unlearn those lies, you experience *meta-noia* or *altered mind*, translated "repentance" in old English. And as you repent, or renew your mind, you will see that the kingdom of heaven is at hand and within and incomparable. As Yeshua taught, *Repent*, (change your mind) *for the kingdom of heaven is here and within you.*

And what is this renewal but becoming like a child once more? What is it but being reborn to see as a child sees with simple faith, united as one with her mother?

Above all, what you need to unlearn are the lies that block your vision of who your Father is and who you are as His son, His daughter. Remove the clouds that block the light already within and around you. Pluck out all the planks of offense that block your vision.

Indeed, renewing the mind is nothing less than wiping out the old operating system of this world and living in a whole new operating system, the one written by Yeshua.

If your heart isn't transformed by childlike trust, you cannot *know* God; you can only know *about* Him. True knowing isn't a function of the brain, as the flesh would have you believe. It is a function of the heart. It is seen and experienced with the *eyes of the heart*.[9] The heart is the seat of either love or fear. It is where you experience either the Father or the lie that has replaced Him.

Grasping for God with the intellect is often the flesh's tricky way of silencing faith. In truth, you are saved from darkness, both in this life and in the life to come, by grace through faith[10], not by grace through the intellect.

Again, *knowing* the Father and Yeshua is a matter of complete, trusting intimacy, not rigid, calculating dogma. And it is experienced with the eyes of the heart. As the Scripture says, *Trust in the Lord with all your heart and lean **not** on your understanding; submit your way to Him.*[11]

The path is clear: trust with the heart, not the understanding; submit your way to Him, however terrifying that might seem to your intellect. His Way, though opposite to the way of the world, will save you from the storm.

Today, become like a child. Set aside all that you think you know so that you might truly *know* Him in spirit and in truth. Today, fall into your Father's arms. Let the chains placed on you by the flesh fall away.

This is the Way of Yeshua.

So become like a child. Let go and trust. You are safe.

CONTEMPLATION

Think of your mind and body as a boat in the troubled sea, and the waves as all that threatens you. Yeshua could calm storms and walk on water.[12] Why do the Scriptures put such an emphasis on this extraordinary demonstration of illogical power? He was surely showing you His Way.

Yeshua calls out to you now. *Come.* But you are afraid of the dark sea because you know what happens when you step out of the boat. The evidence is certain and your understanding is firm: you will drown. This is what the world has taught you.

The boat is the world's plan of salvation from the storms of this life. Thus you have spent your entire life reinforcing the boat, and clinging to it, thinking it will save you. Truly, you worship your boat—your agreements with yourself, your particular philosophy, your intelligence, your possessions, your relationships with family, spouse, and friends. Your faith is in them. And so you do not truly believe in Yeshua to save you in this life.

The boat is the world's plan of salvation from the storms of this life, set up in direct opposition to Yeshua's Way, which is to trust Him beyond all the evidence that the world shows you. You may choose to remain in the bottom of your boat, trembling with fear as the storms rage, or you may let go of what you thought would keep you safe, and trust in Yeshua and so find peace.

Staying in the boat will keep you in misery. Following Yeshua's Way will bring you peace and power over the storms of life. These are your only two choices.

Today you take a major step in remembering who offers you so much. *Come to me all who are weary and burdened with heaviness and I will give you rest,* Yeshua says. *My burden is light and my Way is easy if you will only follow.*[13] Doing so will only cost you all the lies you have believed, whispered by the accuser who would master you.

Today is your day of liberation. Today you have another master, Yeshua, and in Him you are already safe and complete.

PRAYER

Today I will set my mind on You, Yeshua. Fill me with Your Spirit and renew my mind so that I can trust in You rather than in this world, which only enslaves me. So much of what I see intoxicates me with lies. Help me see You instead, because You are the only Way, the only Truth, the only Life.

What a beautiful Savior You are! Without You I would sink beneath the waves and sink into the dark sea. But with You I am saved and made perfect. All the whispers of the flesh are only lies.

Thank You, Yeshua. Thank You for showing me the Way.

ALIGNMENT

That I might know Christ and the power of His resurrection
That I might know Christ and the power of my resurrection in Him

By now you know through your own experience in these meditations that your perception of the world and your identity in the world easily bind you in a false prison of your own making. In truth you are free from the prison, yet you cling to its bars, thinking it will keep you safe from those who come to attack you.

Today, let go of what you think will keep you safe in this world— relationships, wealth, comforts, status, honor, all of it—and trust in Christ in you as a small child would trust. In so doing, you are aligning yourself with who you already are as your Father's risen son, His glorified daughter.

Say this today: *Today, I become like a child as Yeshua showed me. I am reborn in the light and all fear is gone. I trust in who my Father is and who I am in Christ, already safe. My eternal self already knows who she is, and now I align my earthen vessel self with that knowing in Christ.*

I am free from this prison that I thought held me captive! The darkness is gone in this light! I am free, I am free, I am free! I am healed, I am healed, I am healed!

THIRTEEN

BEAUTIFUL, BEAUTIFUL BROTHER AND SAVIOR

*During the days of Yeshua's life on Earth, he offered up
prayers and petitions with fervent cries and tears to the
one who could save him from death,
and he was heard because of his reverent submission.
Son though he was, he learned obedience
from what he suffered and once made perfect, he became
the source of eternal salvation for all who obey him.*

HEBREWS 5:7-9

MEDITATION

The love of your Father has been re-presented to you in these meditations. The glory of Yeshua, His only begotten Son, was revealed when He came to restore you and all of creation into Himself by undoing the great deception of Adam.

You have seen, with new eyes, who you are in Yeshua. He is in you, and through Him you are reunited with your Father, complete. You have risen with Yeshua and are now seated in the eternal realm of the Father.

None of this truth can be seen with natural vision, which has led you into captivity to the systems of this world. New sight is the means to see the kingdom of heaven.

And surrender is the means to that sight.

Though the thought of surrender may strike fear into your heart, that fear is only the flesh whispering its lies once again. In truth you will only surrender feebleness for power, misery for joy, hate for love, death for life, anxiety for peace, jealousy for security, loathing for wonder, terror for boldness, dust for stars.

Above all, you will surrender the last vestiges that fuel your fears of a vengeful Father, because you cannot love what you fear. You cannot be aligned with what you fear, nor can you disobey what you love. As Yeshua said, *If you don't obey me, you do not love me.*[1]

What, then, does it mean to obey?

Obedience can be thought of as alignment. Consider a bolt and a nut. When the bolt's threads match the nut's threads, the bolt aligns properly with the nut and they become joined as one. The bolt "obeys" the nut. Two become one in intimate union. Speaking of Yeshua and you, Paul wrote. *the two shall be joined and shall become one flesh,* as in marriage.[2] Life comes from such a union.

Sometimes the bolt may need to be cleaned or rethreaded to allow for proper alignment. This is the process we call purification—the purging of the chaff in your mind that keeps you from seeing and being who you are in Christ.

Blessed are the pure in heart, Yeshua says, *for they will **see** God.*[3] *Pure* simply means "clean." Or "single-purposed" or "not cross-threaded." Purification of the heart aligns you with the Father so that you can see and know Him and His incomparably great love and power for you as you believe.

It removes all that blinds you to the staggering reality that Yeshua has taken you into His heart. When the clouds that block your vision are removed (purification), the eyes of your heart are opened and you become aware of who you are.

Truly, purification allows you to realize that you are not who you thought you were in the flesh. Like in the story of Superman, it strips away Clark Kent's business suit and reveals his truest identity. In your case, stripping away your old costume reveals that you are, as Paul said, already *clothed in Christ.*[4] Purification, then, allows you to fly. What a beautiful gift it is.

You have heard of your Father's judgment and wrath and anger, and all of these exist, but the meaning of the words have been twisted by the accuser's deception. These have inflamed your fear, which is not from your Father or His Son or His Spirit. There is no fear in love. God is love. He is kind and gentle, even with evil men, as Yeshua said.[5]

Today we will take great strides in removing the fear of such words so that you can love and trust your Father once again.

The purification and "wrath" of your Father are beautiful. They are not like the judgment of your earthly father, who reacts emotionally out of fear that he might lose possession, respect, or authority. Remember, nothing can threaten or even bother your heavenly Father. He is not like the false gods who cringe in fear and scream in anger.

Think of a beautiful valley that you happen upon one day while hiking in the mountains. You see lush, green vegetation, and bright flowers in meadows with tall trees reaching for the sky. It is stunning and you gaze in awe.

Then a ranger comes by and tells you why it's so beautiful. It was a mess of underbrush only ten years earlier, but a forest fire came through and ravaged the valley. The fire cleansed the valley and made way for new growth that resulted in the current awe-inspiring beauty.

The struggles you face are like a fire that is cleansing away all the chaff and underbrush in your life. In the heat of that fire, you feel as though hell has visited you on Earth. But take courage and count it all joy when the fires come, because stunning beauty awaits you in your transformation.[6]

Your Father lovingly prunes away whatever destroys and crushes you. You have only to *surrender* to His love, just like Yeshua did while He was on Earth.

You have in Yeshua an elder brother, as Paul called Him[7], who understands your life. He was tested and stretched in every way you have been and yet did not separate Himself from the Father when the trials came.[8]

And what great *struggle* He felt in His temptation in the desert[9]; what great *fear* haunted Him in the garden[10]; what great *challenges* He faced all through His life.

But Yeshua, because He was fully human, though fully God, learned obedience through His suffering. As it is written, *During the days of Yeshua's life on Earth, He offered up prayer and petitions with fervent cries and tears to the One who could save Him from death, and He was Heard **because of his reverent surrender**. Son though He was, He **learned obedience** from what He suffered and once made perfect, He became the source of eternal salvation for all who **obey Him**.*[11]

In a mysterious and beautiful way, even Yeshua learned obedience to His Father through suffering. He, like you, struggled in every way. Truly, He had no advantage over you while He was on Earth. What a beautiful Savior.

Fear entered the world through Adam in the first garden (of Eden). Yeshua overcame His fear in the second garden (Gethsemane), as the second Adam.[12] There He surrendered His will and restored perfection so that we too may overcome fear, for He has overcome the world. What a beautiful Savior.

Where the first Adam said, *Not your will but mine*, and so plunged the world into darkness, the second Adam, Yeshua, reversed the first Adam's fall, saying instead, *Not my will but yours*,[13] and restored the world to light.

Do you see? Although Yeshua, in His incarnation, struggled between His own human will and His Father's will, He surrendered His will to His Father's. Clearly, Yeshua had no desire to be tortured. His human will was to avoid such a protracted, brutal death. But through tears and anguish He surrendered that will. Thus He prayed, *Not my will, but yours be done.* What a beautiful Savior.

Though being God, Yeshua felt your anguish as His own and had to learn obedience. But His heart shared His Father's will. Was He not fully human *and* fully God? His surrender was to lay down His human will so that His Father's will could fully surface.

Do you see? By learning obedience and submitting to His Father's will, He came into full alignment with His own true will as the Son of His Father. And thus He became the Way for all those who would also align themselves with (obey) the Father.

The same is true for you. Your true self, having been raised with Yeshua, also shares your Father's will. When you surrender the will of your flesh, you can be who you truly are in Him. Then your laments and sorrows are transformed to peace and love.

This doesn't mean you are God, as Yeshua was, but it does mean that you take the same journey He did—learning to align your will with your Father's. *Not my will but yours be done.* His will is beautiful, because it aligns you with your true identity as the son, the daughter of the Father, who has given you incomparably great power for this age, the greatest of which is to love as He loves.

Surrender your will in the flesh so you can be who you are in Christ. And when you feel forsaken in your journey of surrender, have hope, because Yeshua understands that lament and declares that you have not been forsaken.

To obey is to align your heart with the Father's by trusting Him as a little child would trust a father who has never hurt her. To obey is to offer love, joy, and peace to the storms of life.

What a beautiful, beautiful brother and Savior we have in Yeshua. He showed us the Way by taking it Himself. Then, *once made perfect, He became the source of salvation for all who obey Him.*

CONTEMPLATION

Do not follow me or any other man or woman. Follow Yeshua only. See Him in a new way: as one who took the same journey that you are taking. See Him letting go of all encumbrances and temptations so He could be upon that cross for you.

Today, meditate on His glory as one who finally let go of life itself so that you could be reconciled to God. He let go of His will and His body to show you His Way of surrender. He did so for the glory set before Him. And He did it so you might live as a resurrected being now, before your physical death. All you have to do is let go of the mad notion that you are not already risen and glorified as the son, the daughter of the Father.

He is the forerunner who led the new way and showed you how to let go of the old way, making His death and resurrection real for you today.

Meditate on Yeshua and worship Him, for He is worthy.

PRAYER

Yeshua, Lord and Savior, during Your life on Earth You offered up prayer with fervent cries and tears in reverent submission. Son though You were, You learned obedience from what You suffered. And once made perfect, You became the source of my salvation from all troubles. I too will walk in obedience, just as You did.

Because of Your willingness, I no longer have to die. Now only the lies in me have to die, and they will as I follow the Way You showed me while You lived on this earth.

Thank You for You love. Thank You for showing me the Way. Thank You for being that Way. I am in awe of You. It is no wonder every knee will bow before You. It is no wonder every tongue will confess that You are Lord. It is no wonder all of creation will worship You. You are truly a beautiful, beautiful brother and Savior.

ALIGNMENT

That I might know Christ, and the power of His resurrection
And the fellowship of His suffering, being conformed to his death
Philippians 3:10

What joy you will find through your alignment with Christ, who is in you, and you, who are in Him!

It is because Yeshua learned obedience and came into alignment with the Father's will that you can also come into alignment with who you are in Him!

It is because He died that your old self is dead. And so you conform to His death.

It is because He rose that you rose, and it is because He was glorified that you are glorified. And so we are in awe of our elder Brother and Savior today!

Today, sing! Be glad! Christ is the way as we align ourselves with (obey) the truth that Christ is risen and we are in Christ, risen with Him as one.

Say this today: *Today, I surrender my old mind's lies that I am not who Yeshua says I am. Today I align myself with the Way, the Truth, and the Life. He came so that I would experience life abundant in this valley of shadows. He showed me who I am so that my joy might be full!*

Today, I am saved from the valley of the shadow of death and today I will fear no evil.

FOURTEEN
STEP OUT OF YOUR PRISON

No one can serve two masters.
You will hate the one and love the other,
You cannot serve both God and Mammon.
MATTHEW 6:24

If anyone comes to me and does not hate his
own father and mother
And wife and children . . . even his own life
He cannot be my disciple.
LUKE 14:26

Whoever finds their life will lose it,
Whoever loses their life for my sake will find it.
MATTHEW 10:39

If anyone wishes to come after me, he must deny himself
And take up his cross and follow me.
MARK 8:34

MEDITATION

The Way of Yeshua offers complete freedom and peace in your everyday life. Your path on Earth is to glorify God by enjoying Him and all He has made for you. What pleasure and gladness await you!

And yet following His Way is impossible without first being aware of who He made you to be, which is why we have spent so much time looking at our identity in Him.

It is because He surrendered His own human will for His Father's that He was perfected and went willingly to the cross for you.

It is because of His death that you, having died with Him, are now dead to that separation between you and your Father.

It is because He died that He rose again, and you with Him, already.

It is because He rose again that you are now ascended with Him, and so live in the heavenly realm, called the kingdom of heaven.[1]

Yeshua endured the cross for the glory set before Him, but you have that glory already because the Father has given you the same glory He gave Yeshua.[2] This is *because* of Yeshua. This is indeed the good news for all who believe. This we call the gospel.

Blinded, you cannot see who you are. Seeing, you perceive the truth. Surrender is the means by which you can see.

These truths are the foundation of all that remains in your journey. Yes, there are many other truths, but these are the ones that make the accuser cringe, fearing your liberation should you hear and know their truth.

Whenever you believe the truth, you will find yourself full of grace and love and power in Yeshua. Try it and you will see. You will find peace in the storms and walk on the troubled seas of your life. Then, and only then, can you love as He loved.

But when you believe a lie instead of truth, you needlessly suffer the effects of that lie, and find yourself enslaved once more.[3] But today you can surrender those old lies and walk free from your prison once more.

The only reason you ever feel offense instead of love and thus find misery in this life is because you have bound yourself to the deception that you are not already complete and in need of nothing as the son or daughter of God.

The way of the world offers a lie that it can offer you security, though you are perfectly secure already.

The lie that your wealth can save you from irrelevance, though you are royalty already.

The lie that your relationships—with children and spouse and friends—can satisfy your need for acceptance and love, though you are love itself as the light of the world.

The lie that your body or your status or your position can save you from unworthiness, though all that the Father has belongs to you already.

When you bind yourself to such deception, you place your identity in the world that is temporal rather than in Yeshua. Indeed, to the extent you place your primary meaning in *anything* other than the kingdom of heaven, in which you are far more powerful than you can yet imagine, you will find yourself imprisoned by the world.

This is why Yeshua said that the more you invest yourself in the systems of this world (symbolized by mammon or money), the more you serve them. But you cannot serve both God and mammon.[4]

This is why Yeshua said, in one of His most controversial teachings, that you cannot follow Him into the kingdom of heaven beyond the skin of this world unless you *hate* (hold of no account) all of your attachments to this world.[5]

Do you remember His teaching that you must lose yourself for His name's sake to find life?[6] Which self then must you lose? That self which is temporal, that which is seen with your earthly eyes, that which is an earthen vessel—let your attachment to it go. It's a beautiful gift but it isn't who you are.

Do you remember His teaching that you must deny yourself and take up your cross if you want to experience the kingdom of heaven with Him? Again, which self must you deny and place on the cross each day?[6]

Not the self that is risen and eternal, but the earthen vessel that decays, the outer man, the self that is seen as a part of the system of the world, the old man with all of its attachments to the world of mammon.

If you live for what moth and rust destroy and for the body that decays, you will suffer the consequences of that decay. In the same way, if you live for relationships, you will suffer the failings of those relationships. If you live for money, you will be bound by the laws of money. If you live for food, you will worry when there is none, and if you live for pleasure, you will grow sick with that same pleasure.

To the extent these things command your ambition, significance, meaning, and purpose, they enslave you and blind you to who you are, complete and perfectly at peace in Him as the son or daughter of your Father.

THE SIN THAT BLINDS YOU

So many cringe at the word *sin*, and many use it as a weapon to accuse others. But today you will see that it is nothing to fear, only to be avoided, because sin is what blinds you to your staggering light in Yeshua.

Anything in this world that separates you from your intimate experience of the Father is called sin. As Paul wrote, *whatever you do that is not done in faith* (believing in Yeshua), *for you it is sin* (separation).[7] Whatever you do that prevents you from seeing your identity in Yeshua leaves you feeling separated and lost.

And he wrote more: *All things are lawful for me, but not all things are profitable. I will not be mastered by anything.*[8] What blinds and masters one is not necessarily the same as what blinds and masters another, as James wrote.[9]

Think of the many things in this life that distort your vision of your incredible identity as the son or daughter of the Father. All that causes you offense and seems to threaten you, and all that distracts you or fills you with fear of loss. Everything that is not done in faith. When you place your identity in this world with all of its relationships, status, and possessions, you seek your significance in them and so place your faith in them rather than in your true identity.

Thus, it can be said that we all live in sin often, many times each day, whenever we are anxious or angry or do not love those who attack us. Truly, as John wrote: *If we* (Christians) *say that we have no sin, we are deceiving ourselves and the truth is not in us.* Indeed, if you say you have no sin, then pride is your sin.

But do not fear—though your sin dramatically compromises your experience of the kingdom of heaven now at hand and thus leads you to misery, it doesn't make you any less of a son or daughter of the Father. If sin could do that to the sons and daughters of God, we would all be thrown out of our Father's house many times each day. Each time we are distracted by the concerns of the world, we would be cast into the grave, then rise again and be glorified again, only to then be unglorified once more, like a yo-yo, up and down, up and down.

Is your security in Christ so dependent upon your own effort? If so, then you are no better off than those under the law, which will accuse you relentlessly. You will then condemn yourself, which is yet another sin.

Make no mistake, all that is *not* done in faith will lead you into misery in this life, but do not condemn what the Father does not. You are His son, His daughter—so love yourself as He loves you, and flee all that would distract and blind you to this undeniable truth.

When you notice what blinds you to the awareness of your true identity, you will have identified what enslaves you (sin).

And when you surrender that master to Yeshua, you will be free to take great joy in everything that has been given to you as the son of your Father. Each bite of food will be like heaven; the touch of a lover's hand will be like a kiss from your Father; the clothes you wear will be the gift of beauty; you will be like the child in a candy store who relishes every good piece without needing any.

As it is written, you will reap what you sow. If you sow yourself to your own flesh, you will reap the destruction that comes from your identity with the world of flesh. And if you sow to the spirit, you will reap eternal life here and now.[10]

YOU HAVE ONLY TWO CHOICES

You have two choices now, and only two. Choose your master each and every moment. One will give you power and love; one promises the same but lies and leads you into misery.

Think of your mind as divided. Part is caught in the lies of the flesh and your old will; the other part is one with Yeshua, who is the Truth and shares the will of the Father. Your choice is to believe one or the other. You cannot believe both at the same time.

You cannot see two worlds at once, or darkness and light at once.

You cannot serve two masters, as Yeshua said. You cannot serve both God and the system of the world called mammon. You cannot serve both fear and freedom. You cannot serve both offense and forgiveness. You cannot serve both love and judgment. You get to choose one master or the other.

Which will you choose? All of your life comes down to this very simple choice in every moment. What do you choose to see? Who will you put your faith in: your old self, or Yeshua in whom you live and move and have your being? Who will you listen to: the Holy Spirit within you, or the flesh and the accuser of that flesh?

Consider all the schemes that your flesh promised would bring you salvation from the storm. Has listening to the guidance of the flesh ever saved you? Be honest with yourself and you will know the truth.

You will listen to madness, or you will listen to the truth. Two choices. One is your prison; one is your freedom.

But do not judge yourself for your own madness if you cannot hear or see the truth, for now we see only in part.[11] Even awareness of your blindness is a giant step forward in your journey of seeing.

So then, be glad even that you can now *see* your blindness. So few do. Thus, you are blessed and see already.

CONTEMPLATION

In September 1981, a group of eight men in their seventies and eighties entered a monastery two hours south of Boston. They were part of an extensive study on the effects of perception and belief. Their task was simple: they were to actively pretend that they were twenty-two years younger and healthier.

When they arrived, they found the monastery had been transformed to reflect the earlier time period. All news, magazines, memorabilia, clothing styles, music, food, even activities, were taken from the fifties and sixties. For five days the men were immersed in yesteryear, and they embraced that world with abandon.

A second group came the following week, and although the environment was the same, the participants weren't told to pretend they were younger.

At the end of the study, both groups were put through extensive examinations, the results of which were compared to examinations taken before each man entered the monastery.

When the results came in, the researchers were stunned. By all indicators, the men who had pretended to be younger actually became physically and mentally younger. Their posture, height, weight, gait, flexibility, memory, cognition, eyesight, bone length, and blood chemistry had all shifted to reflect slightly healthier, younger versions of themselves.

The control group that had not actively pretended to be younger showed no change.

Far more than you realize, *what you believe (and so perceive) about yourself determines the experience you have in this life*. Truly, these men lost one life to find another through belief alone.

Who do you believe yourself to be today? Or more to the point, who *are* you being today? Your old self living in condemnation and judgment, or your new self, already risen with Christ and seated in heavenly realms?

Even now, after all you've learned, will you continue to cling to the security of that old-self boat, the one you thought would save you from the troubled seas? You can see everything that you thought would keep you safe and give you meaning. There, your religion; there, your family; there, your wealth; there, your status; there, your ministry; there, your clothing; there, your career. Will you put your faith in that boat?

Or will you step out of the boat as the son, the daughter of the Father, and walk in faith with your eyes fixed on Yeshua? Only in Him are you complete. Only in Him do you have real power. Only in Him can you love as He loves.

No one can serve two masters. Today, choose to be who you are in Yeshua, and be free.

PRAYER

Yeshua, today I choose to believe in You once again, that I might be saved. I choose to put my eyes on You and take Your hand. I choose to remember the truth of who I am, because I am in You even as You are in me.

What a beautiful Savior You are to have made me one with You, no longer threatened by any storm. What a beautiful Master. I surrender my sight to You.

I choose You, and in You there is no darkness, only light. I, too, am the light of the world, and I choose to see in the light, not in darkness. I choose You, and I am free from the shackles of my old mind, which only shows me lies.

Now with great relief and peace, I thank You. Thank You, beautiful Master.

Thank You.

ALIGNMENT

That I might know Christ and the power of His resurrection
That I might know Christ and the power of my resurrection in Him

Today the way is made plain. You will align with truth or with a lie.

You will align with love or with fear. You will align with the law of grace or with the law of sin and death. You will align with your resurrection or with the shadow of death. You will align with Christ who speaks truth or with the serpent who whispers and deceives. You will align with your eternal, risen self in Christ, or with the earthen-vessel self still in the grave.

Aligning yourself with the risen self means letting go of your attachment to your old self who has died on that cross with Christ already. This is taking up the cross each day, as Yeshua taught. Lay that old you on the altar and join your identity in Christ, resurrected already.

You can align yourself with only one master: the resurrected self in Christ, or the old self lost in the shadows of death.

The choice is yours. Today, choose Christ and be saved in the valley of the shadow of death.

Say this today: *I choose to align myself with the truth today. I align myself with the law of grace, not the law of sin and death. I align myself with Christ, not with the old self. I align myself with my risen self in Christ, no longer enslaved by the grave in the valley of death's shadow.*

Today, I align myself with who I am.

THE WAY: SUMMARY

In the second section we have entered seven meditations on the *Way* of Yeshua, which is to *see* who you are in the eternal realm of the Father's presence now at hand by surrendering attachment to all other identities.

These constitute the third and fourth declarations of The Forgotten Way.

THE THIRD DECLARATION
Meditations 8-11

Your journey now is to see who you truly are, for you are the light of the world, the son or the daughter of your Father, a new creature flowing with more beauty and power than you have dared imagine possible.

THE FOURTH DECLARATION
Meditations 12-14

You will only see who you are and thus be who you are as you surrender your attachment to all other identities, which are like gods of a lesser power that block your vision of your true identity and keep you in darkness.

III

THE LIFE

Yeshua made it plain: *I am the Way, the Truth and the Life.*

In this final section we will enter seven meditations (15-21) on our *Life* in Yeshua. This is the manifestation of the Father and ourselves on Earth as we are in heaven, evidenced by love, joy, peace and power. And the greatest of these is love.

This constitutes the fifth declaration of The Forgotten Way.

THE FIFTH DECLARATION

Love, joy, and peace are the manifestation of your true identity
and the Father's realm, on Earth as in heaven
through the power of the Holy Spirit.

FIFTEEN

THE EVIDENCE OF YOU IS LOVE

If I speak in the tongues of men and angels, but do not have love, I have become a noisy gong or a clanging cymbal. If I have the gift of prophecy, and know all mysteries and all knowledge; and if I have faith to move mountains, but do not have love, I am nothing.

1 CORINTHIANS 13:1-2

For now we see only a reflection as in a mirror; then we will see face to face. Now I know in part; then I shall know fully, even as I am fully known. And now these three remain: faith, hope and love. But the greatest of these is love.

1 CORINTHIANS 13:12-13 NIV

MEDITATION

In these meditations we have seen the extravagant love of the Father and of Yeshua, the second Adam, who restored us into union with the Father in the eternal realm.

In this life we can *know* (experience) only in part, but in the next life we will *know* (experience) fully.[1] And yet, even knowing in part fills us with love, joy, and peace, which are the fruit of the Spirit, as opposed to grievance, which is the fruit of the fall. It is by our love that we are known as people of the Way of Yeshua.[2]

To *know* the Father is to experience eternal life. And the Father's expression of eternal life on Earth, the will of the Father, is *love*, which sums up all that is written in the Scriptures.[3]

This should come as no surprise, because God—Father, Son, and Holy Spirit—not only loves you, He Himself *is* love. And you who follow Him and call yourself "Christian" will be known for that same love.[4] Thus, the greatest evidence of our union with Christ is our love.

But what kind of love? Surely the same kind of love that Yeshua shows in loving us, a love that Paul eloquently describes in the most well-known passage of all Scripture;

Love is patient. Love is kind.
Love always trusts. Love always hopes.
Love shows no jealousy. Love shows no arrogance.
Love does not seek its own. Love does not dishonor others.
Love keeps no record of wrong. Love is not provoked.
1 Corinthians 13

Are you self-serving? Do you keep any record of wrong? Are you provoked by another person's behavior?

If you are like me, you must say yes. And yes. And yes. Much of the time. And in every one of those times, often throughout the day, it is only because we are not manifesting love as it has been shown to us.

Although united with Yeshua, we often show every evidence but this one, and so find ourselves powerless in this life.

We may speak passionate words in the tongues of men and angels, but if we rise up in anger at our brother when wronged, we only prove that we are without love and so make a mockery of His love.

We may study the Scriptures and vigorously defend our doctrine and write eloquently of our knowledge, but if we don't show kindness to our enemies, we only show that our doctrine is useless.

We may call Him Lord and give all of our possessions to the poor and surrender our body to be burned and have faith to move mountains and heal disease. And yet these will profit us nothing if the evidence of His Spirit called love does not rule our heart.

As Paul wrote, if you say and do all the right things—if you speak the tongues of men and angels; if you proclaim His truth to all; if you fathom all the mysteries and doctrine; if you give all you have to the poor; if you suffer for the Kingdom; if you have faith to move mountains— but don't have the kind of love that holds no record of wrong, then all you believe, say, and do is utterly worthless.[5]

It is impossible for the flesh to love without secretly seeking some self-serving payoff. It is impossible for the flesh to keep no record of wrong, because doing so means not recording wrong in the first place. Thus we fail to love as Christ loves far too often.

And yet this kind of love, expressed through us, is what shows the world the Father's love. Is it any wonder, then, that the world doubts lofty "Christian" rhetoric and, by extension, Yeshua Himself?

Surely the inability to love as the world does not love is the elephant in the room of nearly all who call themselves Christian.

FINDING LOVE ONCE AGAIN

The only way to love as the Father loves is to experience a revelation of who the Father is and who you are as His son or daughter in Christ.

Without grasping your union in Yeshua, risen and glorified with Him, seated in the heavens already, love will always be a frustrating exercise in futility, because you will be trying to love out of the flesh. Only through your identification with Yeshua can you be love in this world.

But take heart, because that revelation is at hand. Hear Yeshua's promise to help you grasp your union with Him.

The Father will give you another Helper . . . that is the Spirit of truth . . . In that day (the coming of the Spirit) *you will know that I am in my Father, and you are in me, and I am in you . . . so that the world may know that* (the Father) *sent me and loved them even as* (the Father) *has loved me.*[6]

Do you see? It could be said that the primary purpose of the Holy Spirit is to reveal that you are one with and in Christ. As you experience your true identity in Christ, you will naturally love as He loves. How can you take offense at the enemy when they are only attacking your earthen vessel? How can you not love the worst in your eyes when you see that they are only blind to the Father's love?

When you love as the Father loves, without condemnation, then the world will know Yeshua was sent by the Father, and that the Father loves all in the same way He loves His Son, as Yeshua said.

But perhaps you are blind to the Father's love for you. It is impossible to truly love yourself or others as yourself unless you have first experienced the Father's love for you.

What, then, is the nature of your Father's love for you? Do you think He asks you to express love in any way He does not?

If He asks you to turn the other cheek, do you think He does not?

If He asks you not to be offended by insults, do you think He can be?

Hear again Paul's description of God's love for you: *Love is patient, love is kind, love is not jealous, love does not dishonor others, friends or enemies.*[7] *Love always trusts. Love always hopes. Love shows no arrogance. Love keeps no record of wrong. Love is not provoked by another person's behavior.*[8]

But of course. Because God, who is infinitely complete, cannot be compromised or threatened or in any way wounded. Indeed, God is the very essence of love itself.

You may look at your life situation and doubt that God is kind to you, but this is only because you have married yourself to the system of the world, which is unkind to you. Trust Him—the life you live on Earth will be over in a blink of an eye, and then you will see how needlessly you lived in fear.

You may look at your life and think He doesn't trust you, but He sees you in His likeness and trusts you to the ends of the earth. So trust Him. It's all going to work out for good.

You may look at the troubles rising against you and think that God is provoked, but your infinite Father cannot be threatened or provoked like an earthly father can be. Neither can you fail the One who is infinitely complete and cannot be compromised. Only the darkness you see blinds you from seeing how innocent and complete you are in His eyes, because He has made you so.

When you listen to the accuser, who whispers lies about the Father's condemnation, you embrace deception and project your own self-condemnation onto the world. Your misery deepens. Your awareness of the Father's love for the world fades.

But today you will see beyond the deception that has blinded you. Today is the day of your liberation from that prison that has held you captive to self-loathing. Today, you see with new eyes how deep is the Father's love for you! Seeing it, you will begin to love yourself as He loves you. And as you love yourself, you will be able to love your neighbor as yourself.

By this all will know that you are in Christ, because only in Him can anyone love with such a staggering love.

The evidence of Yeshua in you is love.

CONTEMPLATION

Imagine a world in which you do not offer yourself or others any condemnation for any reason. Imagine not keeping a record of any wrongs, including those you thought threatened you a decade ago, or a month ago, even only an hour ago.

Imagine living in a world in which no one condemned you for any failure or shortcoming. A world in which everyone loved everyone without blame.

There would be no war. No envy, no strife. No secret thoughts of bitterness against others or yourself. Does this not sound like the will of the Father on Earth as it is in heaven? Would it not be a new earth? And surely that day is coming.

Would it not also be like the Garden of Eden, before the deceiver convinced Adam and Eve that they were *not* created in the likeness of God and could be like Him only by eating of the knowledge of good and evil? They had no grievance or judgment or shame until darkness blocked their vision of the light of their true identity.

But Yeshua, the second Adam, has undone that fall. And you, being reborn in Yeshua and He in you, are the light of the world even as He is the light of the world.

May the eyes of your heart be opened so that you can see the light now shining in you as love. Find your Father and you will have found love. Find your *true self* and you will have found *true love,* because you are one with Christ, who is love.

PRAYER

Father, I come to You stripped of all my preconceived notions of who I thought I was in the flesh. Open my eyes that I might see You in myself and myself in You. Though deception has blocked my sight of Your love, I call upon You to restore my sight.

Holy Spirit, my Comforter and guide in this life, fill me with the full awareness of my Father and my true identity as His child. Fill my heart with gladness and celebration, for I am that prodigal come home to feast at the banquet You have prepared for me in the presence of the enemy, who has no power in the truth.

I worship You, for You have made me whole. And as I stare at myself, I stare at a reflection of You. What a wonder You are. What a magnificent, loving Father who made me like You.

ALIGNMENT

That I might know Christ and the power of His resurrection
That I might know Christ and the power of my resurrection in Him

Today is the day of mirrors. Seek them out. Each time you find one, look closely at the image you see in the glass. What you see is the son, the daughter of God. Look into your eyes, beyond your pupils. What you see is the image of your Creator, beyond the earthen vessel that has hidden her for so long.

Today you see Him as in a mirror.

Look at yourself and dare not condemn the risen son, the glorified daughter of the Father, made in His likeness. Instead, whisper your gratitude in wonder of what you see in the same way a child stares with wonder at a sight that fills her with awe.

Look and stand in wonder, because what you see is only a dim reflection of the wonder your Father has as He gazes upon His son, His daughter.

SIXTEEN

BEING LOVE IN THE DARKNESS

Love the Lord your God with all your heart, and
with all your soul, and with all your strength and
with all your mind; and your neighbor as yourself.
Do this and you will live.

LUKE 10:27-28

Whatever you did not do to the least of these,
you did not do to me.

MATTHEW 25:45 NIV

MEDITATION

The power of love is staggering. In seeing how we are loved, we begin to love ourselves and our Father as He loves us. By loving others as ourselves, we shine Yeshua's light on the blind, and they too see.

The light of the world *is* love.

Love is the expression of the kingdom of heaven on Earth.

Love is the will of the Father expressed on Earth as it is known in heaven.

Love is the currency of God, who knows no fear. He cannot be threatened by anything that would rise up to terrify His sons and daughters.

There is no fear in love; perfect love casts out all fear.

It is said that all evil is rooted in fear. And all fear is only the fear of loss. But there is no fear in love, because love knows no fear of loss.

What do you fear losing?

Why do you fear that loss? Why do you fear the storms that rise up to threaten your sandcastles? Why are you anxious for tomorrow? Why do you worry about the past and fret about who will do what, when, and why?[1]

You fear only when you place your faith in the system of the world rather than in the love of the Father. Only when you place your identity in others and in your outer self rather than in Yeshua and yourself in Him.

When you grasp the length, the depth, and the breadth of Yeshua's love and power, which surpasses all knowledge, your worries will vanish.[2]

You can choose to be enslaved by the system of the world, or you can place your belief in Yeshua, because you recognize yourself as the son, the daughter of the Father in His realm.

And the wonder reaches further, because now as you gaze about, you see that your wife, your husband, your son, your daughter, your mother and father, your neighbor—even those you think of as "the least" in this world darkened by judgment—are also children of the Father.

Remember what Yeshua said when He spoke of those who were cast out by society: *What you did not do to the least of these, you did not do to me. And what you did to the least of these, you did to me.*[3]

Yeshua did not say, "What you do to the least, you do *as if* unto me." He said, "What you do to the least, you do *to* me." As if He was, in some mysterious way, them.

In His time, the *least of these* to which He was referring were the poor and the diseased. Their suffering was considered by most to be God's punishment for sin. To Yeshua's listeners, for Him to equate Himself with such people was shocking and scandalous.

Are you not, like the apostle Paul, who called himself the chief of sinners,[4] not also among the *least of these*? How do you treat yourself, who is the *least of these*? Do you condemn rather than love the one (yourself) who is one in Christ?

And as for your brothers, did Yeshua not say we are to be one with them, in the same way He is one with the Father?[5]

How this mystery can be is beyond us. But as you follow Yeshua by loving others *as* yourself—as you love them *as* Yeshua—you will find your heart filled with peace and power. Then the world will know that you are a Christian, by *that* kind of love.

No matter what you've thought of those you've condemned and cast out, you now get to treat them as the children of the Father. This, too, is to believe in Yeshua. It is not your role, in heart or mind, to condemn others any more than it is your role to condemn yourself.

Remember, what *you* believe about yourself and others doesn't define you or them. Rather, what your *Father* believes defines both you and them. Your belief only defines the experience you have in this life.

So love yourself as the Father loves you, His beloved son or daughter. And then love your neighbor *as* yourself.[6]

The sum of the matter is this: you are in Yeshua and He is in you. You are unified with Him as the son, the daughter of the Father. Love yourself as such and no less, lest you condemn the son, the daughter of God.

Do not think what you might do *for* Yeshua. Rather, follow His teaching and *be* Yeshua to the world. You are His body on Earth.[7]

Does a dog strive to be a dog? Does a tree strive to be a tree? Yet in simply *being*, a tree provides shade for weary travelers and branches where birds can nest.

In the same way, when you see that you already are the son, the daughter of the Father, you will naturally be Yeshua to the world. All of your doing comes naturally out of who you are, and you are one with Him.

As your eyes are opened to this stunning way of being in the world, you will find yourself free of the prison walls that held you captive in self-condemnation and deception. The light that you already are will flood your perception of the world, and you will shout for joy.

CONTEMPLATION

There was once a young girl who went to the river to draw water. Coming to the river, she saw a spider in the tide pool, drowning. So she set down her wooden bucket, dipped her hands into the water, and gently lifted the spider from certain death.

But the spider, being a spider, bit her hand, causing her great pain. She set the spider down, drew her water, and went home, singing.

When she returned to the river with her bucket the next day, she saw the same spider, again drowning. Once again, she dipped her hands into the water and gently lifted the spider to safety.

Once again the spider, being a spider, bit her.

The next day, coming to draw water, she saw the same spider, drowning yet again. So she dipped her hands into the water and once again lifted the spider to safety. But this time the spider spoke to her.

"Why do you save me, knowing that I am a spider who is poisonous and this is what I do?" it asked.

She set it down and smiled. "Because I am the daughter of my Father who is love, and this is what I do."

So ask yourself, *Who am I?*

Are you a dancer, a writer, a mother, a businessman, a truck driver, a teenager, a Christian?

No. These are only *roles* you play. What you *are* is the daughter, the son of the Father. Seeing that, now do whatever you do as that daughter or son. Until you embrace your true identity, you will always struggle in vain to be who you think you should be and do what you think you should do.

When you do see who you are, you will also see others in that same light, and you will give yourself for them.

Then you will spend your life loving the world as the son or daughter of the Father. Then you will love the outcasts on dark streets. Then you will gaze with wonder at the one who serves you in the restaurant, and look with compassion at the politician who stings you or the brother who calls you a sinner.

Seeing *this* kind of love, the world will know that Yeshua was sent by the Father who loves all, the way He loves Yeshua.

God *is* love. And so are you. Now be who you are.

PRAYER

Father, give me eyes to see all those in my world as You see them, so I can love them as You love them. For You love all far more than any earthly father loves his infant son or daughter.

Let me see that same love already within me, beyond my blindness, so that I might love them with my whole heart, knowing how precious they are. In loving them, I know that I am loving You and loving myself.

Holy Spirit, fill me with courage and gratefulness today. Like a mother, You hover over the world, wooing me and all into the Father's love and rest. Your fruit is peace and love and joy, and my heart is full of these because I am in You and You are in me. Let me share our fruit with all who cross my path today.

ALIGNMENT

That I might know Christ and the power of His resurrection
That I might know Christ and the power of my resurrection in Him

Today is another day for your liberation through alignment.

First, return to the mirror and look deeply into your eyes. Imagine there your inner self, as Paul called you. Your risen self. As you do, be in awe of God's great mystery in creating you to live in this earthen vessel. Allow yourself to feel even greater wonder over the mystery that you are, at this very moment, the son, the daughter of the Father.

Now go into your day and look upon those you see in the same way. See them and love them as yourself—it's not your job to judge who they are or aren't. That is for God alone.

Today, not only do you get to align to who you are, but you get to see all in that same light, because what you do to these, you do to Him and so to yourself. As you judge another, you judge yourself. As you love another, you love yourself.

Your pleasure is to treat all who you encounter today not only as Yeshua would, or as *if* they were Him, but *as* Him. This is His way as He said. This is the expression of the Father's will on Earth as it is in heaven. What you do to them and even think about them is what you do and think unto Yeshua, and unto yourself.

If you go by a gas station or to a restaurant, take a few seconds at the counter to love the one serving you. Just offer them thoughts of your gratitude and love. You may or may not say anything other than thank you, but know that your love will bond with the call for love in their own hearts.

Give love to them, because in so doing you are giving love to yourself and to Yeshua. Love the whole world this way and feel the change in you, for you are the beneficiary as much as they.

Go and show this love and the world will know that you are in Christ.

SEVENTEEN

LET ALL YOUR TROUBLES FALL AWAY

How often . . . shall I forgive him?
. . . Seventy times seven.
MATTHEW 18:21-22

Forgive and you will be forgiven; give and it will be
given to you . . .
For with the measure you use it will be
measured back to you.
LUKE 6:37-38 ESV

MEDITATION

We have learned the true nature of the Father's love. We have seen the great love of Yeshua, whose love you share, hidden from you only by your own blindness. That blindness is lifting already as you gaze upon a new life you thought would be possible only after your death. But our hope is for this age, not only for the age to come.

Now we will consider that which blocks your sight of the light and true love. Then we will consider the simple means for removing that block.

Yeshua made it plain: when you judge others, a plank of offense blocks your sight. When you begin to see, you might be surprised to discover that your whole life is full of judgment against people, things, places, nations, groups, and above all yourself.

Why? Because, the flesh was born out of the fruit of the knowledge of good and evil, which is condemnation. Thus the flesh loves grievance and is addicted to negativity, which is its food for survival.

But if you remove that plank of offense against others, you will see clearly.[1] Surrendering judgment frees you from its harsh judgment of you. As Yeshua said, neither He nor the Father accuse you; your only accuser is the system of the world in which your hopes are set.

So stop judging the world and you will have eyes to see. And as much, stop condemning yourself. Would you judge the son of the Father? Don't judge yourself, or you will find yourself judged. Instead, see with the eyes of the Spirit that you are the holy one (saint) in the eyes of the Father. That fallen Adam has died and you have been made new. You are complete, risen, and seated in Yeshua.

In judging yourself and others, you bind yourself to the system of this world, which offers judgment, and so you will be judged by that law. Instead, remove the plank of offense that blocks your perception and so walk in the sovereign presence of the Father's realm where there is no condemnation.

How, you ask? How can I remove the plank that blocks my vision?

Through forgiveness, because forgiveness is the opposite of judgment.

But you have misunderstood forgiveness. Forgiveness isn't absolving another of their crime rather it is letting go of the offense you embraced when that crime was committed against you.

Consider Yeshua's great demonstration of forgiveness. How could He forgive those who were crucifying Him when they knew very well that they were torturing Him? How could He say, *Forgive them, for they know not what they do* while they were yet abusing Him and surely knew it?[2] Why did He hold them to no account? Didn't they deserve judgment? Doesn't any abuser?

And yet Yeshua, having surrendered His own will in the garden of Gethsemane, let go of any offense toward them even while they were brutalizing Him.

To forgive literally means to "let go."[3] Let go of offense to find freedom from that offense. Let go of the whole world of judgment found in the first Adam's embracing of the *knowledge* of good and evil.

Forgive yourself, forgive your children, your spouse, your occupation, your tormentor, your failings, your body, your whole life situation. Let go of everything that you have made a god, thinking it would give you satisfaction or security in this life apart from the realm of the Father in Yeshua.

Let go of your old self. Let go of your need for others to be a certain way so you can feel loved and secure. Let go of your annoyance at even a harsh, disturbing noise down the street, and you will have found the meaning of forgiveness.

To the extent you forgive those who trespass against you, you will find yourself forgiven.

If you are complete, nothing can truly threaten you. There is no longer any need to pretend you aren't already safe, complete, and risen in Yeshua. As such, you are no longer a victim.

The deceiver's greatest lie is that you are *not* who you are, and thus, still a victim. Believing that lie, you will find yourself striving to be freed through whatever other means possible. Be assured, if this is the path you take, failure is guaranteed. Believing his lie guarantees your slavery in a cage made only of that lie.

Instead, don't listen to his lie or all the evidence the flesh might show you to keep you in that lie. The truth is, you are no longer a victim. You are complete and whole, glorified already. See this for only a moment, and you will feel a sudden peace that passes understanding.

Today you will find that as you loose forgiveness on Earth, it will already have been released in heaven.[4] Today you will experience the freedom that is yours through the simple act of love called forgiveness. This is how to walk in the light as the child of light.[5]

CONTEMPLATION

Is it too much to believe that you have the power, at this very moment, to let go of a trauma that has haunted you for many years or months?

Is it too much to believe that you can let go of the fear and worry of what might come tomorrow? Or the anger you feel about the situation you find yourself in now?

There was once a man married to a woman who broke her vows and did not remain faithful. Finding himself dishonored, the man went to his friends and told them of his wounding, and they joined his misery. Then the man, weeping of his great misfortune, found his wife and brought her before his teacher.

"Have you been so wronged?" the teacher asked him in a gentle voice.

"She is a fool who has ripped out my heart!" the husband cried, clawing at his breast.

"Did Yeshua not teach that she is your sister?"

"Then she is a sister who stabs me with her dagger!"

"And did He not teach that to be angry with any sister and call them a fool is to be found guilty of murder?"[6]

The man was inflamed even more. "Have you no sorrow for me? I have been betrayed!"

"So now do you call me, your brother, a fool as well?"

The man caught himself as meaning filled his mind.

The teacher looked at the wife and the husband and arched his brow. "I see before me an adulteress and a murderer. Who then is of the greater sin?"

And so the husband and wife fell to their knees and repented and forgave themselves and each other and so found peace in the midst of that storm that had visited him.

Yeshua came to set both free from their suffering. And you who have been wronged, would you not be free once more?

Whenever you are in misery, it is only because you are identifying with the old you, persuaded that you need protection and justice in the system of the world.

But you can let go of that lie and live in the truth of who you are, right now. Let go of your relationship with the old you and your old story, and rise as the new holy one, united with Yeshua.

Believe in Yeshua and you will be saved from the storms of this life. May God the Holy Spirit, your Comforter, illuminate this single truth in you today.

PRAYER

Father, I lay before You all the hurts and wounds of my past, and I come before You whole and complete as Your beautiful child. For too long I have carried the burden of the past on my shoulders and it has left me secretly bitter. For too long I have allowed my fears of the future to crush me.

But today I release my past and I stand with my elder brother, Yeshua, complete in Him. I stand and declare the wonder of Your love for me exactly as I am, because I am always as I am in that moment.

I am Your child.

I am complete.

I am full of Your glory.

I am in the world but not of it, so I will forgive the world that haunts me and rise again, full of power and peace.

What a wonder that You have given me the glory of Yeshua. Because of His forgiveness I too can forgive myself, my brothers and sisters, my enemies, and my world.

Seal this work in me, Holy Spirit. Comfort me and make me brave and let me fly with You.

I adore You, Father. I adore You, Holy Spirit. I adore You, Yeshua. For I am in You and You are in me.

ALIGNMENT

That I might know Christ and the power of His resurrection
That I might know Christ and the power of my resurrection in Him

There is perhaps no more powerful exercise in alignment than forgiveness, because in letting go of offense against the world, against yourself, or against any other, you are also letting go of your own agreement that they can hold any power over you, the risen son, the glorified daughter of the Father.

Indeed, in aligning with the light rather than the darkness, you are calling that darkness only a shadow that has no power over you. Others might harm your earthen vessel, and they do so only because they walk in blindness to who Christ is and have not awakened to living in Christ.

To return judgment rather than forgiveness is only to join yourself to their blindness and to the darkness they live in. This only keeps you enslaved to the shadows of death.

Today align with the truth of your freedom in the light by considering one person who has wronged you in the past, or who is wronging you now. When you forgive them, you forgive yourself and rise with new power. So then gaze upon them in your mind's eyes and say to them with certainty, *I forgive you, for you know not what you do.*

Say, *You only act out of your own confusion and rage, blinded by darkness, struggling to find your own significance and love. You too were wounded, even as you wounded me. But today I forgive you, for you know not what you do.*

And say even more, *I will not call you a fool and thereby murder you. Instead, I will love, as Yeshua loves, because I am in Him and He is in me.*

Do you feel any lightness come to your spirit? That's the feeling of being saved from the prison of unforgiveness. And how beautiful it is.

Now go and do it again.

EIGHTEEN
GIVING IS RECEIVING

Give, and it will be given to you . . .
For with the measure you use, it will be measured to you.
LUKE 6:38 ESV

Whoever tries to keep their life will lose it,
and whoever loses their life will preserve it.
LUKE 17:33 NIV

MEDITATION

You have heard it said that you will reap what you sow, and this is true. Sow to your spirit and you will reap life. Sow to the flesh, and you will reap death.[1] Nothing you think, say, or do can change this truth. *Everything* you think, say, and do *is* sowing, and you are already reaping what you have sown.

Indeed, you have been unwittingly sowing to the flesh your whole life by secretly clinging to the old mind; by harboring grievance instead of forgiveness; by offering judgment instead of blamelessness. Is it any wonder you sink into the darkness?

But all of that sowing is undone in Yeshua.

Now you will learn another truth about Yeshua's Way that is sure to save you from reaping a harvest of death in this life.

The old mind cringes at any thought of giving, because giving threatens what the flesh thinks must be protected. Think once more of your life as a boat. All that you have in this world you have built into that boat, hoping it will save you from the dark, stormy seas.

The relationships you have, the money you make, the education you've labored for, the career you've built, the status you've attained, the position you hold, the house you live in, the car you drive, the clothes you wear, the face you paint, the hair you fix—all of it is cherished by the flesh as the stuff that gives you meaning and significance.

And all of it is associated with your old identity, as we have seen. Protecting all that you thought you were is the flesh's prime objective. This is its own "plan of salvation" that it presents to you day in and day out, hoping to distract you from your true identity as the son, the daughter of your Father.

When anything threatens to take away your possessions and status and honor and position, which you think gives you security, your flesh cringes. Confronted with the prospect of releasing your grip on the precious boat that you think keeps you safe in this life, your flesh fights panic.

Faced with such a prospect, you secretly hoard all you can. Any thought of giving it away fills you with anxiety (unless you can get praise or status in exchange for giving, but this is only trading in the flesh).

Today is another day of salvation from the lies that have held you captive.

Give as the Father gives, expecting nothing in return. The infinite needs nothing. Nor does the infinite seek it, for there is nothing that can be added to or taken away from God, who is already infinitely complete.

Because you are in Him and He is in you through Yeshua, so you will give from that same place of abundance, expecting nothing in return. Again, when you expect something in return, you are only bartering to gain more flesh.

This is why Yeshua taught so plainly, *Do good and lend, expecting nothing in return, and your reward will be great, and you will be the sons of God, for he Himself is kind to evil men.*[2]

In giving without expecting anything in return, you are giving as He gives, for He would not ask you to do what He does not. He expects nothing in return for His gifts—they are free to you. This is the meaning of true grace.

As Paul wrote, *The wages of sin* (that which separates) *is death* (during this life and in the life to come). *But the gift* (not the barter) *of God is eternal life* (now and forever) *in Yeshua.*[3] *And where sin abounds, grace much more abounds.*[4]

Do you see how the Father loves and gives? When you see, you'll be able to experience His eternal life with each breath you take. He gives you love and peace and joy without condition.

But there is more, because in giving to another who is one with you in Christ, you are giving to yourself. Furthermore, what you do to *the least of these, you do to Yeshua*[5], with whom you are one. Thus you receive, for you are giving to yourself as well as to the other and to Yeshua.

So then, your giving *is* receiving.

When you give joy, you receive more joy. When you give peace to an enemy, you are receiving that same peace.

Indeed, in giving or laying down your whole life, you gain life. But in keeping and protecting your life, you only cling to things that cannot save.

Consider again Yeshua's teaching: *Whoever tries to keep their life will lose life, and whoever gives their life will receive life.*[6] Again, in giving of your life, you receive life.

This is how the last shall be first. This is how the kingdom of heaven, which flows with unlimited power for you, is opposite the way of the world.

Yeshua said, *Give and it will be given you . . . With the measure you use, it will be measured to you.*[7] Though the Father gives you infinite love, you don't often experience it. Indeed, you can only truly experience as much love as you give. With the measure you use, it will be measured to you.

Once more, giving *is* receiving.

Think of the light of Yeshua as the sun that shines in and on you. Sometimes clouds block its rays. These clouds might be your anger or judgment or worry. These clouds might also be money or status or relationships that you cling to, thinking they are your identity.

The act of giving removes those clouds so that the sun, which never stops shining, can reach your awareness and allow you to receive its warmth. To put this truth another way, surrendering and giving are two sides of the same coin.

Give what is imperishable—love and forgiveness—and see the light shining in your life. *In the same measure you give, you receive.*

Give also what is perishable—your time, your money, your resources—and separate the identity this world offers you from the identity Yeshua offers. Give as a gift, without bartering for honor or for material advantage. *In the same measure you give, you receive.*

Then discover this great secret: When you give, you begin to experience the real beauty of what you give, perhaps for the first time. Money, no longer your master, becomes a blessing. Love, no longer connected to offense, keeps no record of wrong.

Giving will allow you to receive joy and peace. Giving will open your sight to your abundance in Yeshua. Giving will save you from the lie that you need whatever you're giving to protect you from the storm.

Giving is receiving. It could be said, *the only thing missing from any situation in this life is what you are not giving to it, most of all forgiveness.*

CONTEMPLATION

Yeshua told this story: A man was traveling on the road alone. Robbers found him, beat him, stripped him of his clothing, and left him dying on the path.

By chance a priest, one who knows the Scriptures well, came by, but he ignored the man and passed by on the other side of the road. Then a Levite, who is a religious worker, came by, and he too ignored the man.

But a Samaritan, considered by Yeshua's audience to be a heretic, also came by. When this heretic saw the man's suffering, he had compassion. So he poured healing oil on the man's wounds and bandaged him and took him to an inn to heal. When the Samaritan left the inn, he left money for the man's care.

Which of the three was following the Way of Yeshua?

The heretical Samaritan, who showed mercy.[8]

The Samaritan had nothing to gain for his giving. Out of his compassion he gave his time, his love, and his wealth. He gained no honor, no earthly reward. He gave only because he had love and healing to give.

Go and do the same.

Let go of your old self's need for compensation. Let go of your expectation for honor. Open your arms and release all that you mistakenly thought would give you value in this world. See your chains falling, and feel yourself rising in new life.

Is this not what it means to let your old life die on the cross so that you might live, risen, in Yeshua? Is this not what it means to take up your cross daily?[9] Is this not what it means to believe in Yeshua instead of your old self?

Now you are receiving the light. Now you are being the light. Now you are flying.

PRAYER

Dear, infinite Father in whom there is no lack, I come to You in awe today, remembering once again how blessed I am to be called Your son, Your daughter. I kneel at Your table in humble, inexpressible gratitude, and yet You offer me a chair, because I am Your son, Your daughter.

Seated here beside You, I experience the limitless love You share with me.

Like You, I will give to the world. I will give love. I will give all that I cling to. And together we will smile, for there is no lack here. I am complete. Nothing can be taken from me.

Yeshua, dear Yeshua, my beautiful Brother and Savior. I can scarcely look at You without weeping. What You have given for me and to me . . . I have no words. Only tears.

As You loved me, I will love the world. I will give. I will give because I am now in You and You are in me and we have no further need but this infinite power and love in the Father's Kingdom.

I will rush to give so that all may know Your love, and the Father's love and my own love, even as I now know that love.

I will rush to give as You have given to me.

Thank You, Yeshua.

Thank You, Father.

ALIGNMENT

That I might know Christ and the power of His resurrection
That I might know Christ and the power of my resurrection in Him

You have only one task today: give to someone. It doesn't matter who they are, just give to them and notice your spirit. Give to them gladly, out of your abundance, which has no limit. Give to them without thought of your loss, knowing now that you can't suffer any real loss. Give to a charity, give to a church. Dig a well for those who thirst for water.

But don't just give materially. Offer love and peace from your heart. And don't give to only one. Give to your wife, your husband, your children, your enemy, your coworker, your neighbor, and expect nothing in return. Give a kind word and notice. Give a smile. When you enter a store, go there to give love, even for five seconds.

Give today and expect nothing in return. Give and notice the joy you feel; then know you are receiving already, because giving is receiving.

In this way you align with the truth that your experience in this life is not defined by what you receive but by what you give. If you look to receive, you only agree with the deception that you are lacking. In giving you are aligning with eternal life.

NINETEEN
ENEMIES AND FRIENDS

Do good to those who hate you, bless those who curse you
Love your enemies . . . expecting nothing in return
And you will be sons of the Most High.
For he, himself, is kind to evil men.
LUKE 6:35

Do not resist an evil person
Whoever slaps you on the right cheek
Turn the other to him also.
MATTHEW 5:39

If anyone comes to me and does not hate
father and mother
Wife and children, brothers and sisters—
even their own life—
He cannot be my disciple.
LUKE 14:26

MEDITATION

So many of the sons and daughters blinded to their Father's love stumble in a darkness of their own making, cringing at the most powerful of Yeshua's teachings and calling them hard. But now you will see the stunning beauty of Yeshua's Way, and how all of that Way is really a simple path—so simple a child can follow it.

Think of what troubles you in this life time and time again. At the root you will find one of two things, both grounded in fear: one, someone (including yourself) who has offended you, so you feel and *fear harm*; two, someone whose love you cherish, so you *fear loss*.

We will call those who have or might offend us *enemies*, and those whose love we cherish, *friends*. The offense of enemies you count as evil. The love of friends you count as good. But both of these enslave you equally, as you will see. And when you see, you will, perhaps for the first time, be able to offer and receive true love.

ENEMIES

Enemies come in two basic guises: the enemy in yourself and the enemy in others. Ultimately they're the same. Both fuel your fear of being harmed. Thus you set about trying to control your world by protecting yourself from them or overcoming them.

The enemy within yourself might be an addiction to food or another substance or activity. It might be your body, which doesn't look or function the way you want it to, or your need for more money. When battling yourself, you go to great lengths to fix what you perceive as the problem, always fretting when you fail and rejoicing when you seem to win for a while. Then another issue crops up, throwing you back into an endless cycle of striving and self-loathing. Soon your body dies, leaving nothing but dust to speak for all your effort.

The enemy outside yourself might be a neighbor, or someone who used to be a friend, or a monster who harmed you or threatened you. When dealing with such enemies, you build up walls to protect yourself, or you attack in self-defense.

Whether within or outside, your only true enemy is fear, because fear is what throws you into misery.

Remember once again Yeshua's teaching about the storm. While crossing a sea known for its ferocious weather, Yeshua fell asleep on the boat. When a storm came up, His disciples cowered in the face of waves and lightning. They woke Yeshua, who looked about at the raging sea and asked what might seem to be an absurd question: *Why are you afraid?*

What? Are you mad? Look! The waves are sure to take our lives!

To which the master surely smiled and gently shook His head. *Oh you of little faith*, He said to the disciples. And then to the chaos of wind and rain: *Peace, be still.*[1]

Was Yeshua a madman? God forbid. Instead He knew to ask that one question that will lead you to the greatest freedom you can experience in this life. *Why are you afraid?*

You fear only because your belief (faith) is in your old flesh-and-bone self (the system of the world) rather than in your true identity in the kingdom of heaven. In the system of the world, the body must be protected; in Yeshua it doesn't matter if the storm takes your flesh and bone, because your true self is spirit. Your body, however wondrous it might be, is only your costume for a short while.

Yeshua's answer for overcoming this world of enemies is twofold. First, let go of your earthen vessel, which you see as threatened. Take up the cross each day and see that you are risen as the son, the daughter of the Father.

Then, offer your world of enemies love. *Do good to those who hate you. Do not judge or resist the evil man. Expect nothing in return . . . and you will be sons of the Most High. For if you love those who love you, what reward do you have?*[2]

Whatever you resist will offer you its own resistance. For every action there is an equal and opposite reaction. You must know that to live by this system of defensiveness is to be enslaved by it, and it offers only death.

We will call this system *living by the sword*, though that sword be wielded in the heart or by the tongue. If your heart lives by that sword, it lives in misery, which is its own kind of death.

So instead of resisting the evil man, turn your cheek.[3] Accept and offer the world what it longs for—love.

Truly, loving those who love you requires no revelation in Christ. As Yeshua said, *If you love someone who loves you, what credit is that to you? Even sinners love those who love them.* Only in loving those who persecute and hate you can you know you have found true love, which is the evidence of your true nature in Christ.

If you do this, *you will be sons of the Most High*.

Yeshua did not say you will *become* the sons of God. He said you will *be* the sons of God. Why? Because this is the kind of love expressed by the son, the daughter of the Father. Loving this way is the only way to be who you truly are, already complete in Yeshua.

In the same way, rather than struggle in vain against your own self-abuse and self-hatred, accept yourself as you are. Offer yourself the Father's love. When you then love yourself as the Father loves you, the behavior and addictions that express themselves as self-abuse will fall away.

If this teaching strikes alarm in you, know that the deception you live in *must* feel alarm. Your old mind knows that it's facing its own death, because you are now aware of its tricks, rooted in a lie.

Truly, it is that lie that brings you great fear in the storms called *enemy*.

No more. Let the lie die. Do not be afraid. Believe instead in Yeshua and your identity in Him. Have faith in Yeshua, and be saved from the storms of this life. Rest in your power through Him to accept and love rather than to resist and attack.

FRIENDS

In the same way that you cling to the need for protection from enemies (even though they cannot hurt the son or the daughter of the Father in

His realm of sovereign power), you also cling to the need for significance and affection from friends. This need is rooted in the fear of loss, which isn't true love. There is no fear in love.

There is perhaps nothing more damaging than fear of loss masquerading as love. Such "love" only enables fear while true love remains in hiding.

How can you love your husband or wife when you need them to be a certain way in order to feel secure? If they don't offer the security or honor you think you deserve from them, you feel wounded. Wounding is what you fear.

Then the one you loved becomes a monster in your house and you feel compelled to either "help" them change (to fulfill your desire for honor and security), or you feel compelled to protect yourself from them—because they've become your enemy.

This doesn't mean you must subject yourself to the physical abuse of another—if necessary, remove your hand from that fire. But do so in love, not in fear or condemnation.

Truly, most of what we call love is little more than addictive clinging. The affection of another person makes us feel good about ourselves, much like a drug that comforts and makes us feel secure. When that person fails us, we get angry at the one we thought we loved.

To call your addictive clinging *love* is an error. As Yeshua made plain, the true measure of love is how well you love someone when they dishonor you, not when they demonstrate love to you. True love is not provoked nor keeps any record of wrongs, as Paul made so clear. There is no fear of loss in love, because love doesn't seek its own needs.[4]

This is why Yeshua insists that you must *hold of no account* your neediness in all of your closest relationships. Hear Him: *If you do not hate* (hold of no account) *father and mother, wife and children, brothers and sisters—even your own life—you cannot be my disciple.*[5]

Some have said that Yeshua means we should love God more than we love others, but these aren't His words. Indeed, sanitizing His words only strips the power from His teaching. He uses the strongest possible terms without comparison—that is, "to hold of no account," which is the meaning of *hate*.

Think about any romantic relationship you've had or have. Isn't it true that your partner holds you *to account*? They expect you to be a certain way in order to satisfy their desire for honor, completion, or significance. As long as their expectations are met and you "love" or honor them as they wish to be "loved" and honored, they are pleased. They have their drug and their addiction is satiated.

But if you fail to meet your partner's expectation in some way, they feel dissatisfied or unappreciated or let down. At times you will surely feel like enemies to each other.

The same is true of your own expectations of them.

Why do you feel so wounded when your partner fails you? Because you have placed your hope *in them* and they have let you down. You have inadvertently turned them into a god, thinking your relationship with them will save you. When they then fail to meet your expectations, your identity is crushed. You feel lost, abandoned, unloved.

You see, you are searching for your meaning and your identity in a relationship by holding those closest to you *to account*. And you are calling this love. Yeshua says no. This is not what it means to follow the Way of love in Him.

Rather, love them by *holding them of no account* (hate) and by *expecting nothing in return*. By turning the other cheek in your heart rather than resisting them, just as you would an enemy. By loving them, even if they persecute you. And if you must, remove yourself from the situation just like you would remove your hand from the fire. But do so in love, without condemnation or holding a record of wrong. The love you find in yourself by following these teachings of Yeshua will stagger you.

Your partner does not define you in the least. You only share a part of this life with that person, and you do so as the son or daughter of God whose identity is firmly rooted in Yeshua alone.

So then, be who you are. Love yourself and your neighbor and your enemy and your children and your partner in this way.

Love your friends, for you are now a friend of Yeshua, your elder brother, in whom your identity is made certain.

CONTEMPLATION

There may be no greater revelation than the revelation of true love. However disturbing Yeshua's teaching on love might at first seem, be glad, because when you begin to love, all of your wounds are healed. Awareness of the truth is the first, giant leap.

You shouldn't condemn yourself for not loving any more than you should condemn another for not loving. Instead, notice the prison you have entered and set your intentions on *being love* to all you meet, because love casts out your own fear.

To be sure, loving as Yeshua loved is not something you will perfect in this life, but the awareness of that true love will radically change your experience in this life.

Imagine being accepted and truly loved exactly as you are at all times by your partner or friends, no matter what you do or don't do. Now imagine your acceptance of them in the same way and focus on this latter state of being.

In such an ideal manifestation of love through the power of the Holy Spirit, no matter what they did, you would look at them without blame, feeling whole. What joy would then live in your heart, you who are unprovoked and keep no record of wrong. What love you would then offer your partner, yourself and the world. How invulnerable you would be, in the world but not of it.

You would hold no record of wrong when they broke their promise to you, in the same way your Father holds no record of your wrong when you, like the prodigal, turn from Him so many times each day.

You would not be annoyed by them. You would not secretly wish they looked differently, or were more appreciative, or were more honoring of you, or made more money. You would simply love them, seeing beyond your need for them to be or not be any certain way.

Will you still be mastered by what cannot save you? Will you continue to look for your salvation in a special relationship? Will you cringe from your enemy and allow your heart to be ruled by fear?

You can only serve one master. Choose to be the son, the daughter of the Father in Yeshua. Let go of all your other gods and masters and find your greatest power in the only identity that saves you and washes you in peace.

PRAYER

Father, how far I have strayed from Your table of delights, seeking love and meaning in a faraway land. But today I come to myself and I remember who I am. I come to You, Father, safe and secure, without the need of anything other than You and Your good gifts. What joy I have as Yours and Yours alone.

Yeshua, holy Savior, my elder brother, despised and rejected by men, what a treasure You are to me. I am forgiven as I forgive. I am released from the madness of this world and its darkness as I release the offenses of all my enemies and friends to fix my eyes only on what is pure and lovely.

Holy Spirit, give me eyes to see the pure and lovely in myself, in my enemies, in my closest friends when they turn their backs on me. Comfort me in my times of distress and fill me with love, with peace, and with joy.

ALIGNMENT

That I might know Christ and the power of His resurrection
That I might know Christ and the power of my resurrection in Him

Today you will face one of the greatest deceptions in this life. The world offers you a savior in the form of relationships. What is beautiful in the sight of the Father has been turned into a master that, in spite of its promises, cannot give you meaning, significance and identity.

Yet we have aligned ourselves with these others to replace our alignment with who we are in Him.

But today you will release your dependence on this master of your own making by holding it of no account. Only then can you love without expecting in return. Only then can you be free to be who you are as the son or daughter of your Father.

Only then can you be the body of Yeshua, expressing true love on Earth as it is in heaven. This is the will of your Father, which you now share.

Close your eyes and love the one who has let you down in any way. Release your need for your child, or partner, or friend, or enemy to be any way other than the way they are.

Do this for even one minute and you will have taken great strides in aligning to your eternal self, complete and risen as the son, the daughter of the Father here on Earth.

TWENTY

FINDING SUPERMAN

Very truly I tell you, whoever believes in me will do the
works I have been doing, and they will do even greater
things than these . . .
I will do whatever you ask in my name,
So that the Father may be glorified in the Son.

JOHN 14:12-13 NIV

If you abide in Me and My words abide in you,
Ask whatever you wish and it will be done for you.
My Father is glorified by this, that you bear much fruit,
and so prove to be My disciples.

JOHN 15:7-8

MEDITATION

Oh what manner of love the Father has lavished upon you, that you should be His son, His daughter. The Father glorified His identity by breathing His likeness into His first son, Adam, whom He placed in the garden of perfection. Then He glorified His identity yet again by breathing His identity into you through Yeshua, the second Adam.

Now you too are the son, the daughter of the Father, united with Yeshua, who undid the fall and placed that garden of beauty in your heart. You now live in the glory of the Father, given to you through Yeshua. He is the light of the world, as are you.

Is this glory manifest in your life today?

Yes, though you might not yet see it clearly. But have great joy. Yeshua came to restore your vision. And as your perception is made clear, your earthly experience will abide in that light of love and power.

In today's meditation, you will see the great promise of power that Yeshua repeated time and again. How plain it is, and how simple the Way, though many sons and daughters have forgotten it.

His declaration is certain: *If you believe in Him, you will do the works He did and greater.* Furthermore, *whatever now you ask in His identity* (name) *He will do.* Why? *So that the Father might be glorified in the Son.*[1]

His declaration is certain: *If you abide in me and my words abide in you, ask whatever you wish and it will be done for you. My Father is glorified by this: That you bear much fruit, and so prove to be my disciples. This I command you so that you love one another.*[2]

You see? There it is again. If you abide in Him and His teaching abides in you, only ask and it is done. Why? Because what you do glorifies the Father by showing His love on Earth in you.

What is the work of Yeshua revealed to you by the Spirit of truth? What is the evidence of the Spirit of truth within you? Many miraculous things, surely, but these are not primary.

The enduring evidence of the Holy Spirit in you is love. As Paul wrote, all manifestations of the Spirit except faith, hope, and love will pass away. And the greatest of these is love. Not the kind of love spun for gain and return, but love that expects nothing in return and holds no account of wrong.

His declaration is certain: *The same glory that the Father gave Yeshua, he gave to you.* Why? *So that the world will know that the Father sent Yeshua and that the Father loves them in the same way he loves Yeshua.*[3]

Again, the Father has glorified His identity on Earth through Yeshua and now through you so that the world might see and know His love.

So you might ask yourself, *Why don't I have the power to love the way Yeshua loves?*

You are now faced with an inner conflict. You know that you are the son, the daughter of the Father. You know you are in Yeshua and He in you. You know that you have the same glory that the Father gave Yeshua. You know that the purpose of this glory is to show the world the Father's manifest power and love through you.

And you know that you have the power to ask anything and have it done to show the Father's glory.

This is your dogma.

But your experience doesn't bear the dogma out. What, then, is the problem?

It can only be one of two things: either you do not actually *believe in Him* (place your full identity in Him), or you are not *asking in His name*.

But don't condemn yourself. Does a child scold himself for not walking and running before he has crawled? No, and neither does the Father.

It could be said that many Christians don't *believe in Yeshua* as it is meant, nor ask anything *in His name* as it is meant.

Instead, we have placed our identity in the system of the world, and we try to love in *that* identity. As much, we ask *using* Yeshua's name, as if it is a magical incantation. Identifying primarily with our earthen vessel, for example, we beg God to heal our bodies, because without it we feel lost and in misery.

Healing is a natural manifestation of the kingdom of heaven—even a cursory exploration reveals it to be true today. But surely we see healing as little as we do because when we do seek it, we seek it out of the flesh, rather than as sons and daughters of the Father who have let go of our attachment to our earthen vessels.

Soon, seeing no great advantage or undeniable good come of our prayers, we stop asking altogether. As James wrote, *You do not have because you do not ask, and when you ask you do not receive, because you ask with wrong motives.*[4]

To believe in the identity of Yeshua is to believe *like* Yeshua.

In that identity, filled with His glory, you will do what the son of the Father does in glorifying the Father, which, above all, is to love as He loves, empowered by the Spirit.

In the same way, to ask *in His name*, means that you ask in His identity. You also ask in *your true* identity, because He is in you and you are in Him. It means you ask as the one who has been grafted into (unified with) Yeshua.

Ask *as* that one.

Instead, you ask in the identity of the fallen Adam, seeking some secret payoff in the flesh, only using Yeshua's birth name. You ask motivated by an identity that is blind to your true identity in Yeshua. Otherwise what you ask *would* be done. Yeshua did not lie.

But, again, do not condemn yourself, because the Father loves you without condemnation, the same way He asks you to love others, holding no record of wrong. Your journey now is to believe in Yeshua, each hour, each day. And as you set your intention to this end, you will find His way, because that way is already in you as Yeshua with whom you are one.

Now your path is certain and the renewing of your mind made clear. This is your journey of transformation. You would gladly let go of all you have to find the treasure in the field, which is Christ and you in Him. For this, you will forgive all that you once thought threatened you on the stormy seas of your life.

For this, you would surrender all that you thought you were, to discover who you really are, and so walk this earth in peace and power as the son, the daughter of God. For this, you would give up your expectation that relationships will give you security and meaning.

Each small step you take in letting go of what masters you announces your freedom in Him who has already saved you.

What will you ask for as the son, the daughter of the Father?

To believe in Yeshua is to believe like Yeshua. As you do, you can do all things through and in Christ.[5]

So, surrender all idle dreams and powerless gods and find true joy. Lay all of your insignificant self-made gifts upon the Father's holy altar, and find a peace that passes understanding.

There, as the son, the daughter, ask anything in the identity of Yeshua, and it will be done so that the glory of the Father already given you will be made manifest on Earth through you, as you, and for you.

There, unattached to the things of this world, the mountain will be moved. The withered hand will be restored, the viper's bite neutralized, and the enemy's accusations silenced.

But above all, there you will rest in love. Love for God. Love for yourself. Love for your neighbor as yourself.

Then your whole body (earthly experience) is filled with light and you are healed.

Then, nothing will threaten you, because you will finally know the truth: you are in Yeshua and He is in you, and all of the world is filled with His gifts to be enjoyed.

CONTEMPLATION

Let's return once again to the analogy of Clark Kent and Superman. The promises of Yeshua are as staggering as the powers of Superman, and yet you have lost hope in those promises for this life. Why? Only because you have forgotten that you already are who He says you are.

But now you know: you don't have to *become* Superman. You already are. The deceiver in all his guises, within and without, hates this truth. He wants to undermine the beauty of Yeshua's incomparable victory over death. So he has convinced you to place your identity in Clark Kent alone.

Take off the Clark Kent costume and see that you are already Superman; you are already clothed in Christ. All you have to do is let go of your attachment to wealth, status, self-serving relationships, even your own life. This is your surrender. Without all those encumbrances you can already fly.

Truly, you have only begun to see the immeasurably great power for those who believe. Truly, the centuries of religious unbelief, which has left the Father's sons and daughters powerless, are finally falling into the grave. Truly, you are awakening to the good news that you can fly with Yeshua, because above all, to fly means to love with a power otherwise unknown by mankind.

The lies of the serpent have been found out. The chains of the knowledge of good and evil have been shattered. New life is in you, and you are in it. All things have become new. Now, open your eyes and see.

Could it be true?

Only the deceiver says differently, and his venom is now a vapor.

PRAYER

Create in me a pure heart, Father, that I might see how true Your Word, Yeshua, is in me. I have been lost, but now I am found at Your table, as Your own, set free from the lies of the deceiver.

I call upon You, Holy Spirit, to fill me with Your comfort as I lay down so many lies and begin to believe once again. Today I will walk in Your love, Your peace, Your joy, because neither You, nor Yeshua, nor the Father knows any fear, so neither will I.

Yeshua, brother and Savior, how precious You are! How glorious Your supremacy! I live because of You. I live in You and You in me. You are the Way, the Truth, and the Life, and apart from You there is no lasting peace or joy.

May the true desires of my heart—to live in You alone, with You in me—be manifested in my life. Because I am the son, the daughter of the Father, and I need only You.

ALIGNING

That I might know Christ and the power of His resurrection
That I might know Christ and the power of my resurrection in Him

Today you align with who you are as the risen glorified son or daughter of the Father. Today align with the one who can "fly."

The world is your sandbox, so build your sandcastles, but never make the mistake of placing your identity in them. Build your sandcastles and take joy in what your hands create, but know that a storm will surely rise to blow it away.

Be a child. Play. Laugh. Leap for joy. Be in awe.

But play as the son or daughter of the Father. Laugh in the delight of your Father and all the world He has made to be enjoyed. Leap for joy, because all of it is here one day and gone the next, yet it is here for your delight.

Say this today: *Today I align myself with who I am. I do so by forgiving all of the shadows who have caused me fear. I do so by surrendering my attachment to everything in this world that I once thought would save me from those shadows and storms in this life. I do so by removing all planks of grievance that block my sight of who I am.*

I do so by loving as He loves, without holding a record of wrong. I do so by giving rather than seeking to receive. I do so by laying my old self on the altar and awakening once more as the risen and glorified one who has been made complete in Christ.

I align myself today that I might know Christ and power of His resurrection. I do so today that I might know the power of my resurrection in Him.

So be it.

TWENTY-ONE
A NEW DECLARATION

Early Christian Hymn

Have this mind in yourselves
which was also in Christ Jesus:
Who, being in the very nature of God,
did not consider equality with God
something to be grasped
But made himself nothing by taking on
the very nature of a servant
And being found in the likeness of a man,
he humbled himself
By becoming obedient unto death, even death on a cross.

PHILIPPIANS 2

MEDITATION

Now we come to the greatest expression of the love in Yeshua. You are set free from the vain imaginations that this world can save you from misery. Now you are clothed in Christ[1]—a son, a daughter of the Father, filled with His glory.

You have traveled far in a short time and saved yourself many years of struggle. You have seen with new eyes and heard the heart of your Father, who does not condemn you.

Once more we will remember and celebrate your joyful union with Yeshua.

You might ask, *How? How can I remember what is so easily forgotten in a world calling me to join in deception and powerlessness? How can I be still and know my Father in all the sounds that scream for my attention? How can I worship Him and set my mind on heavenly things all through the day, remembering that I am seated in the heavens already?*

The way for you today is simple. Start in the awareness that you already have the mind of Christ, risen with Him, and yet what you see in this world too often distracts you from your true identity. His table of delights awaits you even now, each hour and day, but you too often eat the crumbs offered apart from the Father's table, thinking they will give you meaning and significance.

Consider again Yeshua's story of the two prodigal sons, one who left his father's table to search for himself in the pleasures of the world, and one who refused to feast at his father's table because of his judgment.

In the same way, you often find yourself removed from the kingdom of your Father's feast. It is time to return.

Consider Yeshua's story of the master who throws a great feast and invites all to come, yet many refuse, saying they are too busy with wives and houses and lands and the business of the world.[2]

In the same way, you, too, ignore the great feast at your Father's table in favor of all your small distractions in this life. It is time to enter in.

Consider Yeshua's story of the kingdom of heaven recounting ten virgins on the way to a great celebration. Tired of the journey and needing sleep, five let their oil run dry and so could not enter into the feast.[3]

In the same way, you too become tired and favor sleep. But you cannot borrow your neighbor's transformation. Your oil is yours to tend. The time has come to tend to the oil of transformation that lights your way.

All of these feasts are at hand now, in this age as well as the age to come. They are parables of the kingdom of heaven told by Yeshua who loved to compare the kingdom of God to a feast. Today you will enter that Kingdom where you are already one with and in Yeshua and feast on the fruits of love, joy and peace.

When your mind is renewed through a revelation of the Spirit of Truth, you will see that the Father does not judge you and that you are already the light of the world, already at perfect peace and able to love.

Find that part of you—the self that is glorified and eternal—and you will have found yourself at the Father's table in any given moment.

The path Yeshua took is the same path you get to walk each day. You, being made in the likeness of God and restored to Him through and in Yeshua, will align yourself with the Father by surrendering all that blocks your sight of your true self in Him. Let go of all you thought defined you in this world so that you can be who you truly are as the son, the daughter of the Father.

Yeshua called this taking up your cross (dying to your old self) or denying your self. *If anyone wishes to come after me, he must deny himself, and take up his cross daily and follow me.*[4]

So I ask you, which self must you deny? Not your risen self, surely. Rather your attachment to all that is temporal—your earthen vessel and the system of the world—so that you can be who you are in Him, fully empowered. Then and only then will you be able to love yourself and this world as He loves you and the world.

Hear the sum of it all with new ears: *The Forgotten Way of Yeshua is to let go of your attachment to this world to see and experience another, flowing with love, joy, peace, and power in and through Him alone.*

To know (experience) the Father is to know (experience) Him as spirit. And the only way to know yourself as spirit is to "un-know" (stop experiencing) yourself only in this world, because although you are *in* the world you are not *of* it.[5]

To experience the Father who does not condemn you, you gladly surrender your old self of condemnation and fruitless pursuit. You will stop clinging to your experience primarily as an earthen vessel, including your material possessions, your body, your relationships, and your status in this life.

Hold all these things of no account for even a moment and you will find yourself joined with your Father in spirit. Deny your old self. Lose that life. Let it die so that you can live as the son, the daughter, that you already are.

Give up your relationship with your old self and replace it with a relationship between your risen self and your Father in Yeshua—a relationship enabled by the Spirit of Truth, who alone will reveal your union with Yeshua to you.

Do you remember Yeshua's teaching of cutting off your hand? *If your hand causes you to cling to this world, cut it off, for what is a hand in the kingdom of heaven?* Why? Because nothing of the world can compare to knowing the eternal realm called the kingdom of heaven. Now His hyperbole, once seemingly absurd, makes perfect sense.

Why you would surrender the old self is clear to you by now, even as it was clear to Yeshua, not only at the end of His life, but every day, even as He asks you to. Only in doing so can you walk in the awareness of your true identity in Him. Only then can you truly enjoy all that He has given you in this life.

A SIMPLE DAILY PRACTICE

You will worship with others and alone; you will contemplate what has been written; you will hear the good news in your gatherings; you will pray and fast and serve and love and heal and give, because giving is receiving.

But in all of these, it's critical that you actively let go of your old way of thinking and putting on the mind of Christ, which is your true mind.[6] You are transformed by the renewal of your mind. It is your mind that must be transformed, not your identity.

To do this, you must still that old mind each day. And then each hour and each moment. *Be still and know that He is God. Set your mind on things beyond this world of decay. Humble your old self and fall into the light of eternal truth.*

To make way for the mind of Yeshua in you, find a quiet place, enter into stillness and there surrender your old, chattering intellect that can only know about God. Become like a child and know your Father.

In that stillness, humble yourself, even as Yeshua humbled Himself. That is, learn to be self-less. Let your old self fall away. Deny your old self. In such a space of peace, surrender all the roles you have in this life. You are no longer mother, father, student, male or female in Christ.[7] This is to follow Yeshua as He taught.

In that stillness you are no-*thing* (nothing) in this world, because you lay down your whole life even as He did. You are no-*body* (nobody) in this world, because you know Him in spirit, not only in body. You have no offenses, no possessions, nothing that is passing and temporal. In humility, on the altar of your surrender, you will release all of what you thought made you *you*. Only your truest nature in Christ remains.

In that place of worship, the eyes of your heart will be opened to know Him and who you are as the son, the daughter of the Father, having risen with Yeshua, seated now in heavenly places, participating in the glory that the Father gave Yeshua and you.[8]

There, taste and see a revelation of your Father's goodness that will make you weak in the knees. There, you will awaken to love, to peace, to joy.

There, you will love your enemy and your neighbor as your true self, now surrendered. There, all bitterness and anxiety and striving and jealousy and envy and anger and hatred and self-condemnation fade away like a distant, absurd dream.

There, in the eternal realm beyond space and time, you will intimately know the Father and experience eternal life. There, you will worship the Father, for He is spirit, and those who worship Him do so in spirit (because you are spirit as well) and in truth (because Yeshua is Truth, and you are in Him).[9]

There, as you make a space in your awareness for Him, the Holy Spirit will renew you.

Then arise, fully aware that you are a new creature in Yeshua. Arise and see what Yeshua has done in restoring you. Arise and be the body of Christ here on Earth, while you still draw breath. Arise and glorify the triune God—Father, Son, and Holy Spirit—by being His son or daughter and enjoying all He has made for you. Seek His kingdom and all else will be added.

OUR SONG OF SALVATION

Oh, that many would sing *this* song together! Oh, that our halls would be filled with the worship of the sons and daughters of God once more, risen with Christ, full of the Father's glory.

The first son of God, Adam, made in the likeness of God, heard the lie of the serpent that he wasn't created like God, but could be if he consumed the knowledge of good and evil. So the first Adam ate that fruit and fell into the darkness of condemnation, both of himself and his whole world.

But the second Adam, Yeshua, God's only begotten Son, put the deception and grievance of that first Adam to death and rose again. He reversed the fall and made us sons and daughters of the Father once again!

Where God put man into the garden long ago, he has now put the garden into man.

Now His Spirit fills us with love, and joy, and peace because He has saved us from darkness in this life and the life to come. We are His righteousness, His glory, His sons and daughters.

We hold this treasure in earthen vessels for only a short time, seeing Him as in a mirror until this life is over. And soon we will see Him face to face!

Yeshua is beautiful and worthy
As are we, because we are now one with Him
Yeshua is glorified
As are we, because He has given us His glory

Yeshua is risen and seated in the heavenly realm
    As are we, because we are risen with Him and are in Him
Yeshua is the Light of the world
    As are we, and in that light the world will know us by our love.

OUR DECLARATION

Son, daughter of the Father, reborn into a new and living hope: you are not of this world. You are in it to shine the light of Yeshua upon all and manifest the love of the Father on Earth as it is heaven—it is the only way to find peace and power in this life. Remember the Way. Abide in this truth so easily forgotten when the appetites and worries of this world choke out your awareness of who you are, complete in Him.

Now coming to the end of these short meditations, you might continue by starting at the beginning once more. Each reading will open new insights.

Gather together often with those who know His Way and worship in the spirit of Truth. Take the body that was broken for you and the blood that was shed for your union with Him. Do this in remembrance of Yeshua's beautiful life and death. Do this and remember that you now share in His resurrection.

Keep the following declaration of simple truth near to your heart and follow His Way.

THE FORGOTTEN WAY

OUR DECLARATION

THE TRUTH

1. God, who is infinitely good and far more loving and kind to His children than any earthly mother or father imaginable, glorified His identity on Earth by making mankind in His likeness, complete and in union with Him. But the first Adam embraced the knowledge of good and evil, so we were born into darkness, blinded to and separated from fellowship with our Father, who does not condemn us.

2. We, as sons and daughters of the Father, are remade in the likeness of God. Yeshua, the second Adam, came as Light into all darkness and undid what the first Adam did, that we might experience the Father's life right now. This we call eternal life. Even so, we put our identity in and so are mastered by one of two perceptions of reality each day. One is seen in flesh—the passing system of the world, darkened by the knowledge of good and evil, deceiving and enslaving us as we put our faith in it. The other realm is seen in the light through the power of the Holy Spirit—the eternal kingdom of the Father flowing with light and love without grievance.

THE WAY

3. Our journey now is to believe who we truly are, having been raised from the dark grave as new creatures into that realm of light with and in Yeshua. Belief in Yeshua is this: identifying with Him in His death, resurrection, and glory even now, He in us and we in Him. Our true identity is this: we are the sons and daughters of our Father, already made complete and whole; already at peace and full of power though we often forget, each day, whenever we are blinded to our true identity.

4. We will only see who we are, and thus be who we are, as we surrender our attachment to all other identities, which are like gods of a lesser power that block our vision of our true identity and so keep us in darkness. Our surrender is to deny our false selves, to take up the cross, to let go of all that holds us captive in this world, because we are in the world but not of it.

THE LIFE

5. To the extent we place our identity in His, we will be known for our extravagant love, which is the evidence of our true nature, risen with Christ. Walking in the realm of the Father's presence here on Earth—abiding in the vine, who is Yeshua— we will find peace in the storms; we will walk on the troubled seas of our lives; we will not be poisoned by the lies of snakes; we will move mountains that appear insurmountable; we will heal all manner of sickness that twist minds and bodies.

The fruit of the Spirit will flow from us as living waters, because the manifestation of the kingdom of heaven on Earth is love. And when we love, all will know: there goes one who walks in the Spirit and flies on the wings of an eagle.

Selah

For more information on additional small-group resources and speaking engagements

Visit: TheForgottenWay.com

THE SCRIPTURES

REFLECTIONS
BY BILL VANDERBUSH

THE REVELATION OF CHRIST

As we dive into the Scriptures from the meditations, it's important that you understand a few things about how these insights came about.

Jesus gave mankind unimaginable liberty in this world of form, and when we come together as one, nothing is impossible. ***Genesis 11:6*** *The Lord said, "Behold, they are one people, and they all have the same language. And this is what they began to do, and now nothing which they purpose to do will be impossible for them."* We have the freedom to hate, the challenge to love, and enough verses in the Bible to support both vengeance and grace. Using the Bible you can support doctrines of heaven, hell, healing, salvation, sickness, tribulation, dispensation, torment, pleasure, grief, joy, wrath, and grace both universal and conditional.

Have you ever wondered how one book meant to reveal God has been itself such a launching pad for so much conflict and division? Likely because as it reveals Him, it also reveals the conflict within each of us. The Bible reads you far more than you read it. The Word reveals you to yourself, and in doing so it exposes your perspective of your Father.

For many years, the question has persisted, "Who am I in Christ?" The greater question, however, might be, "Who is Christ in me?" Until you have a revelation of who He is, everything you think about who you are is merely a guess. Before you get a revelation of Jesus, you may hold your beliefs in a death grip.

We are obsessed with our own belief. We are proud that we believe in God, and how tightly we hold to that belief. But maybe our belief isn't what matters most. Was there ever an authority figure in your life (a parent, coach, teacher) who said, "I believe in you"? You may not have known exactly what they believed or even what that meant, but you knew that they were in your corner, and that's an empowering feeling. Your heavenly Father believes in you. Think about that. All faith originates with God. It is not a faith you have generated that holds onto God, but a faith that He supplies that holds onto you. This is true rest and security. Pure doctrine and authentic belief are simply saying yes to what God believes about you. God believes some amazing things about you, and what God believes about you defines you and reveals who you truly are.

Being "in Him" is the divine reality that empowers the awakening of your true identity.

Here's why this matters. What you believe becomes the reality that you experience. We are created in the likeness of our Creator to manifest what we believe to be true. This is the power of faith. What we believe, we behold, and what we behold becomes our experience. If you believe you are separated from your Father as a Christian, you will interpret the Bible through that lens of a broken or fragile relationship.

However, if you accept that you are in Him and that there is no distance, no separation, between you and your Father right now, if you believe that you can't stop the endless flood of His mercy for you, then the Bible stops being a confusing book of conflicting commandments and becomes a beautiful revelation of Love Himself. Being in Him doesn't make you God, just as being in you doesn't make Him you. However, you are united as one, together. This is a great mystery, but as with many of God's wonders, your heart can know and delight in what your mind may not yet fully understand.

All of Scripture, all relationships, all of life, all identity, all of time, every mystery is easily understood in the light of this basic revelation. **You are one with God in Christ by the power of the Spirit.** Your Father, God (who is Love, Peace, Joy, Father, Son, Holy Spirit), is one within you right now by His desire and design.

The following reflections are by no means an exhaustive commentary on the verses mentioned. Rather, they simply invite you to revisit something that may be familiar in order to find a treasure that has been buried by confusion. You'll notice that throughout the reflections, this theme of being "in Him" is pervasive, and that's because it was the most prominent collective message in Paul's letters to the churches he planted. For example, the phrases "in Christ" or "in Him" are used twenty-seven times by Paul in his letter to the Ephesians alone.

There's often a disconnect between truth and the manifestation of that reality in our lives. We believe God is only goodness, yet we don't always seem to experience that goodness in our daily lives. So, then, our journey is to discover, experience, and share His goodness in what we call good news.

A gospel that leaves people blind and crushed under the weight of sin, separation, guilt, shame, judgment, and condemnation is hardly good news. In truth, the cure for our disease has been revealed in Christ. So then, how do we put the love of the Father on display?

I have a strong desire to see people walk in the light rather than in darkness, particularly those Christians who live in blindness to their true identity in Christ. In this regard, Paul offered both great encouragement and a warning:

*See to it that no one takes you captive through philosophy and empty deception, according to the tradition of men, according to the elementary principles of the world, rather than according to Christ. For in Him all the fullness of Deity dwells in bodily form, **and in Him you have been made complete**, and He is the head over all rule and authority (Colossians 2:8-10).*

So then, we who believe Jesus' declaration that we are in Him and He is in us, even as He is in the Father, have great cause to rejoice. God is good, and now we too are good, at our very core, because in Him there is no darkness.

THE FORGOTTEN WAY

1. *1 Timothy 1:15* KJV *This is a faithful saying, and worthy of all acceptation, that Christ Jesus came into the world to save sinners; of whom I am chief.*

2. *Romans 8:9* *You are not in the flesh but in the Spirit, if indeed the Spirit of God dwells in you.*

3. *1 Corinthians 13:4* *Love is patient, love is kind and is not jealous; love does not brag and is not arrogant, does not act unbecomingly; it does not seek its own, is not provoked, does not take into account a wrong suffered.*

4. *Ephesians 5:21* NIV *Submit to one another out of reverence for Christ.*

5. *1 Corinthians 13:1* *If I speak with the tongues of men and of angels, but do not have love, I have become a noisy gong or a clanging cymbal.*

6. *1 Corinthians 13:2* *If I have the gift of prophecy, and know all mysteries and all knowledge; and if I have all faith, so as to remove mountains, but do not have love, I am nothing.*

7. *1 Corinthians 13:3* *And if I give all my possessions to feed the poor, and if I surrender my body to be burned, but do not have love, it profits me nothing.*

8. *Matthew 7:22-23* *Many will say to Me on that day, "Lord, Lord . . ." And then I will declare to them, "I never knew you."*

9. **Jesus,** *John 14:21* NIV *Whoever has my commandments and keeps them is the one who loves me.* **John,** *1 John 4:20-21* *If someone says, "I love God," and hates his brother, he is a liar; for the one who does not love his brother whom he has seen, cannot love God whom he has not seen. And this commandment we have from Him, that the one who loves God should love his brother also.* **Paul,** *1 Corinthians 13:2* NIV *If I . . . can fathom all mysteries and all knowledge . . . but do not have love, I am nothing.* **James,** *James 2:19-20* *You believe that God is one. You do well: even the demons also believe, and shudder. But are you willing to recognize, you foolish fellow, that faith without*

works is useless?

10. ***John 1:1-5*** *In the beginning was the Word, and the Word was with God, and the Word was God. He was in the beginning with God. All things came into being through Him, and apart from Him nothing came into being that has come into being. In Him was life, and the life was the Light of men. The Light shines in the darkness, and the darkness did not comprehend it.*

11. ***Matthew 11:28-30*** *Come to Me, all who are weary and heavy-laden, and I will give you rest. Take My yoke upon you and learn from Me, for I am gentle and humble in heart, and you will find rest for your souls. For My yoke is easy and My burden is light.*

It's often taught that the yoke of Jesus is like a team of oxen in a yoke, and we are supposed to rely on His strength in our labors. While the truth of the principle exists, the true meaning of the yoke here is much different. The yoke in rabbinical culture was the way that a particular rabbi interpreted the Scriptures. Many teachers of the law had created personal traditions that placed a heavy burden of religious exercise on people.

Jesus didn't come to complicate the Scriptures and place more burdens upon mankind, but instead to make it possible for "infants" to understand the embrace of the Father, experiencing in love's encounter something that can't be explained by the intellect. This is how the teachings of Yeshua create a place of peace beyond understanding.

12. ***John 14:12, 14*** *Truly, truly, I say to you, he who believes in Me, the works that I do, he will do also . . . If you ask Me anything in My name, I will do it.* ***Matthew 21:22*** *And all things you ask in prayer, believing, you will receive.*

13. ***Matthew 5:21-22*** *You have heard . . . "Whoever commits murder shall be liable . . ." But I say to you that everyone who is angry with his brother shall be guilty.* ***1 John 3:15*** *Everyone who hates his brother is a murderer; and you know that no murderer has eternal life abiding in him.*

14. ***John 14:15, 20.*** *The Father . . . will send you a helper . . . that is the Spirit of truth . . . In that day you will know that I am in the Father, and you in Me, and I in you . . .* ***John 17:22-23*** *The glory which You have given Me I have given to them, that they may be one, just as We are one; I in them and You in Me, that they may be perfected in unity, so that the world may know that You sent Me, and loved them, even as You have loved Me.*

15. ***Ephesians 2:4-6*** *But God, being rich in mercy, because of His great love with which He loved us, even when we were dead in our transgressions, made us alive together with Christ (by grace you have been saved), and raised us up with Him, and seated us with Him in the heavenly places in Christ Jesus.*

16. ***2 Corinthians 5:17*** *Therefore if anyone is in Christ, he is a new creature; the*

old things passed away; behold, new things have come.

17. **Galatians 2:20** *I have been crucified with Christ; and it is no longer I who live, but Christ lives in me; and the life which I now live in the flesh I live by faith in the Son of God, who loved me and gave Himself up for me.* **1 Timothy 1:15** *Christ Jesus came into the world to save sinners, among whom I am the foremost of them all.*

18. **Colossians 2:10** *In Him you have been made complete.*

19. **Colossians 3:3** *For you have died and your life is hidden with Christ in God.*

20. **Philippians 1:21** *For to me, to live is Christ and to die is gain.*

21. **Romans 8:1** *Therefore there is now no condemnation for those who are in Christ Jesus.*

22. **Galatians 2:20** *I have been crucified with Christ and I no longer live, but Christ lives in me.*

23. **John 14:6** *I am the way, the truth, the life.*

24. **Luke 17:21** *The Kingdom of God is among you (some translations: within you).*

25. **Luke 11:34** *The eye is the lamp of your body; when your eye is clear, your whole body also is full of light; but when it is bad, your body also is full of darkness.*

26. **Matthew 5:14-16** *You are the light of the world. A city set on a hill cannot be hidden; nor does anyone light a lamp and put it under a basket, but on the lampstand, and it gives light to all who are in the house. Let your light shine before men in such a way that they may see your good works, and glorify your Father who is in heaven.*

27. **Matthew 6:10** *Your kingdom come, Your will be done on Earth, as it is in heaven.*

28. **Luke 17:21** KJV *Neither shall they say, Lo here! or, lo there! for, behold, the kingdom of God is within you.*

29. **John 17:3** *This is eternal life, that they may know You, the only true God, and Jesus Christ whom You have sent.*

The word *know* here is the Greek word *ginosko*. It's an awareness that comes through your senses. This means that to *ginosko* someone or something requires encounter, interaction, or to touch and taste. It is a union so intimate that it's hard to see where one begins and the other ends.

30. **Matthew 18:3** *Truly I say to you, unless you are converted and become like children, you will not enter the kingdom of heaven.* **Matthew 11:25** *Jesus said, "I praise You, Father, Lord of heaven and earth, that You have hidden these things from the wise and intelligent and have revealed them to infants."*

31. **Psalm 34:8** KJV *O taste and see that the Lord is good.*

32. **John 5:22, 45** ESV *The Father judges no one, but has given all judgment to the Son . . . Do not think that I will accuse you to the Father. There is one who accuses you: Moses, on whom you have set your hope.*

33. **Matthew 8:26** *He said to them, "Why are you afraid, you men of little faith?"*

Then He got up and rebuked the winds and the sea, and it became perfectly calm.

34. **Luke 6:42** *Or how can you say to your brother, "Brother, let me take out the speck that is in your eye," when you yourself do not see the log that is in your own eye? You hypocrite, first take the log out of your own eye, and then you will see clearly to take out the speck that is in your brother's eye.*

35. **Ephesians 1:18-19** *I pray that the eyes of your heart may be enlightened, so that you will know what is the hope of His calling, what are the riches of the glory of His inheritance in the saints, and what is the surpassing greatness of His power toward us who believe.*

36. **Colossians 2:10** *In Christ you have been made complete.*

37. **Ephesians 3:20-21** *Now to Him who is able to do far more abundantly beyond all that we ask or think, according to the power that works within us, to Him be the glory in the church and in Christ Jesus to all generations forever and ever.*

38. **Hosea 3:5** *They will come trembling to the Lord and to His goodness in the last days.* **Jeremiah 33:9** *They will fear and tremble because of all the good and all the peace that I make.*

39. **2 Timothy 3:5** *Holding to a form of godliness, although they have denied its power.*

40. **Matthew 7:14** *For the gate is small and the way is narrow that leads to life, and there are few who find it.*

41. **1 John 4:17** *By this, love is perfected with us, so that we may have confidence in the day of judgment; because as He is, so also are we in this world.*

42. **1 Corinthians 12:27** *Now you are Christ's body, and individually members of it.*

43. **Galatians 3:26-28** *For you are all sons of God through faith in Christ Jesus. For all of you who were baptized into Christ have clothed yourselves with Christ. There is neither Jew nor Greek, there is neither slave nor free man, there is neither male nor female; for you are all one in Christ Jesus.*

44. **1 John 4:18** *There is no fear in love; but perfect love casts out fear, because fear involves punishment and the one who fears is not perfected in love.*

45. **Romans 12:2** *And do not be conformed to this world, but be transformed by the renewing of your mind, so that you may prove what the will of God is, that which is good and acceptable and perfect.*

YOUR JOURNEY FORWARD

46. ***John 1:1-5*** *In the beginning was the Word, and the Word was with God, and the Word was God. He was in the beginning with God. All things came into being through Him, and apart from Him nothing came into being that has come into being. In Him was life, and the life was the Light of men. The Light shines in the darkness, and the darkness did not comprehend it.* ***Hebrews 4:12*** *For the Word of God is living and active and sharper than any two-edged sword, and piercing as far as the division of soul and spirit, of both joints and marrow, and able to judge the thoughts and intentions of the heart.* ***Colossians 2:8-10*** *See to it that no one takes you captive through philosophy and empty deception, according to the tradition of men, according to the elementary principles of the world, rather than according to Christ. For in Him all the fullness of Deity dwells in bodily form, and in Him you have been made complete, and He is the head over all rule and authority.*

In the same way your word is the expression of your thoughts, the Word of God is the manifestation of God's intention, expressed in and as Christ, not mere words in any human language that point to Him. It is important to remember that when the apostles' letters and the Gospels were written, there was no New Testament. These passages aren't referring to other letters and writings, but to Christ Himself. He is understood primarily through revelation of the Holy Spirit, whereas the written word is often understood through our cognitive interpretation, that is, our intellect.

Having said that, the Word (Christ) can be revealed to us through the written word, which points to Him. Too often, however, we mistake our own limited interpretation as the conclusive revelation Word. When we do this we are operating according to the "traditions of men according to the principles of the world." We must rely on more than the intellect of man to quicken our understanding of the written word.

47. ***Matthew 11:28-30*** *Come to Me, all who are weary and heavy-laden, and I will give you rest. Take My yoke upon you and learn from Me, for I am gentle and humble in heart, and you will find rest for your souls. For My yoke is easy and My burden is light.*

48. ***Matthew 18:3-4*** NIV *Truly I tell you, unless you change and become like little children, you will never enter the kingdom of heaven. Therefore, whoever takes the lowly position of this child is the greatest in the kingdom of heaven.* ***Matthew 4:17*** *Jesus began to preach and say, "Repent, (metanoia, change your minds) for the kingdom of heaven is at hand."* ***Luke 17:21*** *For behold, the kingdom of God is within you.*

To see the kingdom of God, become as a child, trusting in your Father's voice, love, strength, and goodness. This is rest. This is entering into eternal life. This is how we begin to know the Father.

49. ***1 John 4:18*** *There is no fear in love; but perfect love casts out fear, because fear*

involves punishment, and the one who fears is not perfected in love.

50. **Luke 6:35** *But love your enemies, and do good, and lend, expecting nothing in return; and your reward will be great, and you will be sons of the Most High; for He Himself is kind to ungrateful and evil men.*

Is it surprising to you that your Father is kind to those bent toward evil? Have you ever heard a parent defend a misbehaving child beyond reason? Perhaps you have done it yourself. You do it because you believe in the heart of goodness that exists in your child even when they can't see it in themselves. How much kinder is our Father than any earthly parent who might stand up for their child. There is more goodness within you than you can imagine.

51. **Matthew 25:1-9** *Then the kingdom of heaven will be comparable to ten virgins, who took their lamps and went out to meet the bridegroom. Five of them were foolish, and five were prudent. For when the foolish took their lamps, they took no oil with them, but the prudent took oil in flasks along with their lamps. Now while the bridegroom was delaying, they all got drowsy and began to sleep. But at midnight there was a shout, "Behold, the bridegroom! Come out to meet him." Then all those virgins rose and trimmed their lamps. The foolish said to the prudent, "Give us some of your oil, for our lamps are going out." But the prudent answered, "No, there will not be enough for us and you too; go instead to the dealers and buy some for yourselves."*

52. **Luke 8:5-8** *"The sower went out to sow his seed; and as he sowed, some fell beside the road, and it was trampled under foot and the birds of the air ate it up. Other seed fell on rocky soil, and as soon as it grew up, it withered away, because it had no moisture. Other seed fell among the thorns; and the thorns grew up with it and choked it out. Other seed fell into the good soil, and grew up, and produced a crop a hundred times as great." As He said these things, He would call out, "He who has ears to hear, let him hear."*

THE MEDITATIONS

ONE
LOOK! HOW MAGNIFICENT IS YOUR FATHER!

1. *Genesis 1:26 Then God said, "Let us make man in Our image, after Our likeness."*

Man was made to live in an intimate communion with God, glorified with the very image and identity of God, animated by His very breath, the empowering holiness of His Spirit. You were made to live in God, and He in you. He is our life, our breath, our love, our joy, our peace. It is God Himself who defines who you are. The work of Jesus is to restore us to this identity.

2. *Jeremiah 1:5 Before I formed you in the womb I knew you. Ephesians 1:3-4 Blessed be the God and Father of our Lord Jesus Christ, who has blessed us with every spiritual blessing in the heavenly places in Christ, just as He chose us in Him **before the foundation of the world**, that we would be holy and blameless before Him.*

Before God even said, "Let there be light," we existed in the mind of God. This is a profound and wonderful mystery, because it means that you existed as the pure and creative knowledge of God even before the formation and fall of the cosmos.

3. *Ephesians 1:5-7 In love He predestined us to adoption as sons through Jesus Christ to Himself, according to the kind intention of His will, to the praise of the glory of His grace, which He freely bestowed on us in the Beloved.*

4. *John 1:1-5 In the beginning was the Word, and the Word was with God, and the Word was God. He was in the beginning with God. All things came into being through Him, and apart from Him nothing came into being that has come into being. In Him was life, and the life was the Light of men. The Light shines in the darkness, and the darkness did not comprehend it.*

5. *Acts 17:28 In Him we live and move and exist, as even some of your own poets have said, "For we also are His children."*

Your origin and identity are in Him. To be able to see yourself in Him is a challenge if you have grown up to believe that you and God are separated. Are you separated from Christ? Our brother Paul would say emphatically no. Jesus Himself expressed this in **John 14:20**: *In that day you will know that I am in My Father and you in Me and I in you.*

6. *1 John 3:1-2 See how great a love the Father has bestowed on us, that we would be called children of God; and such we are. For this reason the world does not know us, because it did not know Him. Beloved, now we are children of God, and it has not appeared as yet what we will be. We know that when He appears, we will be like Him, because we will see Him just as He is.*

Is there any more secure meditation than this reality that God would grant us an identity as His children? It wasn't the result of your ability to impress Him. It's a gift of great love.

TWO
THERE IS NO FEAR IN LOVE

1. *John 17:3 This is eternal life, that they may know You, the only true God, and Jesus Christ whom You have sent.*

2. *Matthew 18:3 Truly I say to you, unless you are converted and become like children, you will not enter the kingdom of heaven. Matthew 11:25 Jesus said, "I praise You, Father, Lord of heaven and earth, that You have hidden these things from the wise and intelligent and have revealed them to infants."*

3. *Psalm 34:8 O taste and see that the Lord is good; How blessed is the man who takes refuge in Him!*

When you truly experience (know) your Father, you will see that He is very good. There is a great difference between information and revelation.

4. *1 John 4:18 There is no fear in love; but perfect love casts out fear, because fear involves punishment, and the one who fears is not perfected in love.*

Love and fear are two of the most powerful motivators of human behavior. I've heard of people who are scared *of* falling in love, but once the love comes, the fear goes. I have never heard of anyone who was scared *into* falling in love. Yet I have spoken with many people whose relationship with God was motivated by a fear of hell rather than a love of God. And for many that fear is what motivates them to this day.

How is it for you? If you are like many others who first responded to God out of fear, you may find that over time, cold, mechanical distance seems to separate you from God. I pray every sense of unhealthy fear is replaced with an awe-inspired love for your Father in whom there is no fear, because there is no fear in love.

5. *Psalm 111:10* ESV *The fear of the Lord is the beginning of wisdom; all those who practice it have a good understanding.*

There are a few Hebrew terms for *fear.* One is *Pachad,* which is "fear whose objects are imagined." We all have the defensive power to anticipate what may be and can become afraid of something that doesn't even exist. A completely opposite term, the word used in Psalm 111:10, is *Yirah,* which is "the fear that overwhelms us when we suddenly find ourselves in the presence of (or in possession of) considerably more power (wealth, authority, or influence) than we are used to."

6. *Psalm 103:10-13 He has not dealt with us according to our sins, Nor rewarded us according to our iniquities. For as high as the heavens are above the earth, So great is His lovingkindness toward those who fear Him. As far as the east is from the west, So far has He removed our transgressions from us. Just as a father has compassion on his children, So the Lord has compassion on those who fear Him.*

How far is the east from the west? This is not a description of distance, but a metaphor that transcends any measurable space. To put it simply, your transgressions no longer exist. Did you notice that this is in the Old Testament? David caught sight of the mercy of God in the middle of one of the most dysfunctional family dynamics in history. Even prior to Jesus' arrival in the flesh, David sees the heart of the Father. The only thing God intends to separate us from is our sin. The love of your Father is so great that He desires to remove every barrier to your union with Him.

7. *John 14:9 Jesus said to him, "Have I been so long with you, and yet you have not come to know Me, Philip? He who has seen Me has seen the Father." John 10:30 I and the Father are one. John 5:18 For this cause therefore the Jews were seeking all the more to kill Him, because He not only was breaking the Sabbath, but also was calling God His own Father, making Himself equal with God. Colossians 2:9 For in Him all the fullness of Deity dwells in bodily form. 2 Corinthians 5:19 God was in Christ*

reconciling the world to Himself, not counting their trespasses against them, and He has committed to us the word of reconciliation.

This is such a beautiful mystery. In the same way that Jesus was one with the Father, in Him you are rejoined with the Father.

8. ***Matthew 23:9*** *Do not call anyone on Earth your father; for One is your Father, He who is in heaven.* ***1 Corinthians 8:6*** ESV *Yet for us there is one God, the Father, from whom are all things and for whom we exist, and one Lord, Jesus Christ, through whom are all things and through whom we exist.* ***Ephesians 4:6*** ESV *One God and Father of all, who is over all and through all and in all.* ***Romans 8:15*** *For you have not received a spirit of slavery leading to fear again, but you have received a spirit of adoption as sons by which we cry out, "Abba! Father!"*

No matter how your father in this world has been, ultimately in God we have a very good Father.

9. ***Romans 8:38-39*** *For I am convinced that neither death, nor life, nor angels, nor principalities, **nor things present, nor things to come**, nor powers, nor height, nor depth, nor any other created thing, will be able to separate us from the love of God, which is in Christ Jesus our Lord.*

Did you notice what's missing here? The one thing not included in this list is the past, and that's because your past isn't even relevant. Your Father loves you so deeply that He refuses to allow your past, your failures, your sins, your offenses, to dictate to Him whether He can love you. There is nothing in the present and nothing in the future that can threaten your Father's love for you. Let the eternal reality of your Father's love erase any foreboding anticipation of the unknown. This reality is your rest. You are loved by your Father right now, where you are, as you are.

THREE
THE STORY OF YOUR FATHER

1. ***Luke 15:31-32*** *"My son," the father said, "you are always with me, and everything I have is yours. But we had to celebrate and be glad, because this brother of yours was dead and is alive again; he was lost and is found."* ***1 John 4:19*** *We love, because He first loved us.*

When the son crests the hill in the distance the father runs toward him. Even before the son can get his rehearsed repentance speech out of his mouth, the father declares him restored. That's what your heavenly Father is like. Your behavior cannot manipulate God or dictate to Him whether He loves you or not. See your Father and see yourself. As you behold how loved you are by Him, you will understand what it means to love.

Your love for your Father will never be greater than your perception of how loved you are *by* your Father. When you see how loved you really are, your heart will respond, for even the love you have for Him is a gift of love from Him. He has fully supplied to you all the love you need, in Himself.

2. *John 5:22* ESV *The Father judges no one, but has given all judgment to the Son.*

So is the Son going to judge you? Though He certainly has the power to, this is what He said a few verses later: *John 5:45 Do not think that I will accuse you before the Father; the one who accuses you is Moses, in whom you have set your hope.*

The law of Moses (as well as all systems of the world) unveils our sinfulness but has no power to do anything about it. Jesus reveals His heart toward us in that He has not come to accuse us, but to find and save us. This is the Father's heart.

John 3:17-18 For God did not send the Son into the world to judge the world, but that the world might be saved through Him. He who believes in Him is not judged; he who does not believe has been judged already, because he has not believed in the name of the only begotten Son of God.

Does condemnation exist for you? Yes, but its source is not God. Condemnation is from the accuser and from yourself, and it began at the fall. Do you remember what God asked Adam? *Who told you that you were naked?* They had always been naked and without shame because God did not judge the nakedness of His creation. We live under the weight of our own condemnation, and in condemning one another we condemn ourselves. But neither the Father nor the Son condemn you, for you are in Christ and He in you.

Romans 8:1-4 Therefore there is now no condemnation for those who are in Christ Jesus. For the law of the Spirit of life in Christ Jesus has set you free from the law of sin and of death. For what the Law could not do, weak as it was through the flesh, God did: sending His own Son in the likeness of sinful flesh and as an offering for sin, He condemned sin in the flesh, so that the requirement of the Law might be fulfilled in us.

You are legally obligated to be free, in Him. We are all legalists as such, and our liberation in Christ is our new law.

3. *Romans 5:20 The Law came in so that the transgression would increase; but where sin increased, grace abounded all the more so that as sin reigned in death, even so grace would reign through righteousness to eternal life through Jesus Christ our Lord.*

4. *Hebrews 8:7* NIV *For if there had been nothing wrong with that first covenant* (the law of Moses) *no place would have been sought for another* (the law of grace in Christ's death and resurrection). *Hebrews 7:18-19* NIV *The former regulation* (the

law of Moses) *is set aside* (canceled) *because it was weak and useless (for the law made nothing perfect) and a better hope is introduced* (the new law of grace) *by which we draw near to God* (know Him). **Hebrews 8:13** NIV *By calling this covenant "new" he has made the first one* (the law of Moses) *obsolete.* **Romans 8:1-3** *Therefore there is now no condemnation for those who are in Christ Jesus, because through Christ Jesus the law of the Spirit who gives life* (through grace) *has set you free from the law of sin and death. For what the law was powerless to do because it was weakened by the flesh, God did by sending his own Son in the likeness of sinful flesh to be a sin offering. And so he condemned sin in the flesh in order that the righteous requirement of the law might be fully met.*

The fulfillment of the law is grace in Christ. The law showed the world how powerless we are to attain righteousness through a system of rules and sacrifices—these only trap us in a never-ending cycle of failure. But in Christ we are free from the law of sin and death.

5. **Hebrews 12:6** NIV *The Lord disciplines the one he loves, and he chastens everyone he accepts as his son.*

6. **Jeremiah 1:5** *Before I formed you in the womb I knew you.*

Your Father has known you far longer than you can imagine. You existed in Him before you were ever formed in flesh. What did He think of when He dreamed of you? It was perfect, good, pure, a righteous reflection of His own holiness. The One who knew you before you could be known is the only One qualified to define you. He truly knows you better than you know yourself. See now what He sees, for you are in Christ, and Christ is in you.

7. **Luke 11:34** *The eye is the lamp of the body; when your eye is clear, your whole body also is full of light, but when it* (your perception) *is bad, your body also is full of darkness.* Your beliefs and perceptions determine your earthly experience, as we will see in greater depth later.

8. **1 Samuel 12:22** *For the Lord will not abandon His people on account of His great name, because the Lord has been pleased to make you a people for Himself.*

Your Father's heart has always been for you and not against you. His promise silences a deep fear in us that we could be left alone, lost, or forgotten. The word for *name* in Hebrew means much more than something to be called. It speaks of identity and nature. Because of who He is, because of the very essence of His nature, He will not abandon you. That is the relentless affection of your Father.

Psalm 136:1-5 *Give thanks to the Lord, for He is good, For His lovingkindness is everlasting. Give thanks to the God of gods, For His lovingkindness is everlasting. Give thanks to the Lord of lords, For His lovingkindness is everlasting. To Him who alone does great wonders, For His lovingkindness is everlasting. To Him who made the heavens with skill, For His lovingkindness is everlasting.*

A revelation of your Father's goodness will generate gratitude. King David writes in the Psalms a repeated phrase that was a foreign and unfolding concept in the Old Testament: that God would care to express love, that He would be kind, and that He is good. These were concepts that David understood because his heart was awakening to its authentic identity. He was a man after God's own heart. In spite of his sins and failures, he could find grace and intimacy in the presence of God. David perceived the goodness of God in ways that many of us, thousands of years later, struggle to see.

9. ***Psalm 91:1-2*** NIV *He who dwells in the shelter of the Most High will abide in the shadow of the Almighty. I will say of the Lord, "He is my refuge, my fortress, my God, in whom I trust."*

Trust is born out of union and intimacy. How do you trust God? Let go of all judgment, all offense, all grievance. These are not what define you. You are who your Father says you are.

FOUR
THE STORY OF YOU

1. ***Genesis 1:26-27*** *Then God said, "Let Us make man in Our image, according to Our likeness; and let them rule over the fish of the sea and over the birds of the sky and over the cattle and over all the earth, and over every creeping thing that creeps on the earth." God created man in His own image, in the image of God He created him; male and female He created them.* ***Genesis 2:7*** *Then the Lord God formed man from the dust of the ground, and breathed into his nostrils the breath of life.*

We are made in the likeness of God. In breathing life into Adam, God also infused him with His identity. There are only two times in the Scriptures where it is said that God breathed on man. The first is here in Genesis, and the second is in John 20:22 after the resurrection of Christ. There, He breathes upon the disciples and says, "Receive the Holy Spirit." The first breath infused us with the identity of the Holy Spirit of God. The second does no less. His breath restored us to the deepest possible intimacy with our Father.

In essence, the One who created mankind in the beginning came once more to re-create you through His own death and resurrection. What a powerful story.

2. ***John 12:28*** *"Father, glorify Your name." Then a voice came out of heaven: "I have both glorified it, and will glorify it again."* ***Luke 3:38*** *Adam, the son of God.*

This context of Adam being called a son of God beautifully compares that first Adam with Jesus, who is called the last Adam in 1 Corinthians 15:45. Adam failed to resist the tempter in the garden, but Jesus successfully resisted the tempter in the wilderness. Just as Adam's failure was imparted to you, so now Christ's victory is yours as well. Mankind's broken communion with the Father has been restored in the mystery of the reconciliation of Jesus Christ.

3. *John 1:1-4 In the beginning was the Word, and the Word was with God, and the Word was God. He was in the beginning with God. All things came into being through Him, and apart from Him nothing came into being that has come into being. In Him was life, and the life was the Light of men.*

It might seem perplexing to reference this verse at this point in the study, but see here that John begins his account of Jesus with a parallel to the story of Creation. In Genesis 1 God makes us in His likeness, yet here in John 1 something important is clarified: Christ was there at the beginning, doing the creating. So to be made in the likeness of God is to be made in the likeness of Yeshua. In as much, you have been remade in that same likeness through Yeshua. Think about this.

The image you're created in is God in Christ Jesus, for you are made in the image and likeness of the Word, and the Word is who created you. Jesus demonstrates to us the most authentic way to be human. In His likeness you are intelligent, relational, creative, eternal, glorified, spiritual. His life is our life, and His light is our light. You are not God, and He is not you. But you are *in* Him, and He is *in* you. This beautiful mystery of union is the basis of your identity.

4. *1 John 1:5 God is Light, and in Him there is no darkness at all.*

5. *Genesis 3:9-13 Then the Lord God called to the man, and said to him, "Where are you?" He said, "I heard the sound of You in the garden, and I was afraid because I was naked; so I hid myself." And He said, "Who told you that you were naked? Have you eaten from the tree of which I commanded you not to eat?" The man said, "The woman whom You gave to be with me, she gave me from the tree, and I ate." Then the Lord God said to the woman, "What is this you have done?" And the woman said, "The serpent deceived me, and I ate."*

Fear of our own shame (self-judgment) causes us to judge others. This knowledge of good and evil is the fruit of the fall, and we eat it every day. When we choose fear over love we go blind to authentic identity—ours and everyone else's. In Yeshua you are restored to your original identity. That is who you are and how deeply you are loved by your Father.

6. *John 1:4-5 NIV In him was life, and that life was the light of all mankind. The light shines in the darkness, and the darkness has not overcome it.*

The contrast between dark and light is clear as John describes the confused weakness of darkness and the overpowering invasion of light. The illusion that darkness has substance is only convincing if no light is present. But in truth, the light has come into all darkness, not just into a small corner of it, not just in half the atoms or half of the world. The darkness has not overcome it, anywhere. God is not only partially victorious. Neither is His Son.

7. **John 12:28** *"Father, glorify Your name." Then a voice came out of heaven: "I have both glorified it, and will glorify it again."*

8. **Psalm 22:1** *My God, my God, why have You forsaken me?* **Matthew 27:46** *About the ninth hour Jesus cried out with a loud voice, saying, "Eli, Eli, lama sabachthani?" that is, "My God, My God, why have You forsaken Me?"*

9. **John 19:30** *Therefore when Jesus had received the sour wine, He said, "It is finished!" And He bowed His head and gave up His Spirit.*

10. **Romans 8:1-2** *Therefore there is now no condemnation for those who are in Christ Jesus. For the law of the Spirit of life in Christ Jesus has set you free from the law of sin and of death.*

There has been much division in the church over the question of whether we're under law or under grace. But this doesn't need to be so, because as Paul understood it here, we are clearly still under law, just not the *old* law. Every student of law understands the concept of an overturned law. When a new law overturns an old one, the new law becomes the standard. The old standard is no longer legal or relevant.

In Christ there is a new law, and it's called "the law of the Spirit of life in Christ." The result of this is that you are at a place of perfect liberty; that is what grace is. The Spirit of God has unveiled a limitless horizon before you. He has empowered you to dream and to do according to the infinite ability of an absolutely good Father. Now, the most authentic "legalists" are the ones who recognize their true freedom. Grace has become the higher law.

11. **Isaiah 9:2** *The people who walk in darkness Will see a great light; Those who live in a dark land, The light will shine on them.* **John 8:12** *I am the Light of the world.* **Matthew 5:14** *You are the light of the world.*

Who is the "you" in that last verse? Meditate on the powerful beauty of this mystery. What does it mean to be the light of the world? This can only be understood when you know that all distance and separation that once existed between you and Christ have been eliminated.

12. **John 12:28** *"Father, glorify Your name." Then a voice came out of heaven: "I have both glorified it, and will glorify it again."* **Romans 3:23-24** *For all have sinned and fallen short of the glory of God, being justified as a gift by His grace through the redemption which is in Christ Jesus.*

Have you ever read those three verses together? You were made to shine with the glory of God, but sin created the darkness of separation between you and Him.

But the Father planned to glorify His identity once more through the death and resurrection of the second Adam, and Paul makes it clear in Romans.

Most of the time Romans 3:23 is quoted all by itself, giving the impression that the end of the verse is the end of the thought. But this isn't the case. This Scripture doesn't make the case for your guilt, but for your innocence. You no longer fall short of the glory of God in Christ. He has now glorified His name again in you. Now Jesus' prayer begins to make much more sense.

John 17:22-23 The glory which You have given Me I have given to them, that they may be one, just as We are one; I in them and You in Me, that they may be perfected in unity, so that the world may know that You sent Me, and loved them, even as You have loved Me.

Without Him you would most certainly be nothing. Thankfully you are not without Him. You began in the mind and heart of God. So before you can discover who you truly are, turn your affection to the origin of your identity and see your Father as He truly is. Whatever has your positive attention also has your affection, and in encountering your Father, you will discover an affirming revelation of yourself. You were created to radiate the goodness of God.

13. *Romans 5:17-18, 20 For if by the transgression of the one, death reigned through the one, much more those who receive the abundance of grace and of the gift of righteousness will reign in life through the One, Jesus Christ. So then as through one transgression there resulted condemnation to all men, even so through one act of righteousness there resulted justification of life to all men . . . The Law came in so that the transgression would increase; but where sin increased, grace abounded all the more.*

Whatever Adam's sin did to condemn you, Yeshua's grace has done much more. This is a great and wonderful mystery. You haven't outrun or run out of the grace of God. Sin will never exhaust the righteousness of truth, for truth is not an opinion of man. Truth is the person of Jesus Christ.

14. *1 Corinthians 13:12 For now we see in a mirror dimly, but then face to face; now I know in part, but then I will know fully just as I also have been fully known.*

15. *Ecclesiastes 3:11 He has made everything appropriate in its time. He has also set eternity in their heart, yet so that man will not find out the work which God has done from the beginning even to the end. Isaiah 57:15 ESV For thus says the One who is high and lifted up, who inhabits eternity, whose name is Holy: "I dwell in the high and holy place, and also with him who is of a contrite and lowly spirit, to revive the spirit of the lowly, and to revive the heart of the contrite."*

Some say God is outside of time but can see the whole spectrum from beginning to end. Some say God operates within time and limits Himself so that He doesn't see what is going to happen, yet still remains involved. Both possibilities may have elements of truth.

But it is clear that God created all things, including time, and His eternal realm is not defined by the time He created. Before there was time, there was God: *2 Timothy 1:9 NIV He has saved us and called us to a holy life—not because of anything we have done but because of his own purpose and grace. This grace was given us in Christ Jesus before the beginning of time.* Time is a beautiful creation that gives us the opportunity to observe and understand the good work that our Father is doing within us, for He has never stopped creating. We will forever be awakening to what has always been, and what has always been is love.

16. *Ephesians 1:4 NIV For he chose us in him before the creation of the world to be holy and blameless in his sight. In love he predestined us for adoption to sonship through Jesus Christ, in accordance with his pleasure and will—to the praise of his glorious grace, which he has freely given us in the One he loves.*

God Himself is your point of origin. You began in His heart and mind, by His sovereign will. Even before the foundation or fall of the world He saw you as His son, His daughter, the incarnation of the Godhead on Earth as it is in heaven.

FIVE
SEEING WHO YOU ARE

1. *1 Corinthians 6:19 Do you not know that your body is a temple of the Holy Spirit who is in you, whom you have from God, and that you are not your own?*

There is a difference between the body and the Spirit. Your body is a temple, but *only* a temple. It is not who you are. It is merely a costume, a vessel that contains the eternal you. So treat it with great respect, but do not mistake it for more than it is. It is a beautiful but decaying vessel. Paul asks his question rhetorically: Isn't it really self-evident that we are created to be the dwelling place of God? Keep in mind that the churches Paul is writing to had no New Testament and little or no access to Old Testament Scriptures. They had nothing but the gospel Paul shared with them and the indwelling power of the Holy Spirit. Yet Paul finds it hard to believe that they don't understand their union with God in Christ by the power of the Holy Spirit. I wonder if Paul would be just as surprised by our lack of belief today.

2. *Matthew 5:48 Therefore you are to be perfect, as your heavenly Father is perfect. 1 John 4:17 As He is, so also are we in this world.*

The Greek word for "be" (*Esomai*) here is different than the word "become" (*Ginomai*). *Esomai* is not an assignment commanding you to strive to become something. It's a prophetic revelation of your present identity. This is Yeshua's declaration of Christ in you, the hope of glory. *Perfect* and *holy* are who you are right now. For you are as He is.

2 Corinthians 5:21 He made Him who knew no sin to be sin on our behalf, so that we might become the righteousness of God in Him.

Our blindness to how our Father sees us keeps us in a behavioral cycle of consistent failure. Holiness is the natural response of a heart at rest in the grace of God. Righteousness is not something you become. It is who you are.

3. *Galatians 2:20 I have been crucified with Christ; and it is no longer I who live, but Christ lives in me; and the life which I now live in the flesh I live by faith in the Son of God, who loved me and gave Himself up for me.*

Paul was making a personal application (I myself have been crucified) to unveil a divine revelation of his identity. To receive what God says about you means you have to be willing to listen to God speak about you in this way. It's as if Paul heard Jesus say, *You have been crucified with me, and it is no longer you who live, but I who live in you; and the life you now live in the flesh you live by faith in me, who loves you and gave myself for you.*

4. *Ephesians 2:4-6 God, being rich in mercy, because of His great love with which He loved us, even when we were dead in our transgressions, made us alive together with Christ (by grace you have been saved), and raised us up with Him, and seated us with Him in the heavenly places in Christ Jesus.*

The result of your co-crucifixion and co-resurrection is that you are currently, right now, present in this world of form and dimension of time, and simultaneously present in the dimension of eternity. It's far too grand for our minds to grasp as long as we believe that all we see is all there is. But our spirits know far more truth than our minds currently understand.

5. *Romans 8:29-30 For those whom He foreknew, He also predestined to become conformed to the image of His Son, so that He would be the firstborn among many brethren; and these whom He predestined, He also called; and these whom He called, He also justified; and these whom He justified, He also glorified.*

6. *1 Timothy 1:15-16 It is a trustworthy statement, deserving full acceptance, that Christ Jesus came into the world to save sinners, among whom I am foremost of all. Yet for this reason I found mercy, so that in me as the foremost, Jesus Christ might demonstrate His perfect patience as an example for those who would believe in Him for eternal life.*

Philippians 3:8-15 More than that, I count all things to be loss in view of the surpassing value of knowing Christ Jesus my Lord . . . so that I may gain Christ, and may be found in Him, not having a righteousness of my own derived from the Law, but that which is through faith in Christ, the righteousness which comes from God on the basis of faith, that I may know Him and the power of His resurrection and the fellowship of His sufferings, being conformed to His death; in order that I may attain to the resurrection from the dead. Not that I have already obtained it or have already become perfect (fully experienced the perfection of union in Christ in this life), but I press on so that I may lay hold of that for which also I was laid hold of by Christ Jesus. Brethren, I do not regard myself as having laid hold of it yet; but one thing I do: forgetting what lies behind and reaching forward to what lies ahead, I press on toward the goal for the prize of the upward call of God in Christ Jesus. Let us therefore, as many as are perfect, have this attitude.

1 Corinthians 12:7-8 Because of the surpassing greatness of the revelations, for this reason, to keep me from exalting myself, there was given me a thorn in the flesh, a messenger of Satan to torment me—to keep me from exalting myself! Concerning this I implored the Lord three times that it might leave me. And He has said to me, "My grace is sufficient for you, for power is perfected in weakness."

7. *2 Corinthians 5:17 Therefore if anyone is in Christ, he is a new creature; the old things passed away; behold, new things have come.*

The Greek word translated "creature" here is *kitisis*, which simply means "creation." To make something new is not like fixing something that was broken, but rather like making something for the very first time, as if the broken had never even existed. Only one who is the master of time could do such a thing. *Romans 8:1 Therefore there is now no condemnation for those who are in Christ Jesus. Colossians 2:10 In Him you have been made complete.*

Is there any question of who you are in Christ? Thus the words of Jesus from the cross: *It is finished!*

8. *2 Corinthians 4:7 NIV But we have this treasure in jars of clay, to show that this all-surpassing power is from God and not from us. 2 Corinthians 5:1 ESV For we know that if the tent that is our earthly home is destroyed, we have a building from God, a house not made with hands, eternal in the heavens. 2 Corinthians 4:18 NIV So we fix our eyes* (perception) *not on what is seen, but on what is unseen, since what is seen is temporary* (including the body you see) *but what is unseen is eternal* (your true spiritual self)*. 2 Corinthians 5:16 Therefore from now on we recognize no one according to the flesh; even though we have known Christ according to the flesh, yet now we know Him in this way no longer.*

Do you ever think about your spirit? Do you know that you are a spiritual being? Try something today: think of the body as a costume we are all wearing. Ignore everybody's costume and ask your Father to reveal to you what He believes about them. Each person is a much-loved child of God made in His image and likeness. Remember, that is who you are too.

9. *James 2:19* *You believe that God is one. You do well; the demons also believe, and shudder.*

10. *2 Timothy 3:5* *For men will be lovers of self . . . holding to a form of godliness, although they have denied its power.*

11. *Colossians 2:8* *See to it that no one takes you captive through philosophy and empty deception, according to the tradition of men, according to the elementary principles of the world, rather than according to Christ.*

12. *Ephesians 2:8* *For by grace you have been saved through faith; and that not of yourselves, it is the gift of God.* *Hebrews 11:1-3* *Now faith is the assurance (substance) of things hoped for, the conviction (evidence) of things not seen . . . By faith we understand that the worlds were prepared by the word of God, so that what is seen was not made out of things which are visible.*

In Western culture, we protect ourselves from deception by putting our faith only in that which we first understand. But there are things in Christ that require faith before we can understand. Even then, your spirit knows what your mind can't yet fully grasp. Surrendering what you think you know, in order to be who you truly are (loved, whole, secure, complete, at rest, in Him), requires the very faith that God Himself freely gives you.

13. *Acts 26:17-18* *I am sending you to open their eyes so that they may turn from darkness to light and from the dominion of Satan to God, that they may receive forgiveness of sins and an inheritance among those who have been sanctified by faith in Me.*

Our brother Paul was confronted by the Light, left in the tomb of his own blindness for three days, then commissioned to turn mankind from darkness to light. How much more can a person be identified with the mission of Christ?

14. *John 5:22* ESV *The Father judges no one but has given all judgment to the Son.* *Matthew 7:1* *Do not judge so that you will not be judged.* *John 5:45* *Do not think that I will accuse you before the Father; the one who accuses you is Moses, in whom you have set your hope.*

Six
The Great Mystery

1. ***1 John 5:7*** *KJV For there are three that bear record in heaven, the Father, the Word, and the Holy Ghost: and these three are one.*

Yeshua demonstrated what it truly means to be human. The relationship of love and trust that you have with your Father is possible because you are united by the power of the Spirit.

2. Quantum science is revealing a realm that defies the mechanical laws of Newtonian physics we all grew up understanding. Surely our children's children will have a much better understanding of nature than we do, even as we now have a better understanding than those who once believed the world was flat. In the quantum world, particles both exist as material and don't at the same time. They can be in two places at once, and they are not bound by space and time. This has been proven over and over, and yet no one knows how it works.

God consistently frustrates human wisdom that exalts itself apart from God. Trying to understand God fully through the lens of the physical world without the help of the Spirit (as science had tried to do for years) is like my dog trying to understand the Internet. There are dimensions that we can't even begin to comprehend, and now even science is embracing the mystery of it all, in large part because of quantum physics. In fact, at times it seems that science is ahead of traditional religion when it comes to contemplating things like two things being one at the same time in the quantum realm.

3. ***John 14:20*** *ESV In that day you will know that I am in My Father, and you in Me, and I in you.*

Take a moment and consider the staggering implications of this statement. If you believe Jesus' words to be true, then the reality is both overwhelming and inevitable, and available for you to know now. God (Father, Son, Spirit) is fully resident and present within you now. The notion that "Christ lives in us" has perhaps been overstated to the point that we are desensitized to the truth of it. But how beautiful to know that we are not merely the expendable and deteriorating home of God. No, He is also the home we live within.

4. ***Matthew 25:40*** *Truly I say to you, to the extent that you did it to one of these brothers of Mine, even the least of them, you did it to Me.*

The least of them that Jesus was referring to were those considered sinners in His day. What we do to others, including outcasts and sinners, we are actually doing to Christ. So then let us treat all of our brothers and sisters in this world as we would treat Christ. Jesus chooses the least to call His brothers. He puts no effort of theirs on display as qualification. It is not their badness on display but rather His goodness. Why are we so quick to look at our brothers and be angry at what they have or have not done? We judge those who offend us and our ego demands justice, but treating others as Christ is the beginning of being the light of the world.

5. *John 17:3 This is eternal life, that they may know You, the only true God, and Jesus Christ whom You have sent.*

6. *John 15:5-11 I am the vine, you are the branches; he who abides in Me and I in him, he bears much fruit, for apart from Me you can do nothing. If anyone does not abide in Me, he is thrown away as a branch and dries up; and they gather them, and cast them into the fire and they are burned.*

To the extent that you hold onto the perspective that you are separated from Him, you will find yourself in suffering.

If you abide in Me, and My words abide in you, ask whatever you wish, and it will be done for you.

It is in the context of being in Him that all things are possible.

My Father is glorified by this, that you bear much fruit, and so prove to be My disciples. Just as the Father has loved Me, I have also loved you; abide in My love. If you keep My commandments, you will abide in My love; just as I have kept My Father's commandments and abide in His love. These things I have spoken to you so that My joy may be in you, and that your joy may be made full.

The fruit of the vine here is love. If you read these words and your heart isn't filled with love and joy, you missed the true message.

7. *Genesis 3:22-24 KJV And the Lord God said, Behold, the man is become as one of us, to know good and evil: and now, lest he put forth his hand, and take also of the tree of life, and eat, and live for ever: Therefore the Lord God sent him forth from the garden of Eden.*

In the garden the tree of life is seen as a source of eternal life for those who eat of its fruit. In the New Testament, Christ is the source of eternal life for all who believe. He is the tree of life. In *Psalm 34:8* we're encouraged to approach God in a radical way: *taste and see that the Lord is good.* Then in *John 6:56* Jesus makes a most shocking claim, establishing Himself as our tree of life. *He who eats My flesh and drinks My blood abides in Me, and I in him.*

If Jesus is the tree of life for us, and you are in Him, then who are you? You are the branches directly attached to the vine (the trunk and root system that sources life).

Ezekiel 47:12 By the river on its bank, on one side and on the other, will grow all kinds of trees for food. Their leaves will not wither and their fruit will not fail. They will bear every month because their water flows from the sanctuary, and their fruit will be for food and their leaves for healing.

Here's a verse about you. **Psalm 1:3** *He will be like a tree firmly planted by streams of water, Which yields its fruit in its season And its leaf does not wither; And in whatever he does, he prospers.*

Finally in Revelation the tree of life appears again. Its function directly relates to Yeshua's mandate to us to bring healing to the broken. **Revelation 12:22** *On either side of the river was the tree of life, bearing twelve kinds of fruit, yielding its fruit every month; and the leaves of the tree were for the healing of the nations.*

In Him, you are revealed as the tree of life for the nations. In you He is revealed as the ultimate Savior.

8. **Ephesians 5:28-32** ESV *In the same way husbands should love their wives as their own bodies. He who loves his wife loves himself. For no one ever hated his own flesh, but nourishes and cherishes it, just as Christ does the church, because we are members of his body. "Therefore a man shall leave his father and mother and hold fast to his wife, and the two shall become one flesh." This mystery is profound, and I am saying that it refers to Christ and the church.*

While Paul's advice can be applied to marriage, that's not what he's really talking about. He's painting a picture of you and God in Christ. The intimacy of human marriage is a metaphor for your union with God. Christ loves you the way He loves Himself. Why? Because you are His body.

9. **John 17:22-23** ESV *The glory that you have given me I have given to them, that they may be one even as we are one, I in them and you in me, that they may become perfectly one, so that the world may know that you sent me and loved them even as you loved me.*

You carry the presence of the glorious One with and within you. Therefore you are, by association, glorious. It's illogical to claim that Yeshua lives within you and at the same time claim that you are not glorious. When understood, there's no pride in that reality. Just gratitude.

10. **Romans 8:29-30** *For those whom He foreknew, He also predestined to become conformed to the image of His Son, so that He would be the firstborn among many brethren; and these whom He predestined, He also called; and these whom He called, He also justified; and these whom He justified, He also glorified.*

This can be difficult to understand unless you (a) realize that you are joined together with Christ and (b) see yourself from an eternal perspective. Being glorified was your destiny before the invention of time itself. It has been thought that being glorified is impossible without being sanctified (declared holy). But what if you've already been sanctified?

John 17:19 For their sakes I sanctify Myself, that they themselves also may be sanctified in truth.

Apart from Yeshua your sanctification is impossible. Your union with righteousness Himself overcomes your sin nature by grace. For this reason, Paul can say with confidence in *2 Corinthians 5:21 He made Him who knew no sin to be sin on our behalf, so that we might become the righteousness of God in Him.*

SEVEN
SONS AND DAUGHTERS OF THE FATHER

1. *Galatians 3:26 For you are all sons [and daughters] of God through faith in Christ. Galatians 4:6* NIV *Because you are his sons [and daughters], God sent forth the Spirit of his Son into our hearts, the Spirit who cries out, "Abba, Father!" Romans 8:19* NIV *For the creation waits in eager expectation for the children of God to be revealed.*

Creation is literally waiting for us to awaken to who we really are.

2. *Matthew 23:9 Do not call anyone on Earth your father; for One is your Father, He who is in heaven.*

As you continue to study the Scriptures, read them from a perspective of being "in Him." You'll begin to realize that the mysteries and hard sayings of the Bible are clarified. Your earthly father may have failed you, but have no fear, for he is not your Father in Christ. There is no need to make God in his image.

3. *Luke 14:26 If anyone comes to Me, and does not hate his own father and mother and wife and children and brothers and sisters, yes, and even his own life, he cannot be My disciple.*

In Christ, you're not rejecting anyone. If the teachings of Jesus could be summed up in a single phrase, it would be, "Let go." Surrender who you think you are so that you might be who you truly are.

4. *Romans 8:29 For those whom He foreknew, He also predestined to become conformed to the image of His Son, so that He would be the firstborn among many brethren.*

EIGHT
THE TALE OF TWO KINGDOMS

1. *John 17:3 This is eternal life, that they may know You, the only true God, and Jesus Christ whom You have sent.*

2. *1 Corinthians 13:12 For now we see in a mirror dimly, but then face to face; now I know in part, but then I will know fully just as I also have been fully known. 1 Corinthians 2:16 "Who has known the mind of the Lord, that he will instruct him?" But we have the mind of Christ. 1 John 2:20 But you have an anointing from the Holy One, and you all know.*

Though we don't experience the spiritual dimension fully now, we know more about it than we understand. That is, we have intimate union with our Father, even as a child knows its mother without being taught everything about her. Like that child, we don't yet understand all that we know. But we can rest assured in this revelation, that God is infinitely good and complete.

3. *Luke 17:20-21 Now having been questioned by the Pharisees as to when the kingdom of God was coming, He answered them and said, "The kingdom of God is not coming with signs to be observed; nor will they say, 'Look, here it is!' or, 'There it is!' For behold, the kingdom of God is in your midst."*

We look outside of ourselves for what we believe we don't possess. But everything we need in God is already within reach, as we will discover when we seek His kingdom above all else. All of our longings can be summed up as a longing for a relationship with God Himself, in Christ through the power of the Holy Spirit.

4. *John 1:4-5 In Him was life, and the life was the Light of men. The Light shines in the darkness, and the darkness did not comprehend it.*

Light is not offended, worn out, or overpowered by darkness. As long as a light is shining, it doesn't even know the darkness exists. It can't, for the source of light sees nothing but what it illuminates. It doesn't have to fight against the darkness. It simply does what it was created to do. It shines.

5. *Colossians 1:17 He is before all things, and in Him all things hold together.*

There is nothing that exists apart from Him, without His knowledge, or without His involvement. This doesn't mean that God is behind evil. In our blindness we abuse the creation we have been given to steward. To abuse means to use something for a purpose other than that for which it was intended. A hammer was created to pound a nail. Have you ever hit your thumb with a hammer? When a creation forgets its purpose, brutal consequences can result. Wisdom recognizes purpose in creation and works with it to bring about the best possible outcome.

6. **Psalm 139:8** *Where can I go from Your Spirit? Or where can I flee from Your presence? If I ascend to heaven, You are there; If I make my bed in Sheol, behold, You are there.*

Is there anywhere that God is not present, if He is indeed omnipresent? The trees are not God, but He clearly exists in them because He is everywhere. If Christ, as the Light of the world, is interwoven even on a subatomic level with matter, why does He seem so distant? Because we have been led to believe that He is. Much modern church passion is tied to a desire to find God or be close to God. But the psalmist realized that God is not hard to find. You can't get away from the One who holds all things together.

7. **John 17:3** *This is eternal life, that they may know You, the only true God, and Jesus Christ whom You have sent.*

When does eternal life begin? Because the entire concept of *eternal* transcends linear time, it is impossible for eternal life to have a beginning. You are a multidimensional being, able to be in both time (here in this world of form) and eternity (seated in heavenly places now) at the very same time. So your eternity has already begun by this very realization. In Him you live and move and have your being.

From our perspective God appears to work with and within time, for it is the existence that we know. But the dimension of heaven may be to us as difficult to comprehend as the universe is to a baby. Consider that God's timelessness may perhaps be best seen in His ability to move freely throughout time to ultimately make all things work together for good for you. Whatever theories we come up with, God will always exceed our expectations, for God is better than we think, and we cannot imagine Him to be better than He is.

8. **2 Corinthians 4:17** *We look not to the things that are seen, but to the things that are unseen. For the things that are seen are transient, but the things that are unseen are eternal.*

9. **Mark 12:30-31** *"Love the Lord your God with all your heart, and with all your soul, and with all your mind, and with all your strength . . . You shall love your neighbor as yourself." There is no other commandment greater than these.*

Compare this with the following verse. **Luke 14:26** *If anyone comes to Me, and does not hate his own father and mother and wife and children and brothers and sisters, yes, and even his own life, he cannot be My disciple.*

Followers of Yeshua's Way are awakening to this reality. Our authentic identity, which we embrace, is "in Him." Our false identity is every label that we have been identified with that is other than "in Him." Yeshua tells us to "hate" these roles (child, parent, spouse), which means we must hold them of no account in our search for identity.

As Paul wrote in **Galatians 3:28** *There is neither Jew nor Greek, there is neither slave nor free man, there is neither male nor female; for you are all one in Christ Jesus.* Your nationality, your gender, and your cultural position are not who you truly are. Nor is your job title, your résumé, or your social status. When you surrender who you think you are to who you truly are—a child of your Father—then the divine nature of your Father (who is Love) will be the very Spirit that you put on display. This is how our fruits are known.

10. **2 Corinthians 4:16, 18** *Therefore we do not lose heart, but though our outer man is decaying, yet our inner man is being renewed day by day . . . while we look not at the things which are seen, but at the things which are unseen; for the things which are seen are temporal, but the things which are not seen are eternal.*

11. **2 Corinthians 5:13** NIV *If we are "out of our mind," as some say, it is for God; if we are in our right mind, it is for you.*

The bliss of union with God can cause joy to erupt from within you like a person who has fallen in love. Paul lets people know that he'll hold it together when he's around them, but otherwise he may seem out of his mind. What could cause such a joy that transcends human intelligence? The realization that you are one with God in Christ by the power of the Holy Spirit. And that your unity with Him is the result of His desire and design, not your worthiness. This is grace.

12. **2 Corinthians 5:16** ESV *From now on, therefore, we regard no one according to the flesh. Even though we once regarded Christ according to the flesh, we regard him thus no longer.*

It is impossible to know Yeshua without realizing this truth. You are, at the eternal core of your being, spirit, not body.

John 4:24 *God is spirit and those who worship Him must worship in spirit and in truth.*

God is spirit and so are you. Your costume, beautiful as it may be, is temporal. We commune in this world of flesh and form, but don't mistake anyone's external costume, nor all of its labels, for the true person you see before you. See what your Father sees in others and in yourself.

NINE
WHAT DEFIES EARTHLY EYES

1. *John 20:27 Then He said to Thomas, "Reach here with your finger, and see My hands; and reach here your hand and put it into My side; and do not be unbelieving, but believing."*

2. *1 Corinthians 15:44 It* (the body) *is sown a natural body, it is raised a spiritual body. If there is a natural body, there is also a spiritual body.*

1 Corinthians 15:50 Now I say this, brethren, that flesh and blood cannot inherit the kingdom of God; nor does the perishable inherit the imperishable.

3. *John 17:11 I am no longer in the world; and yet they themselves are in the world, and I come to You. Holy Father, keep them in Your name, the name which You have given Me, that they may be one even as We are.*

Where is Jesus while He's praying this? Clearly He's standing on Earth. But He said He's not in this world, and He spoke truth. How can this be? He was with them, but their perspective of this life didn't match His yet. Does ours?

John 17:15-16 I do not ask You to take them out of the world, but to keep them from the evil one. They are not of the world, even as I am not of the world.

In Him, you are here in form, but your authentic identity is in Him seated in heavenly places. We are learning to reflect the light of heaven in the darkness of this world, for you are the light of the world.

4. *2 Corinthians 5:16-17 Therefore from now on we recognize no one according to the flesh . . . Therefore if anyone is in Christ, he is a new creature; the old things passed away; behold, new things have come.*

You are not a refurbished wreck. You are a creation that has never been seen before. An entirely new creature that has no other point of reference for being than the One in whose image and likeness you are created. With this in mind, you *must* see Him in order to know who you are.

5. *2 Corinthians 4:7 ESV But we have this treasure in jars of clay, to show that the surpassing power belongs to God and not to us.*

2 Corinthians 5:1 ESV For we know that if the tent that is our earthly home is destroyed, we have a building from God, a house not made with hands, eternal in the heavens.

After the resurrection, Jesus is recognized in physical form, even showing the scars of the crucifixion. But in his Revelation, John also sees Jesus, and though He is still recognizable in a body, this form is unlike anything John has ever seen before. He can barely describe the glory of it (Revelation 6:11-16). However we will be known in the realm of heaven, it won't be by this mortal flesh we now inhabit, which is subject to age, decay, injury, pain, and disease. Care for this costume you wear, for you are a dwelling place of the Spirit of God, but know that you won't be dragging this body and its issues into eternity. Your body is not you. Who you are is far more beautiful.

2 Corinthians 4:18 NIV *So we fix our eyes* (perception) *not on what is seen, but on what is unseen, since what is seen is temporary, but what is unseen is eternal.*

2 Corinthians 5:16 *Therefore from now on we recognize no one according to the flesh; even though we have known Christ according to the flesh, yet now we know Him in this way no longer.*

Do you ever think about your spirit? Do you know that you are a spiritual being? Try something today. Ignore everybody's costume and ask your Father to reveal to you how He sees the people you encounter. When it comes to a person's costume, refuse to be offended by anything temporal. Love them as God loves them. See that what you do to the least in your eyes, you do to Christ. If you don't know who a person really is, start here: everyone is a much-loved child of God made in His image. Remember, that is who you are, too.

6. *Colossians 3:1-3* NIV *Since then you have been raised with Christ, set your hearts on things above* (beyond), *where Christ is, seated at the right hand of God. Set your minds on things above, not on Earthly things. For you have died and life is now hidden with Christ in God.*

7. *Matthew 6:24* *No one can serve two masters; for either he will hate the one and love the other, or he will be devoted to one and despise the other. You cannot serve God and mammon.*

8. *Genesis 1:26* ESV *Then God said, "Let us make man in our image, after our likeness. And let them have dominion over the fish of the sea and over the birds of the heavens and over the livestock and over all the earth and over every creeping thing that creeps on the earth."*

How do you define *dominion*? Is it "to rule, control, and dominate" or "to love, protect, and serve"? How did Jesus demonstrate the Father's nature here on Earth? Whatever power, intelligence, and inventive brilliance we exercise here must have love as its foundation, or it's of no value.

Psalm 115:16 *The heavens are the heavens of the Lord, But the earth He has given to the sons of men.* The restoration of your authentic identity will open your eyes to care for this world entrusted to you. See the beauty of this world around you as a gift from your Father. Bless it and do not curse it, for you are restored in Him.

9. *Matthew 11:28-30 Come to Me, all who are weary and heavy-laden, and I will give you rest. Take My yoke upon you and learn from Me, for I am gentle and humble in heart, and you will find rest for your souls. For My yoke is easy and My burden is light.*

As we've seen earlier, the *yoke* in rabbinical culture referred to the way that particular rabbi interpreted the Scriptures. The teachings of Yeshua are complex, but not complicated. Think of a beautiful diamond with many facets. A geologist can study the diamond for its complexity, and a bride can admire it for its worth and brilliance, but a child can hold the diamond and equally enjoy its beauty without a full understanding of its makeup or its value.

Psalm 62:1-2 My soul waits in silence for God only; From Him is my salvation. He only is my rock and my salvation, My stronghold; I shall not be greatly shaken.

10. *John 16:33 These things I have spoken to you, so that in Me you may have peace. In the world you have tribulation* (trouble), *but take courage; I have overcome the world.*

Have you spent your life trying to crucify your flesh, or are you living the joy of the resurrected life as a child of your victorious Father? It has been said that peace is not the absence of conflict, but the presence of Jesus. Every word Jesus said was to impart peace into you. If the words of Jesus frightened you or caused your heart any response other than peace, you have missed the point. Go back and ask Him to reveal His peace to you through His Spirit and His Word.

Romans 8:37 ESV No, in all these things we are more than conquerors through him who loved us.

How can you be *more* than a conqueror? It's like being the wife of a champion boxer; when the fight is over, he hands you the check. You didn't swing a single punch, but you reap the full benefits of a victory that someone else won. Or you can think of it like an inheritance, in which you receive a wealth that someone else worked for and passed on to you out of love. It's the inexplicable wonder of the love and grace of your Father. In this way Yeshua died for your sin.

11. *Matthew 7:7 Ask, and it will be given to you; seek, and you will find; knock, and it will be opened to you.* Compare that verse to *James 4:3 You ask and do not receive, because you ask with wrong motives, so that you may spend it on your pleasures.* Then meditate on *Mark 11:24 Therefore I say to you, all things for which you pray and ask, believe that you have received them, and they will be granted you.*

The key here is the phrase "when you pray." To pray is to give your attention to the presence of God. What are the desires that arise in your heart when you're in His presence, fully aware of Him? Give attention to those.

1 John 5:14-15 This is the confidence which we have before Him, that, if we ask anything according to His will, He hears us. And if we know that He hears us in whatever we ask, we know that we have the requests which we have asked from Him.

TEN
SEEING IN THE DARK

1. ***John 3:1-3*** *Now there was a man of the Pharisees, named Nicodemus, a ruler of the Jews; this man came to Jesus by night and said to Him, "Rabbi, we know that You have come from God as a teacher; for no one can do these signs that You do unless God is with him." Jesus answered and said to him, "Truly, truly, I say to you, unless one is born again he cannot see the kingdom of God."*

Yeshua offers an answer to a question that hasn't even been asked yet. He reveals that your awakening in Him (the new birth) is what opens your eyes to see the kingdom of God.

2. ***Matthew 6:22-23*** *The eye is the lamp of the body; so then if your eye is clear, your whole body will be full of light. But if your eye is bad, your whole body will be full of darkness. If then the light that is in you is darkness, how great is the darkness!*

Notice that Yeshua said "eye" not "eyes." He wasn't talking about the eyes in your head, but your perception of reality. When attention is given to the fullness of light, that spiritual perspective has a dramatic effect on our experience in bodily form. Could it be that a key to healing can be found in how we see?

3. ***Matthew 5:29*** *If your right eye makes you stumble, tear it out and throw it from you; for it is better for you to lose one of the parts of your body, than for your whole body to be thrown into hell.*

4. ***Matthew 13:14*** NIV *You will be ever hearing but never understanding; you will be ever seeing but never perceiving.*

5. ***1 John 1:5-10*** *God is Light, and in Him there is no darkness at all. If we say that we have fellowship with Him and yet walk in the darkness, we lie and do not practice the truth; but if we walk in the Light as He Himself is in the Light, we have fellowship with one another, and the blood of Jesus His Son cleanses us from all sin.*

If we say that we have no sin, we are deceiving ourselves and the truth is not in us.

Sin is missing the mark; all that would separate us from the experience of our true identity as the sons and daughters of God. Do you have the capability to sin? Yes. In fact, most live in sin most of the time. But don't assume that your ability to miss the mark means that it is your truest nature to do so because it is risen with Christ. Missing the mark, however, is all your lower nature knows to do.

When we become aware of who we are, that is, when we walk in the light, then our minds are cleansed of all notions of separation in Christ and the lower nature is silenced.

You can choose sin, and as you do, you suffer its consequences in your life. But that sin doesn't change your identity. Letting go of false identities and surrendering to who we are *in Him* awakens us to the reality of our purity by His grace. That purity is a gift and is not partial. It's complete.

If, on the other hand, we say that we have no sin (anything that separates us from our intimate awareness of who we are), we are only being self-righteous because we all lose sight of who we are far too often. But, again, that does change who we are. We are the sons and daughters of the Father in Christ.

6. *Matthew 8:26 He said to them, "Why are you afraid, you men of little faith?" Then He got up and rebuked the winds and the sea, and it became perfectly calm.*

Yeshua could rest within the storm because there was no storm within Him. There is no need for a storm within you. Let go of your fear as you hear your Father speak peace to the waves. Join Him in this declaration and say what He is saying. "Peace, be still." To say what the Father is saying is to exercise the faith of Christ.

When there is no storm in you, nothing will have the power to threaten you. Yeshua released the dimension of heaven from within Him to affect the world around Him.

ELEVEN
SEEING IS BELIEVING

1. *Matthew 6:25, 31 Do not be worried about your life, as to what you will eat or what you will drink; nor for your body, as to what you will put on. Is not life more than food, and the body more than clothing? Do not worry then, saying, "What will we eat?" or "What will we drink?" or "What will we wear for clothing?'*

2. *Matthew 25:24-30 And the one also who had received the one talent came up and said, "Master, I knew you to be a hard man, reaping where you did not sow and gathering where you scattered no seed. And I was afraid, and went away and hid your talent in the ground. See, you have what is yours." But his master answered and said to him, "You wicked, lazy slave, you knew that I reap where I did not sow and gather*

where I scattered no seed. Then you ought to have put my money in the bank, and on my arrival I would have received my money back with interest. Therefore take away the talent from him, and give it to the one who has the ten talents." For to everyone who has, more shall be given, and he will have an abundance; but from the one who does not have, even what he does have shall be taken away. Throw out the worthless slave into the outer darkness; in that place there will be weeping and gnashing of teeth.

Here we find a parable on the reality of reaping what you sow and the harsh system of the world. The harsh taskmaster is life, not God, and to cringe in fear at your lot in life and not use what is given you like this servant did is only to suffer deeply in this life, cast out in utter darkness.

Instead, live life full of light and be bold with what is given you.

3. *John 16:33 These things I have spoken to you, so that in Me you may have peace. In the world you have tribulation, but take courage; I have overcome the world.*

When you hear the authentic gospel, when the Word speaks, your soul is empowered to respond with courage and reflect the peace of heaven. Peace is the fruit of the gospel.

4. *Luke 6:42 NIV How can you say to your brother, "Brother, let me take the speck out of your eye," when you yourself fail to see the plank in your own eye? You hypocrite, first take the plank out of your eye, and then you will see clearly to remove the speck from your brother's eye.*

In the context of love and humility, correcting our brothers and sisters is beautiful, because it unites and empowers rather than divides and controls.

5. *Genesis 3:9-13 Then the Lord God called to the man, and said to him, "Where are you?" He said, "I heard the sound of You in the garden, and I was afraid because I was naked; so I hid myself." And He said, "Who told you that you were naked? Have you eaten from the tree of which I commanded you not to eat?"*

This is one of the rare moments when God asks a question. He doesn't do this because He doesn't know where Adam is, but to expose that the man was now living in a self-generated perspective of separation from God.

The man said, "The woman whom You gave to be with me, she gave me from the tree, and I ate." Then the Lord God said to the woman, "What is this you have done?" And the woman said, "The serpent deceived me, and I ate."

Judgment is the fruit of the fall, and with it, guilt and shame.

6. *Matthew 5:14-16 You are the light of the world. A town built on a hill cannot be hidden. Neither do people light a lamp and put it under a bowl. Instead they put it on its stand, and it gives light to everyone in the house. In the same way, let your light shine before others, that they may see your good deeds and glorify your Father in heaven.*

7. *John 5:22, 45 NIV The Father judges no one . . . Neither will I accuse you before the Father. Your accuser is Moses (the law) in whom your hopes are set.*

8. ***Luke 6:37*** ESV *Judge not, and you will not be judged.*

Why? Because your judgment is what judges you. The law of judgment (Moses), which is the natural system of the world, is what judges you, not your Father or Jesus.

9. ***Hebrews 8:13*** ESV *In speaking of a new covenant, he makes the first one obsolete. And what is becoming obsolete and growing old is ready to vanish away.*

10. ***John 8:12*** *Then Jesus again spoke to them, saying, "I am the Light of the world; he who follows Me will not walk in the darkness, but will have the Light of life."*

11. ***Ephesians 1:17-22*** *That the God of our Lord Jesus Christ, the Father of glory, may give to you a spirit of wisdom and of revelation in the knowledge of Him.*

Authentic wisdom is a revelation of Jesus Christ.

I pray that the eyes of your heart may be enlightened, so that you will know what is the hope of His calling, what are the riches of the glory of His inheritance in the saints, and what is the surpassing greatness of His power toward us who believe. These are in accordance with the working of the strength of His might which He brought about in Christ, when He raised Him from the dead and seated Him at His right hand in the heavenly places, far above all rule and authority and power and dominion, and every name that is named, not only in this age but also in the one to come.

The implications of this are amazing beyond words. The cross did far more than deal with the sin and eternity issue. Yeshua restored you to your original design, beyond even what Adam experienced in the garden. You are indeed a new creation, one that has not been before.

And He put all things in subjection under His feet, and gave Him as head over all things to the church, which is His body, the fullness of Him who fills all in all.

You are created to be the mansion that God has chosen to fill with His presence.

TWELVE
SEE LIKE A CHILD AND BE FREE

1. ***Matthew 11:25*** *At that time Jesus said, "I praise You, Father, Lord of heaven and earth, that You have hidden these things from the wise and intelligent and have revealed them to infants."*

Because the letter kills and the Spirit gives life, anyone surrendered to the Holy Spirit can know the Word. It is not a function of intellect. If our study of the letter alone were the key to "knowing" God, we would have not killed Him when He came in the flesh.

2. ***Matthew 18:3*** NIV *Truly I tell you, unless you change and become like little children, you will never enter the kingdom of heaven.*

The childlike heart is vulnerable, teachable, joyful, creative, and filled with wonder. There's a difference between being childish and childlike. Childishness is a posture of stubborn challenge. Childlikeness is a perspective of hopeful curiosity. Every question you ever ask is one of challenge or curiosity. Let childlike wonder awaken in you again as you let go of all offense at the past and fear of the future.

3. ***John 14:8-10*** *Philip said to Him, "Lord, show us the Father, and it is enough for us." Jesus said to him, "Have I been so long with you, and yet you have not come to know Me, Philip? He who has seen Me has seen the Father; how can you say, 'Show us the Father'? Do you not believe that I am in the Father, and the Father is in Me?"*

4. ***Matthew 6:10*** *Your kingdom come. Your will be done, On earth as it is in heaven.*

Jesus reveals the will of the Father so this world can reflect His world. He desires that this dimension will bear the image of that dimension in every way. When you desire the same thing, you invite the Father to reveal to you the dimension in the Holy Spirit filled with love, joy, and peace. The first step into seeing that world is to simply accept that there is no distance between you and your Father right now. Yes, right now.

5. ***Luke 14:28*** ESV *For which of you, desiring to build a tower, does not first sit down and count the cost, whether he has enough to complete it?*

Jesus makes the point that every investment requires sacrifice. Count the cost and compare it to the reward. In the case of choosing to follow Yeshua's Way, the joy of the return makes the sacrifice of letting go insignificant, though it might not seem so at the time. Letting go always requires faith, but after a while, letting go becomes natural. But just because you've mastered the art of letting go doesn't mean you have to be okay with loss. Some losses hurt deeply, yet the joy to come is priceless.

6. ***Matthew 16:26*** *For what will it profit a man if he gains the whole world and forfeits his soul?*

7. ***Matthew 13:44-46*** *The kingdom of heaven is like a treasure hidden in the field, which a man found and hid again; and from joy over it he goes and sells all that he has and buys that field. Again, the kingdom of heaven is like a merchant seeking fine pearls, and upon finding one pearl of great value, he went and sold all that he had and bought it.*

The kingdom of heaven is the realm of the King's domain, and that kingdom is always within reach. The realm of the kingdom is priceless beyond description and closer than you can imagine.

8. **Romans 12:2** *Do not be conformed to this world, but be transformed by the renewing of your mind, so that you may prove what the will of God is, that which is good and acceptable and perfect.*

Learning a new revelation almost always requires that you unlearn an old one. To love learning is to also embrace the process of unlearning. The world is full of common sense, because, well, it's common. But a renewed mind sees beyond what is common sense.

9. **Ephesians 1:18** *I pray that the eyes of your heart may be enlightened, so that you will know what is the hope of His calling, what are the riches of the glory of His inheritance in the saints.*

Hope is the joyful expectancy of good. There is a difference between expectation and expectancy. Expectation creates a box that must be filled with a certain thing a certain way in order for us to be happy. Expectancy has no boxes. It simply assumes that good is coming and is happy about it before it even shows up. The eyes of your heart are enlightened when you're filled with joy at the thought of your Father's voice before you've even heard it.

10. **Ephesians 2:8** *For by grace you have been saved through faith; and that not of yourselves, it is the gift of God.*

11. **Proverbs 3:5-6** NIV *Trust in the Lord with all your heart and lean not on your own understanding; in all your ways submit to him, and he will make your paths straight.*

There is no rest apart from trust, and trust is appropriately placed only in Him. Pay attention to the reality of His presence in all your ways. We are lost and our ways go wrong when we perceive God as distant and separate from us.

12. **Matthew 8:24-26** *And behold, there arose a great storm on the sea, so that the boat was being covered with the waves; but Jesus Himself was asleep. And they came to Him and woke Him, saying, "Save us, Lord; we are perishing!" He said to them, "Why are you afraid, you men of little faith?" Then He got up and rebuked the winds and the sea, and it became perfectly calm.* **Matthew 14:25** *And in the fourth watch of the night He came to them, walking on the sea.*

13. **Matthew 11:28-30** *Come to Me, all who are weary and heavy-laden, and I will give you rest. Take My yoke upon Me and learn from Me, for I am gentle and humble in heart, and you will find rest for your souls. For My yoke is easy and My burden is light.*

THIRTEEN
BEAUTIFUL, BEAUTIFUL BROTHER AND SAVIOR

1. *John 14:23-24 Jesus answered and said to him, "If anyone loves Me, he will keep My word; and My Father will love him, and We will come to him and make Our abode with him. He who does not love Me does not keep My words."*

Obedience is simply alignment. It is to surrender to union with God in Christ by the power of the Holy Spirit. Obedience is not about rules, but about the relationship of love found in the presence of your Father. Look at Paul's letters of instruction to the churches. He never itemizes all the commands of Jesus, emphasizing obedience to those. Instead he capitalizes upon this revelation of union with Christ and then addresses specific issues a church is dealing with. Paul knows that unless we get a revelation of how much we are in Christ, we'll just become religious.

But once we awaken to that reality of being in Him, the secure love of our Father will become our life source. We will then love as He loves us, and love is the sum of all Jesus' commandments: love God by aligning with Him in the vine, and love our neighbors as ourselves.

2. *Mark 10:6-8 From the beginning of creation, God made them male and female. "For this reason a man shall leave his father and mother, and the two shall become one flesh"; so they are no longer two, but one flesh. What therefore God has joined together, let no man separate.*

This is Jesus speaking about marriage and divorce. Keep this in mind when you read the next verse, written by Paul.

Ephesians 5:30-32 We are members of His body. "For this reason a man shall leave his father and mother, and the two shall become one flesh." This mystery is great; but I am speaking with reference to Christ and the church.

Paul interprets the Genesis passage through the lens of union with Christ. Paul understands that the union of marriage here on Earth is only a shadow of the reality of loving union that we have with God in Christ.

3. *Matthew 5:8 Blessed are the pure in heart, for they shall see God.*

The pure heart is manifest by gratitude for the grace that accomplished what you could have never done on your own. The only way a heart can be pure is if the One who is holy steps into it.

4. *Galatians 3:26-28 You are all sons of God through faith in Christ Jesus. For all of you who were baptized into Christ have clothed yourselves with Christ. There is*

neither Jew nor Greek, there is neither slave nor free man, there is neither male nor female; for you are all one in Christ Jesus.

It is baptism that "clothes" you in Christ. Is baptism to mean more than we may have thought?

Matthew 28:19 Go therefore and make disciples of all the nations, baptizing them in the name of the Father and the Son and the Holy Spirit.

This is not simply a scripted line to be recited over someone as the minister plunges them under the water. To baptize is to immerse or saturate. In Hebrew culture, someone's name is equivalent to his identity. So the revelation meant to be imparted in water baptism may be better understood if it said, "Be immersed in the identity of Father, Son, and Holy Spirit." Baptism is a physical reflection of a spiritual reality, namely, that you are clothed and complete in Him.

The objective isn't to give anyone a new label, such as "Christian", as much as to make them disciples of the way of Yeshua, a way we too often forget each day.

5. *Luke 6:35 But love your enemies, and do good, and lend, expecting nothing in return; and your reward will be great, and you will be sons of the Most High; for He Himself is kind to ungrateful and evil men.*

6. *James 1:2-4 Consider it all joy, my brethren, when you encounter various trials, knowing that the testing of your faith produces endurance. And let endurance have its perfect result, so that you may be perfect and complete, lacking in nothing.*

7. *Romans 8:29 NIV For those God foreknew He also predestined to be conformed to the image of His Son, that He might be firstborn among many brothers and sisters. Hebrews 2:10-11 NIV In bringing many sons and daughters to glory, it was fitting that God, for whom and through whom everything exists, should make the pioneer of their salvation (Jesus) perfect through what He suffered. Both the one (Jesus) who makes people holy, and those who are made holy (you) are of the same family. So Jesus is not ashamed to call them brothers and sisters.*

What do you usually get from your older brother when you're a kid? Well, usually you get hand-me-down clothes. Read *John 17:22* and find out how much more you get from Jesus: *The glory which You have given Me I have given to them, that they may be one, just as We are one.*

8. *Hebrews 4:15 NIV For we do not have a high priest (Jesus) who is unable to empathize with our weaknesses, but we have one who has been tempted in every way, just as we are, yet he did not sin.*

He was tempted just as we are, and the way we are tempted in this life is over and over again, every day—that's what makes it difficult. His temptation wasn't a one-time affair but was just as continual as our own, all the way to His death.

9. ***Matthew 4:1-2*** *Then Jesus was led up by the Spirit into the wilderness to be tempted by the devil. And after He had fasted forty days and forty nights, He then became hungry.*

10. ***Mark 14:33-35*** *And He took with Him Peter and James and John, and began to be very distressed and troubled. And He said to them, "My soul is deeply grieved to the point of death; remain here and keep watch." And He went a little beyond them, and fell to the ground and began to pray that if it were possible, the hour might pass Him by.*

11. ***Hebrews 5:7-9*** NIV *During the days of Jesus' life on Earth, He offered up prayers and petitions with fervent cries and tears to the one who could save Him from death, and He was heard because of His reverent submission. Son though He was, He learned obedience from what He suffered and, once made perfect, He became the source of eternal salvation for all who obey Him.*

To truly obey means to align yourself with someone, not just in deed but in thought and nature. Jesus said in ***John 12:49*** *For I did not speak on My own initiative, but the Father Himself who sent Me has given Me a commandment as to what to say and what to speak.*

He is demonstrating a lifestyle of relationship with the Father. He is showing us what it is like to live in union with God by the power of the Holy Spirit.

12. ***1 Corinthians 15:45*** *So also it is written, "The first man, Adam, became a living soul." The last Adam became a life-giving spirit.*

Jesus does exactly the opposite of the first Adam, and Paul makes clear that Jesus is the last Adam. There is not another.

13. ***Luke 22:42*** *Father, if You are willing, remove this cup from Me; yet not My will, but Yours be done.*

In the garden of Eden, Adam chooses his own will over God's and eats of the tree of the knowledge of good and evil. In that act man said to God, "Not thy will, but my will be done." Yeshua, the last Adam, in the second garden, sweats blood from a brow that will be pierced with a crown of thorns and thistles, and through the sweat and blood He says to the father, "Not my will, but thy will be done." And so reverses the first Adam's choice.

FOURTEEN
BE FREE FROM YOUR PRISON

1. ***Ephesians 2:4-9*** *But God, being rich in mercy, because of His great love with which He loved us, even when we were dead in our transgressions, made us alive together with Christ (by grace you have been saved), and raised us up with Him, and seated us with Him in the heavenly places in Christ Jesus, so that in the ages to come He might show the surpassing riches of His grace in kindness toward us in Christ Jesus. For by grace you have been saved through faith; and that not of yourselves, it is the gift of God; not as a result of works, so that no one may boast.*

If you died and rose and now are seated in heavenly places, you ascended with Christ. You are a multidimensional being, able to be in both time (here in this world of form) and eternity (seated in heavenly places now). You are a divinely created convergence of heaven and earth, made with a will to love so that you can fully participate in a relationship with your Father, who both made and inhabits you in and through the Spirit. So your eternity has already begun. In Him you live and move and have your being. Now.

Colossians 3:1-4 NIV *Since, then, you have been raised with Christ, set your hearts on things above, where Christ is, seated at the right hand of God. Set your minds on things above, not on Earthly things. For you died, and your life is now hidden with Christ in God. When Christ, who is your life, appears, then you also will appear with him in glory.*

We are made to observe, learn, and reflect, and whatever we behold, we become like. So we set our affection and attention on things above. The word *when* in the above verse is a progressive state of being (such as *whenever*) rather than a singular calendar event. So the verse is understood like this: Whenever Christ appears, you appear. Whenever Jesus is revealed, so are you.

2. ***John 17:22*** *The glory which You have given Me I have given to them.*

It is being in Christ that gives you access to His glory. Nothing of God originated with us or is carried by us independent of His presence. What a beautiful gift the Father has given us in Christ.

3. ***Hebrews 4:2*** *For indeed we have had good news preached to us, just as they also; but the word they heard did not profit them, because it was not united by faith in those who heard.*

God's belief is for you and not against you. But unbelief easily blinds Christians to the good news of who they are. When you believe a lie, you empower it to take a foothold in your mind, will, and emotions. A lie is a disease to your soul, as powerful in its effect on your experience of life as is the truth. An encounter with God empowers you with the faith of Christ and puts your soul at rest.

4. *Matthew 19:24 Again I say to you, it is easier for a camel to go through the eye of a needle, than for a rich man to enter the kingdom of God.* It is not wealth or status or all this world has to offer that is evil, as is often quoted. Rather it is the *love* of wealth that is the root of all evil (1 Timothy 6:10). What we love reveals who we believe we are, because the affection of our hearts defines our identity in this world.

5. *Luke 14:26 If anyone comes to Me, and does not hate his own father and mother and wife and children and brothers and sisters, yes, and even his own life, he cannot be My disciple.*

6. *Luke 9:23 If anyone wishes to come after Me, he must deny himself, and take up his cross daily and follow Me.*

Matthew 16:25 For whoever wishes to save his life will lose it; but whoever loses his life for My sake will find it.

You will never seek and find yourself outside of a revelation of Yeshua—only in Him can you be found. To see Him is to come to know who you truly are.

7. *Romans 14:23 Whatever is not from faith is sin.*

Consider that sin is whatever creates a perspective of distance between you and God. Faith is the pure river of life flowing from the oasis of our united relationship with Christ.

8. *1 Corinthians 6:12 All things are lawful for me, but not all things are profitable. All things are lawful for me, but I will not be mastered by anything.*

Just because all things are lawful for you, like Paul, doesn't mean that all serves you. Anything that blinds you to your identity in Christ is missing the mark or is sin, and that thing may be different for you than for your brother. That blindness (sin) doesn't change who you are, but it changes your experience of life and necessarily leads to misery. So seek to be mastered by nothing except Christ in you and you will experience true freedom.

9. *James 1:14 But each one is tempted when he is carried away and enticed by his own lust.*

It has been said that the same sun that melts ice hardens clay. What carries you away? What blinds you? Whatever creates a sense of a barrier between you and God will blind you to who you truly are.

10. *Galatians 6:8 For the one who sows to his own flesh will from the flesh reap corruption, but the one who sows to the Spirit will from the Spirit reap eternal life.*

11. *1 Corinthians 13:12 For now we see in a mirror dimly, but then face to face; now I know in part, but then I will know fully just as I also have been fully known.*

FIFTEEN
THE EVIDENCE OF YOU IS LOVE

1. *1 Corinthians 13:12 For now we see in a mirror dimly, but then face to face; now I know in part, but then I will know fully just as I also have been fully known.*

Is there any time when God has not known you? Is there any time when God forgot why He made you? Do you think you have disappointed your Father? You haven't. How can you disappoint someone who knows everything and loves you still? God doesn't manipulate you with His love. His love is an invitation for you to see what He has always seen in you and to know what He has always known about you: that you are both forgiven and innocent.

2. *Romans 14:17 The kingdom of God is not eating and drinking, but righteousness and peace and joy in the Holy Spirit. Galatians 5:22-23 The fruit of the Spirit is love, joy, peace, patience, kindness, goodness, faithfulness, gentleness, self-control; against such things there is no law.*

John 13:35 By this all men will know that you are My disciples, if you have love for one another.

3. *Mark 12:28-31 One of the scribes came and heard them arguing, and recognizing that He had answered them well, asked Him, "What commandment is the foremost of all?" Jesus answered, "The foremost is, 'Hear, O Israel: The Lord our God, the Lord is one. And you shall love the Lord your God with all your heart and with all your soul and with all your mind and with all your strength.' The second is this: 'You shall love your neighbor as yourself.' There is no other commandment greater than these."*

The core of love is often contrasted with wrath and judgment, as if these are equal and necessary opposing forces. But the Scriptures give love uncompromising importance. They never declare that God is wrath, but it is written that God *is* love. Wrath and mercy are not equal weights that create a healthy balance. All of what we think of as wrath is only purifying that which inhibits love in our lives. As such, it is healing, like an antibiotic that kills disease. When dis-ease is gone, ease and rest come.

4. *John 13:35 By this all men will know that you are My disciples, if you have love for one another.*

Mankind is blinded by division. Our awareness of our union with God in Christ by the power of the Holy Spirit will awaken the world.

5. *1 Corinthians 13:1-3 If I speak with the tongues of men and of angels, but do not have love, I have become a noisy gong or a clanging cymbal. If I have the gift of prophecy, and know all mysteries and all knowledge; and if I have all faith, so as to remove mountains, but do not have love, I am nothing. And if I give all my possessions to feed the poor, and if I surrender my body to be burned, but do not have love, it profits me nothing.*

It's possible to exercise spiritual gifts, perform supernatural miracles, have enviable intellect, and accomplish great works of social service that don't require God's involvement. But the only thing that gives us or any work we do value is the pure love of God. If you haven't figured this out by now, love is a big deal in the Bible. Without love, we and our works are nothing.

6. *John 14:16, 17, 20; 17:23 I will ask the Father, and He will give you another Helper, that He may be with you forever; that is the Spirit of truth, whom the world cannot receive, because it does not see Him or know Him, but you know Him because He abides with you and will be in you . . . In that day you will know that I am in My Father, and you in Me, and I in you . . . I in them and You in Me, that they may be perfected in unity, so that the world may know that You sent Me, and loved them, even as You have loved Me.*

7. *1 Corinthians 13:4 Love is patient, love is kind and is not jealous; love does not brag and is not arrogant.*

Love is not a feeling, a concept, an idea, or a philosophy. Love is a person. Love is Jesus Christ. So if you are confused about who Jesus is, read 1 Corinthians 13 and replace the word *love* with *Yeshua*. Because you are in Him, this passage becomes a beautiful description of who you truly are.

8. *1 Corinthians 13:4-8 Love is patient, love is kind and is not jealous; love does not brag and is not arrogant, does not act unbecomingly; it does not seek its own, is not provoked, does not take into account a wrong suffered, does not rejoice in unrighteousness, but rejoices with the truth; bears all things, believes all things, hopes all things, endures all things. Love never fails.*

In 2 Corinthians 5:18, Paul describes the boundless goodness of the reconciliation of Jesus to mankind. God doesn't count our trespasses against us. Isn't this the same love as defined in 1 Corinthians 13? In reconciling us to Him, Jesus doesn't seek His own, Jesus is not provoked, He does not take into account a wrong suffered, He does not rejoice in unrighteousness, He rejoices in the truth. Jesus bears all things, believes all things, hopes all things, and endures all things. Jesus never fails because Jesus is God and God is love and love does not fail.

SIXTEEN
BEING LOVE IN THE DARKNESS

1. ***Matthew 6:34*** *So do not worry about tomorrow; for tomorrow will care for itself. Each day has enough trouble of its own.* ***1 Peter 5:6-7*** *Therefore humble yourselves under the mighty hand of God, that He may exalt you at the proper time, casting all your anxiety on Him, because He cares for you.*

To worry is to meditate on the power of a negative circumstance. We have no ability to "let go" by ourselves. Only when we see that we are held, loved, and cared for by our Father can we rest in the peace of Yeshua. Humility is not humiliation. In surrendering to the embrace of the Father you will find that He lifts you up. Rather than being humiliated, you are exalted. Every fear, worry, and anxiety is burned away in the consuming fire of His love. Your Father tells you not to worry because releasing anxiety is both possible and beneficial. Worry is only faith in the storm. Rest is the reward of trust.

2. ***Ephesians 3:17-19*** *That you, being rooted and grounded in love, may be able to comprehend with all the saints what is the breadth and length and height and depth, and to know the love of Christ which surpasses knowledge, that you may be filled up to all the fullness of God.*

Your Father is perfect. He's better than you think, and you can't imagine Him to be better than He is. When you surrender to His embrace, you can fully rest in the knowledge that He will love you into complete wholeness, no matter how broken you think you have become.

3. ***Matthew 25:40*** *Truly I say to you, to the extent that you did it to one of these brothers of Mine, even the least of them, you did it to Me.*

2 Corinthians 5:14-16 *For the love of Christ controls us, having concluded this, that one died for all, therefore all died; and He died for all, so that they who live might no longer live for themselves, but for Him who died and rose again on their behalf. Therefore from now on we recognize no one according to the flesh.*

Galatians 3:28 *There is neither Jew nor Greek, there is neither slave nor free man, there is neither male nor female; for you are all one in Christ Jesus.*

4. ***1 Timothy 1:16*** NIV *But for that very reason I was shown mercy so that in me, the worst of sinners, Christ Jesus might display his immense patience as an example for those who would believe in Him and receive eternal life.*

5. ***John 17:22*** *The glory which You have given Me I have given to them, that they may be one, just as We are one.*

6. *Mark 12:30, 31 "Love the Lord your God with all your heart, and with all your soul, and with all your mind, and with all your strength." . . . "You shall love your neighbor as yourself." There is no other commandment greater than these.*

God is complete, never divided. Yet He lives in you fully and completely. Though in this world of form we appear to be in different costumes, Christ is never divided. Therefore we are indeed one in spirit. That spirit realm is eternal, and this physical dimension is temporal. See yourself as one with the person you are blessing, giving to, loving, and you will see that the grace you release comes into you. This is why judging is so deadly. For we are one, even with those we hate.

7. *1 Corinthians 12:27* ESV *Now you are the body of Christ and individually members of it. Romans 12:5 We, who are many, are one body in Christ, and individually members one of another.*

SEVENTEEN
LET ALL YOUR TROUBLES FALL AWAY

1. *Luke 6:42 How can you say to your brother, "Brother, let me take out the speck that is in your eye," when you yourself do not see the log that is in your own eye? You hypocrite, first take the log out of your own eye, and then you will see clearly to take out the speck that is in your brother's eye.*

2. *Luke 23:34 But Jesus was saying, "Father, forgive them; for they do not know what they are doing." And they cast lots, dividing up His garments among themselves.*

3. *Colossians 3:12-14 So, as those who have been chosen of God, holy and beloved, put on a heart of compassion, kindness, humility, gentleness and patience; bearing with one another, and forgiving each other, whoever has a complaint against anyone; just **as the Lord forgave you**, so also should you. Beyond all these things put on love, which is the perfect bond of unity.*

To love is to forgive. If we could forgive our enemies without loving them, Jesus would have never given the command to love our enemies. To forgive someone isn't to say that what they did was okay. It's to extend mercy in spite of what was done. This is bearing with one another, just as Christ has done for us. True forgiveness is to set someone free from your judgments and punishments.

4. *Matthew 18:18 Truly I say to you, whatever you bind on Earth shall have been bound in heaven; and whatever you loose on Earth shall have been loosed in heaven.*

Look closely here at the wording. "Shall have been" indicates that what happens here in time reflects what already is in eternity. The standard of heaven is not lowered by our blindness, sin, failure, and darkness here on Earth. Rather, we are to shine with the radiant love of a superior kingdom. So we are not on a mission to bring Earth to heaven, but heaven to Earth. The way we do that is to recognize what already exists in heaven and reflect it here on Earth.

5. *1 Thessalonians 5:4-5 But you, brethren, are not in darkness, that the day would overtake you like a thief; for you are all sons of light and sons of day. We are not of night nor of darkness.*

6. *Matthew 5:21-22 You have heard that the ancients were told, "You shall not commit murder" and "Whoever commits murder will be liable to the court." But I say to you that everyone who is angry with his brother* (or sister) *will be guilty . . . And whoever says, "You Fool!" shall be guilty . . .*

Just as Jesus taught that lust was essentially the same as adultery, here He makes the case plain that what people think is ultimately as ruinous as what they do, because both thought and action separate them from their true identity. To be angry with someone who has wronged you may seem unavoidable, but according to Jesus you only join them in their darkness.

EIGHTEEN
GIVING IS RECEIVING

1. *Galatians 6:8 For the one who sows to his own flesh will from the flesh reap corruption, but the one who sows to the Spirit will from the Spirit reap eternal life.*

2. *Luke 6:35 But love your enemies, and do good, and lend, expecting nothing in return; and your reward will be great, and you will be sons of the Most High; for He Himself is kind to ungrateful and evil men.*

3. *Romans 6:22-23 But now having been freed from sin and enslaved to God, you derive your benefit, resulting in sanctification, and the outcome, eternal life. For the wages of sin is death, but the free gift of God is eternal life in Christ Jesus our Lord.*

Being enslaved to God may sound negative, but remember that the Son has set you "free indeed" and, in that freedom, find a beautiful liberty, sanctification, and eternal life in your union with God in Christ.

4. *Romans 5:20 The Law came in so that the transgression would increase; but where sin increased, grace abounded all the more.*

5. *Matthew 25:40 Truly I say to you, to the extent that you did it to one of these brothers of Mine, even the least of them, you did it to Me.*

6. *Luke 9:24 For whoever wishes to save his life will lose it, but whoever loses his life for My sake, he is the one who will save it.*

7. *Luke 6:37-38 Do not judge, and you will not be judged; and do not condemn, and you will not be condemned; pardon, and you will be pardoned. Give, and it will be given to you. They will pour into your lap a good measure—pressed down, shaken together, and running over. For by your standard of measure it will be measured to you in return.*

This verse is often used to uphold the principle of giving in terms of money, but if you read the verse in context, you can clearly see that the context is not money, but the giving of non-judgment, which is grace.

8. *Luke 10:36-37 "Which of these three do you think proved to be a neighbor to the man who fell into the robbers' hands?" And He said, "The one who showed mercy toward him." Then Jesus said to him, "Go and do the same."*

Our compassion unifies us. In this story, Jesus uses the outcast to illustrate a love that is for all mankind. Our position, reputation, heritage, religion, or nationality have no power to justify a lack of compassion for another person made in the image and likeness of God.

9. *Luke 9:23 Take up your cross daily and follow me.*

NINETEEN
ENEMIES AND FRIENDS

1. *Mark 4:39-40 He got up and rebuked the wind and said to the sea, "Hush, be still." And the wind died down and it became perfectly calm. And He said to them, "Why are you afraid? Do you still have no faith?"*

2. **Luke 6:35** *But love your enemies, and do good, and lend, expecting nothing in return; and your reward will be great, and you will be sons of the Most High.*

Take a moment to meditate on this perspective of your Father. There is none higher. Nothing is above your Father in greatness, in glory, in power, in strength, in all of time and eternity. And He has raised you, His son, His daughter, up with Him. This is resurrected life.

Matthew 5:46 For if you love those who love you, what reward do you have?

3. *Matthew 5:39 Do not resist an evil person, but whoever slaps you on the right cheek, turn the other to him also.*

Grace and mercy do not say that evil behavior is okay. It is saying that there is no storm, no wave, that can rise above the love of Christ alive within you. The kindness of God is the very light that leads the blind toward sight.

4. *1 Corinthians 13:5* (Love) *does not dishonor others, it is not self-seeking, it is not easily angered, it keeps no record of wrongs.*

5. *Luke 14:26 If anyone comes to Me, and does not hate his own father and mother and wife and children and brothers and sisters, yes, and even his own life, he cannot be My disciple.*

Let no other person be empowered to define your identity. Do not even try to define it yourself. That alone is reserved for your Father. It is from that identity of love Himself that you can reflect His divine nature to be a father, husband, wife, brother, or sister in this life. Only in this way can you love as He loves.

TWENTY
FINDING SUPERMAN

1. *John 14:12-13 Truly, truly, I say to you, he who believes in Me, the works that I do, he will do also; and greater works than these he will do; because I go to the Father. Whatever you ask in My name, that will I do, so that the Father may be glorified in the Son.*

Have you ever seen a believer do greater works than Jesus? Think of the works Jesus did. And now He says you will do greater? And in doing greater, you will be expressing the glory of the Son on Earth as it is in heaven. As His son, His daughter, this is your inheritance in this life.

2. *John 15:8, 16-17 ESV By this my Father is glorified, that you bear much fruit and so prove to be my disciples . . . I chose you and appointed you that you should go and bear fruit and that your fruit should abide, so that whatever you ask the Father in my name, He may give it to you. These things I command you, so that you will love one another.*

You can't bear fruit apart from union with Christ. It is the abiding presence of Christ's love within you that makes fruit naturally come forth.

3. *John 17:22-23 The glory which You have given Me I have given to them, that they may be one, just as We are one; I in them and You in Me, that they may be perfected*

in unity, so that the world may know that You sent Me, and loved them, even as You have loved Me.

Our union with God and with each other is the key that opens the locked door that stands between the world and the love of the Father. Could it be that the world is blind because we have put on display division and judgment rather than unity and grace? Meditate on this phrase, "that the world may know."

4. ***James 4:2-3*** *You do not have because you do not ask. You ask and do not receive, because you ask with wrong motives, so that you may spend it on your pleasures.*

By "spend it on your pleasures," James means all that would satisfy the old mind, the flesh-body divorced from Christ. So much of what we ask for is motivated by our identification with our bodies and our relationships. Is it any wonder then that we ask amiss?

5. ***Philippians 4:11-13*** *I have learned to be content in whatever circumstances I am. I know how to get along with humble means, and I also know how to live in prosperity; in any and every circumstance I have learned the secret of being filled and going hungry, both of having abundance and suffering need. I can do all things through Him who strengthens me.*

This passage is not just about enduring challenges, and it's not about placing mind over matter. Paul is revealing the power of the renewed mind to transform reality by seeing this world from divine perspective.

Luke 1:37 *For nothing will be impossible with God.* ***Mark 10:27*** *Looking at them, Jesus said, "With people it is impossible, but not with God; for all things are possible with God."* ***Mark 9:23*** *And Jesus said to him, "'If You can?' All things are possible to him who believes."*

TWENTY-ONE
A NEW DECLARATION

1. ***Galatians 3:27*** *For all of you who were baptized into Christ have clothed yourselves with Christ.*

2. ***Luke 14:18-20*** *But they all alike began to make excuses. The first said to him, "I have bought a field and I must go out and see it. Please have me excused." And another said, "I have bought five yoke of oxen and I go to examine them. Please have me excused." And another said, "I have married a wife and therefore I cannot come."*

*3. **Matthew 25:1-9** Then the kingdom of heaven will be comparable to ten virgins, who took their lamps and went out to meet the bridegroom. Five of them were foolish, and five were prudent. For when the foolish took their lamps, they took no oil with them, but the prudent took oil in flasks along with their lamps. Now while the bridegroom was delaying, they all got drowsy and began to sleep. But at midnight there was a shout, "Behold, the bridegroom! Come out to meet him." Then all those virgins rose and trimmed their lamps. The foolish said to the prudent, "Give us some of your oil, for our lamps are going out." But the prudent answered, "No, there will not be enough for us and you too; go instead to the dealers and buy some for yourselves."*

*4. **Matthew 16:24** Jesus said to His disciples, "If anyone wishes to come after Me, he must deny himself, and take up his cross and follow Me."*

*5. **John 17:16** They are not of the world even as I am not of the world.*

*6. **Mark 9:43** NIV If your hand causes you to stumble, cut it off. It is better to enter life maimed than with two hands to go into hell (Gehenna) where the fire never goes out.*

*7. **1 Corinthians 2:16** "Who has known the mind of the Lord, that he will instruct him?" But we have the mind of Christ.*

*8. **Galatians 3:28** There is neither Jew nor Greek, there is neither slave nor free man, there is neither male nor female; for you are all one in Christ Jesus. **Colossians 3:9-11** Do not lie to one another, since you laid aside the old self with its evil practices, and have put on the new self who is being renewed to a true knowledge according to the image of the One who created him—a renewal in which there is no distinction between Greek and Jew, circumcised and uncircumcised, barbarian, Scythian, slave and freeman, but Christ is all, and in all.*

In Paul's letter to the Colossians, he even becomes more radical with this thought. He includes here the Scythians who were violent, hostile and rejected by the society and culture of the day. Think of the most hated, rejected, and outcast subcultures in our world today, and insert that group in place of "barbarian." Now understand how stunning this statement is. And yet you are none of these labels. You are in Christ and He is in you.

*9. **Ephesians 2:4-8** But God, being rich in mercy, because of His great love with which He loved us, even when we were dead in our transgressions, made us alive together with Christ (by grace you have been saved), and raised us up with Him, and seated us with Him in the heavenly places in Christ Jesus, so that in the ages to come He might show the surpassing riches of His grace in kindness toward us in Christ Jesus. For by grace you have been saved through faith; and that not of yourselves, it is the gift of God. **John 17:22-23** The glory which You have given Me I have given to them, that they may be one, just as We are one; I in them and You in Me, that they may be perfected in unity, so that the world may know that You sent Me, and loved them, even as You have loved Me.*